WRITING AND PSYCHOANALYSIS

WRITING AND PSYCHOANALYSIS

A Reader

John Lechte

Senior Lecturer in Social Theory, Macquarie University, Australia

A member of the Hodder Headline Group
LONDON • NEW YORK • SYDNEY • AUCKLAND

First published in Great Britain in 1996 by
Arnold, a member of the Hodder Headline Group
338 Euston Road, London NW1 3BH
175 Fifth Avenue, New York, NY10010

Distributed exclusively in the USA by
St Martin's Press Inc.,
175 Fifth Avenue,
New York, NY 10010

British Library Cataloguing in Publication Data
A catalogue entry for this book is available from the British Library

Library of Congress Cataloging-in-Publication Data
Writing and psychoanalysis : a reader / [edited by] John Lechte.
    p.   cm.
  Includes bibliographical references and index.
    ISBN 0–340–64561–X. — ISBN 0–340–62498–1 (pbk.)
    1. Criticism.   2. Psychoanalysis and literature.   I. Lechte,
John.
PN98.P75W75   1995
809' .93353—dc20
                                        95–34257
                                        CIP

ISBN 0 340 64561 X (hb)
ISBN 0 340 62498 1 (pb)

Typeset in 10/11 pt Times by Anneset, Weston-super-Mare, Avon
Printed and bound in Great Britain by J. W. Arrowsmith Ltd, Bristol

Contents

Acknowledgements

Leslie Hill and Murray Domney helped me out of a number of difficulties with my translation from the French of Foucault and Kristeva. I am sincerely grateful to them but, of course, take full responsibility for any remaining errors. Helen Easson helped in the final stages of the preparation of the manuscript – and I thank her for it. I thank Christopher Wheeler of Arnold for suggesting this project, and for his extreme patience as a number of deadlines slipped by. And, as always, Gill deserves all my thanks – for everything!

The editor and publisher would like to thank the following publishers for permission to use copyright material, and for giving permission to reproduce material for which they hold the rights: Athlone Press and Columbia University Press for Gilles Deleuze, *Difference and Repetition*, trans. Paul Patton (London: Athlone Press, New York, Columbia University Press, 1994, pp. 96–116), copyright (©) 1994 The Athlone Press Limited. Reprinted with permission from Columbia University Press. The Johns Hopkins University Press for Jeffrey Mehlman, 'How to Read Freud on Jokes: The Critic as *Schadchen*', *New Literary History*, vol. VI, no. 2 (Winter 1975), pp. 439–61. Reprinted with permission from The Johns Hopkins University Press. The Johns Hopkins University Press for Jacques Derrida, 'My Chances/*Mes Chances*: A Rendezvous with Some Epicurean Stereophonies', trans. Irene Harvey and Avital Ronell, in Joseph H. Smith and William Kerrigan, eds, *Taking Chances*: *Derrida, Psychoanalysis and Literature* (Baltimore, MD and London: The Johns Hopkins University Press, first published 1984, paperback edition 1988, pp. 1–32), copyright (©) Forum on Psychiatry and the Humanities. Reprinted with permission from The Johns Hopkins University Press.

Éditions Gallimard, Tavistock Publications, and Georges Borchardt for Michel Foucault, 'Introduction' [to Section III], in *Histoire de la folie à l'âge classique* (Paris: Gallimard 'TEL', 1972, pp. 363–72), copyright (©) 1961 by Librairie Plon. Copyright (©) by Random House. Reprinted with permission from Tavistock Publications and Georges Borchardt, Inc. Éditions Gallimard for Michel Foucault, 'La Folie, l'absence d'œuvre', in *Histoire de la folie à l'âge classique* (Paris: Gallimard, 'Bibliothèque des histoires', 1972, pp. 575–82, copyright (©) Éditions Gallimard, 1972. Librairie Anthème Fayard for Julia Kristeva, 'Nom de mort ou de vie', in Jacques Sédat, ed., *Retour à Lacan* (Paris: Fayard, 1981, pp. 163–82), copyright (©) Librairie Arthème Fayard, 1981.

Random House UK for 'Dostoevsky and Parricide' and 'Psychopathic Characters on the Stage'. Sigmund Freud Copyrights, The Institute of Psycho-Analysis and The Hogarth Press Ltd for permission to quote from *The Standard Edition of the Complete Psychological Works of Sigmund Freud,* translated and edited by James Strachey. HarperCollins for 'Dostoevsky and Parricide' from *The Collected Papers, Volume 5* by Sigmund Freud, edited by James Strachey. Published by BasicBooks, Inc. by arrangement with The Hogarth Press Ltd and The Institute of Psycho-Analysis, London. Reprinted by permission of BasicBooks, a division of HarperCollins Publishers, Inc.

City Lights Books for Jacques Lacan, 'Homage to Marguerite Duras', trans. Peter Connor, in *Duras on Duras* (San Francisco: City Lights, 1987, pp. 122–9). English translation copyright (©) 1987 by City Lights Books. Leslie Hill for Leslie Hill, 'Lacan with Duras', *Journal of the Institute of Romance Studies*, 1 (1992), pp. 405–24. Reprinted with permission of the author. Virago Press and Harvard University Press for Jacqueline Rose, 'She', in *The Haunting of Sylvia Plath* (London: Virago Press, 1991, ch. 1, pp. 11–28), copyright (©) Jacqueline Rose 1991. Published by Virago Press 1991. Reprinted with permission from Harvard University Press. Éditions Gallimard and Columbia University Press for Julia Kristeva, 'La Sensation est-elle un langage?', in *Le Temps sensible: Proust et l'expérience littéraire* (Paris: Gallimard, 'NRF essais', 1994, pp. 280–306), copyright (©) Éditions Gallimard. Reprinted with permission from Columbia University Press.

Every effort has been made to trace copyright holders of material, and those who hold the rights to the reproduction of this material. Any rights not acknowledged here will be acknowledged in subsequent printings if notice is given to the publisher.

Preface

The selection of writings for this collection was largely governed by two principles. The first was that each text should be the result of an engagement with writing, rather than simply being a theorisation of the relationship between writing and psychoanalysis. Of course there are essentially theoretical issues raised by the relationship between writing and psychoanalysis; and some of these have been explicitly addressed in Section One. However, even here, in the more explicitly theoretical section, the theorising is based on an engagement with key literary works. The engagement, then, rather than the theorisation – or psychoanalysis – of the link between writing and psychoanalysis is what I have aimed to bring out.

The second principle is that, as far as possible, I have chosen texts which use a psychoanalytic framework to bring out the nature of the 'writerly' or literary aspect – and not just the clinical aspect – of texts. I have thus chosen pieces which clearly treat the works being analysed or interpreted as 'subject' rather than object. This issue is highlighted sharply, I believe, in Section Two, 'Writing and Madness'.

What, however, about the specific items in this collection? The general Introduction, and the specific introduction to each piece, should clarify this from a theoretical point of view. Let me say here, however, that I wanted, as far as possible, to offer material that would be of deep interest to readers, but would not have been so readily available before. I am particularly pleased, for example, to be able to present translations of works by Foucault and Kristeva which have until now been unavailable in English, and which do throw new light on madness, literature and psychoanalysis.

Finally, let me say that I have included two important examples of Freud's own writing on literature as a mark of where we have come from on the theme of this collection, and also as a source to which we may still – in the 1990s – profitably return.

John Lechte
Sydney
1995

Introduction

[P]sychoanalysis cannot be deployed as pure speculative knowledge or as a general theory of man. It cannot span the entire field of representation, attempt to evade its frontiers, or point towards what is more fundamental, in the form of an empirical science constructed on the basis of careful observation; that breakthrough can be made only within the limits of a praxis in which it is not only the knowledge we have of man that is involved, but man himself — man together with the Death that is at work in his suffering, the Desire that has lost its object, and the language by means of which, through which, his Law is silently articulated.

(Michel Foucault, *The Order of Things*)

Philosophy and Psychoanalysis

Although Freud's texts date from the 1920s and the remainder in this collection were written between 1965 (Lacan on Duras) and 1994 (Kristeva on Proust), the themes of these works go to the very heart of intellectual and aesthetic (fictional) enterprises as these are understood and practised in today's 'postmodern' society. Within a postmodern experience it is no longer possible for those engaged in the seriousness — and joy — of thinking to remain aloof from issues of subjectivity and objectivity, of method, of the rhetoric of prose, of the truth value of texts and the nature of their expressive power, of the essence of writing — of literature — and of the social and psychological context of writing. This state of affairs is best characterised by saying that, everywhere, a drive for a heightened reflexivity is on the agenda, and that for certain theorists of the contemporary scene this is in keeping with a historical tendency towards ever more concerted and complex social forms of individuality and differentiation.[1]

Many people might expect, then, that psychoanalysis would be one of the major instruments of a heightened reflexivity: it would lead people to see, for instance, that subjectivity is more than what is available to immediate experience, or even more than is available to the philosopher of the psyche — or to the philosopher of the *cogito*. The defiles of subjectivity would now be knowable only after a rigorous process of analysis which, in the end, might show that subjectivity as such, in its totality, is unknowable, and that a certain kind of ignorance is the price we pay for 'being' subjects. But even if we concede that psychoanalysis is one of the most refined instruments of reflexivity available — one that may be used for gaining an insight into subjectivity – does this not still imply, especially in the wake of certain kinds of psychoanalytic practice, that subjectivity holds the key to knowledge, well-being, and thus to the secret of artistic practice? If we really know who we are as subjects, does not much else fall into place? Will we not know, for example, how to see the objective world anew, and be at least alerted to the power of illusion, even if we cannot overcome it? With psychoanalytic practice, though, the ego as identical with itself – the ego we feel comfortable with because it seems to be identical with consciousness – has been dealt a solid blow by the theory of the unconscious; and the acknowledgement of language as formative of subjectivity has effectively challenged biologistic explanations of human social and mental life. But are we really any closer to cutting loose from reductionism – or from forms of metaphysics – when we attempt to follow a psychoanalytic path?

Our question must, it would seem, be answered partly in the negative, if only because certain thinkers and writers of feminist persuasion have shown the phallocentric nature of Freudian theory, even in its more recent and sophisticated Lacanian version. From one quarter, at least, then, psychoanalysis has been found wanting for not being sufficiently aware of its own presuppositions or of its own specific historical and social (political?) heritage. It is as though, quite simply, psychoanalysis were not reflexive enough! If it were, however, would it even be possible to say what psychoanalysis is? Could it still constitute itself as a discourse or as an institution? Could it have an identity? Such questions lie behind Jacques Derrida's opening statement in his commentary on Lacan's reading of Poe's 'The Purloined Letter'[2]: 'La psychanalyse, à supposer, se trouve.' ['Psychoanalysis, supposedly, is found' – or: 'finds itself'.][3] A claim to identity, on the other hand, is equivalent to the claim to a certain mastery founded on unity – the unity of One. This is also the basis of the symbolic order; and if the latter were all there was in the psychoanalytic arsenal, it would be much easier to pin it down and say: 'It is pure metaphysics, after all!' A number of people have made such a claim.

The view I would like to defend here is that psychoanalysis is not to be pinned down so easily – whatever the market value of its therapy might be today. I would want to say that psychoanalysis exists at the heart of the fold between mastery (identity) and dissolution. Psychoanalysis, in effect, is barely a discourse, barely an institution, when its specificity is seriously considered; and in this way, it resembles writing in the fullest sense – the sense that I would presently like to outline. With Derrida in philosophy, however, comes the view that although psychoanalysis might constitute an important therapeutic practice – although it might be the most highly developed form of reflexive theoretical practice (as far as the nature of the subject is concerned) – it is necessary to ask whether subjectivity – its form and its content – is really at the heart of epistemological, scientific and, of course, aesthetic problems? Could it not be that, today, faith in psychoanalysis – in the theory – is an overreaction to a positivism which, in principle, excluded subjectivity from the knowledge equation? Certainly, a philosophical critique of a Heideggerian kind is likely to challenge the claim that psychoanalytic theory can be separated from humanism. Indeed, for the philosopher of Being, it would join other humanisms (including the one based on Nietzsche's 'will to power') with its claim to have discovered truth in an aspect of the human subject – in this case, in the psyche. Heidegger's reservation about psychoanalysis might well be the one he made when writing of Nietzsche's 'will to power': 'Modern metaphysics, as the metaphysics of subjectness, thinks the Being of that which is in the sense of will.'[4] Is psychoanalysis effectively another version of the 'metaphysics of subjectness'? Might it not be forced to concede to philosophy on this point? With regard to an issue which will concern us here, Heidegger cites Nietzsche's aphorism from the *Will to Power* – 'Art is *worth more* than truth'[5] – as being indicative of the metaphysics of the 'will' characteristic of the reduction of everything to 'subjectness'. Even if, at an institutional level, the analyst is called to be analysed – even if, then, there could well be a psychoanalysis of psychoanalysis – it remains a matter of debate whether *psycho*analysis – the analysis of the psyche – is where all interest should be focused.

Psychoanalysis: Yesterday and Today

Let us agree that the confrontation between psychoanalysis and philosophy is an important and productive one. The reader of this collection should therefore be aware that it is sometimes a philosopher (Derrida, Deleuze) who makes the running in discussions relating to psychoanalysis and writing, and that when psychoanalysis is viewed cautiously here, this often stems from an uneasiness related to a perception that psychoanalysis might lead to the closure of thought, one caused by a blindness to the limits of (its) reflexivity.

That said, however, we can also recognise that throughout its history, psychoanalysis has transformed itself from a relatively positivist, nineteenth-century theory and practice, with all the medical pretensions that this entailed, to the highly nuanced and poetic discourse it has often become in the wake of Jacques Lacan. It may well be, as Leslie Hill suggests, that Freud was fascinated by the nineteenth-century Gothic tale or the Romantic short story, and that psychoanalysis has found it difficult to throw light on more modern literary genres. Nevertheless, with a more modern frame of reference in mind, it is interesting to note how Freud's – at times – 'applied' approach to Jensen's *Gradiva* pivots around the phenomenon of displacement. First of all, the story, *Gradiva, qua* fiction, is a diversion, a source of pleasure. Thus, if a message is there for the analyst's clinical gaze, it is masked, indirect, present only in a displaced form. Second – and this is the most interesting aspect – the story itself turns out to be about displacement: the historical Gradiva from Pompeii turns out to be a figure from the hero's own childhood; and, even more than this, the hero's 'escape' into archaeology, resulting in the repression of erotic sensuality through a turning away from the present, is itself an allegory of displacement. Repression, in a word, leads to displacement (and therefore to fiction of a realist kind), thus giving rise to the hero's vivid imagination. Freud comments: 'This division between imagination and intellect destined him to become an artist or a neurotic; he was one of those whose kingdom was not of this world.'[6] Even with the most clinical of intentions, through the notion of repression, and thence of displacement, Freud cannot fail to reveal to us how writing (fiction) and psychoanalysis, or writing and subjectivity, have a similar structure. Therefore, although Freud's interpretative aspirations and preferred literary genre may, in particular studies, have limited him, it is not so clear that the conceptual arsenal of psychoanalysis is equally limiting. For the Foucault of *The Order of Things*,[7] the logic of the psychoanalytic theory of the unconscious, to the extent that one is extant, entails turning away from other social sciences and refusing every general theory of humanity. The human, on this reading, is never a given, but is always to be constituted. At the level of individuality, the human is also other. (This is what made Hegel so cross with women. They wreck the community because they stand for individuality.) Most of all, though, Foucault argues that psychoanalysis cannot be a general theory of man because it includes the living, active – subjective – side within its theoretical and therapeutic framework. Where is the psychoanalyst situated? And to what effect? These are the key questions of an essentially reflexive disposition.

More recently, Julia Kristeva's work has developed the notion of subjectivity as an open system, where semiotic drive activity is taken in charge by an ever-changing, and ever more complex, symbolic order,[8] and where, as a result, individuality is what 'calls for thinking' (Heidegger). This view of subjectivity gives psychoanalysis an essentially dynamic status. Concepts, symbolic forms of all kinds, together with psychoanalytic practice, would always be in a process of evolution and formation. Psychoanalysis, on this account, becomes an attempt to institutionalise the openness fundamental to the analytic process. True, this openness in part entails a focus on the formation of subjectivity; true, the limits to thought are seen – perhaps too readily – to be limits to subjectness; and, true, writing and artistic endeavour are linked to the broader principles of the psychoanalytic canon. On the other hand, the limits to – and possibilities of – thought often do stem from factors related to subjective states. The blank page (or screen) – inseparable from a particular psychical state – is a real element in the writing process, even if we do not wish to reduce the possibility of writing to this. But in Kristeva's use of the psychoanalytic framework, writing as fiction is linked to identification so strongly that it (writing) can become equivalent to a kind of transubstantiation. In effect, through identification, I *become(s)* the other (recall: 'I is an other' – Rimbaud); I open myself up to the other so unconditionally that it is as though my own self were to disappear in the wake of the other. This is what Kristeva, in her reading of Joyce in particular, calls 'transubstantiation'.[9]

Kristeva, as analyst, has tapped into the permeability of the subject–object relation, one that is fundamental to the process of identification. In her discussion of the 'borderline' patient in this volume, she shows that, in contradistinction to Aristotelian logic, one is almost simultaneously in- and outside language – both 'father and son', 'actor and impresario', author and fictional character – split, in short, between One

and other – and that this recognition constitutes a blow to classical humanism, which sees the subject as a necessarily indivisible unity. As a result,
psychoanalysis cannot be reduced to a means of discovering the nature
of an individual psyche through the discourse of an analysand – this is
the humanist view – but shows that discourse itself, in a fundamentally
objective way – and because of this objectivity – is not at all available to
the ego, and that the latter cannot be reduced to the subject proper.

This point is further developed in Kristeva's study of Proust, included in
this collection, where Proust's writing is progressively seen as both fictional and constitutive of a distinctive subjectivity formed through a specific interaction between perception and intellection, between the semiotic
and the symbolic. On this view, subjectivity, in its singularity, is not exclusively on one side of the equation or the other. This is why the study of it
can be quite destabilising.

American ego psychology, on the other hand – as illustrated by Hanna
Segal's work – sees knowledge and aesthetic practice as being for the
ego, or for the 'self', a self that appears to be always-already constituted
rather than always in a process of formation. For Hanna Segal and ego
psychology, therefore, the main question is to know what the object is and
does for an already existing ego-self. Where does this ego come from?
(and where is it going?), we need to ask.

Writing, Surrealism and Madness

Transubstantiation in relation to writing and identification brings us directly
to the issue of writing and psychoanalysis. I say 'writing' here, not literature, although literature is surely involved. The institution of literature,
based on a canon of works and on a (relatively) well-formed discourse, is
too narrowly focused for our purposes. Indeed, it is precisely psychoanalysis, I suggest, which forces us to broaden our horizon, and to see
that writing and identification transcend the purely literary. This is not to
say that writing in the fullest sense will not become literature; but it is to
say that memory as writing, the unconscious as writing, codes as a form
of writing, writing and everyday life, writing as a form of identification, writing as the act of writing, show the term 'literature' to be much too circumscribed. Madness, too, tends to be excluded from literature – although
not from writing or fiction.

To understand this more fully, we recall that the members of Dada and
the Surrealists challenged the whole institution of literature and gave vent,
as they saw it, to the creativeness of madness. Jacques Vaché's bizarre
letters were thus published in the review *Littérature* in July 1919. A passage from one of these reads: 'Mon rêve actuel est de porter une
chemisette rouge, un foulard rouge et des bottes montantes – et d'être
membre d'une société chinoise sans but et secrète en Australie.'[10] As
Elisabeth Roudinesco has argued, surrealist writing, instead of being analytical, attempted to become an analogue of madness[11] – the most telling
example of this being, of course, *Magnetic Fields (Les Champs magné-
tiques)* by André Breton and Philippe Soupault.[12] There, the goal was to

open writing up to unconscious desire, and thereby escape the constraints of conscious reason.

Even if the surrealist attempt to imitate a certain kind of madness by consciously liberating the unconscious in writing now seems naïve, the exercise itself prompts us to think about how one might be mad in relation to language, and what might constitute a psychoanalytic approach to writing and madness. Lacan was much taken by this question in his thesis on paranoia (1932) – a thesis which addresses the issue of delirium and breaks with the conventional 'wooden prose' of a medical thesis. Lacan, as Roudinesco says, 'proposed a *writing* of madness' where he would 'recount his heroine's adventures with the pen of an authentic writer.... That in fact,' concludes Roudinesco, 'is the greatest originality of this innovative book...'.[13]

From another angle, the fictional writings of the subject of his case study, Aimée, allow Lacan to argue that Aimée unconsciously fictionalises her relation to the external world, a world which became an externalisation of her ideal self, and writes truly in her fiction. Her writing becomes continuous with her everyday life, so much so that Lacan judges it useful for providing information about Aimée's personality and state of mind – including her delirium.[14] The act of attacking a well-known actress with a knife, allegedly because the actress had stymied Aimée's stage career, becomes meaningful for the assailant – to the point of delirium – and has to be interpreted. Lacan, fascinated by Dalí's 'paranoid–critical method', begins to see that paranoia is not a hallucinatory delusion which leaves reason and logic behind, but is, rather, based on a surfeit of reason and interpretation. In a certain sense, paranoia leads to a radical overinterpretation of a text. Umberto Eco almost describes it when, writing about overinterpretation, he says:

> The paranoiac is not the person who notices that 'while' and 'crocodile' curiously appear in the same context: the paranoiac is the person who begins to wonder about the mysterious motives that induced me to bring these two particular words together. The paranoiac sees beneath my example a secret, to which I allude.[15]

Through the notion of paranoia, madness is not so much in the writer but in the reading. We can thus ask how close such paranoia comes to being a delirium of rationality and interpretation rather than a delirium where meaning and reason would be entirely absent. On this account, Freud himself might at times be on the edge of madness – the kind of madness coming, for instance, from the elimination of chance from the world: 'What we call chance in the world outside can, as is well known, be resolved into laws. So, too, what we call arbitrariness in the mind rests upon laws, which we are only now beginning dimly to suspect.'[16] Let me briefly summarise the above by saying that, from Surrealism to Lacan, two kinds of delirium are at issue for the reader of writing: one is the delirium that aims to be an analogue of madness because a calculating, self-conscious writing is deemed to be stultifying. This is a writing that aims for a kind of loss of self; it thus borders on mysticism. The other kind of delirium, uncovered by Dalí, is one that derives from a heightened reflexivity and the discovery of meaning in the most 'innocent' of places. This is the delirium of an excess of meaning and consciousness. Here, an apparently acute awareness of the self and the world leads to a paranoid delirium. Most importantly, the reader's position, as Eco points out, is potentially one of paranoid delirium. Through the work of a theorist like Julia Kristeva, psychoanalysis takes on the task of weaving a path somewhat apart from the excesses of either position. Let us now elaborate on what is at stake here.

Since Foucault rewrote the history of madness, it is no doubt a mark of the master's blindness to think that the task of psychoanalysis could be to speak the truth of the madness supposedly manifest in the writing before it. Versions of applied psychoanalysis did, of course, proceed in precisely this way. Freud himself was tempted. The piece on Dostoevsky attempts to use the writer's work – in particular *The Brothers Karamazov* – as a means of confirming the author's neurosis, a neurosis which hinders the ego's struggle for unity, as though this struggle were somehow a defect and quite separate from successful artistic endeavour. As Sollers asks: 'What would have become of Dostoevsky's art if his "ego" had succeeded in making a synthesis, a unity?'[17] For Sollers, Freud does not understand that neurosis and writing might be continuations of each other – that madness might be a source of writing strength.

Nevertheless, apart from concepts like 'displacement', Freud's word is complex and often ambivalent because his thought is always explicitly evolving: consequently, he is never sure at any given moment that he has got everything right. Uncertainty is part of his discourse – to the point where uncertainty is built into the very epistemological foundation of psychoanalysis. At stake here is the relationship of pathology to individuality – which raises the issue of oft-repeated opposition of the normal and the pathological.

Foucault, perhaps better than anyone, has discussed how the phenomenon of madness was gradually overcome in the modern era by the concept of mental illness. Thus, Rameau's Nephew signals the end of the experience of a madness that is able to know itself as such before a more clinical gaze stifles it to produce mental illness. The mentally ill patient rarely knows himself as mentally ill. Mentally ill patients are rarely dreamers intervening in their own dilemma. All the intervening – that is, all the objectifying – would now be done exclusively by an other. While madness had a certain autonomy, mental illness is a condition of dependence. What we need to ask is this: How can we account today for an Artaud, a Nietzsche, a Van Gogh, or a Raymond Roussel, or even a Joyce? How can we read their writing today? Largely, by denying their madness – and so by denying the madness of reading paranoia – and certainly by denying that their works are those of a mentally ill person.

Writing as Such

As implied above in the discussion of madness, the issue of reading raises questions about how psychoanalysis relates to writing. Writing must be understood here in its broadest sense: as a mark on a surface. How this mark becomes the vehicle of significance is what interests us, and the way psychoanalysis becomes embroiled in the process of significance interests us too. A fully 'applied' psychoanalysis sees writing as the object to be worked on in order that the psychological obsessions of an author may be revealed, or certain shibboleths of psychoanalytic theory confirmed. Readings around Edgar Allan Poe's 'The Purloined Letter' demonstrate what is at stake here. Marie Bonaparte, for instance, detects Poe's secret obsessions behind his writing;[18] while Lacan, at the other end of the spectrum, sees the story itself as a purloined letter — that is, as the embodiment of a pure signifier susceptible of taking on a wide range of meanings. The letter is a signifier — a virtual object, as Deleuze shows (see Section One below) — in Poe's story precisely because its text is not available to the protagonists. So while a quasi-medicalisation of the story by Marie Bonaparte implies that there is a fundamental meaning (a signified) lurking in the background — or even in the foreground — the story, as writing, is a series of marks, a signifier, capable of taking on a whole gamut of different meanings. In Lacan's reading, writing is fundamentally of the order of the signifier. To be confronted, therefore, by enigmatic marks on a cave wall, marks organised in a particular way, is to be confronted — to the extent that their conventional meaning is *un*known — by the signifier. The realm of the signifier, then, is the realm of uncertainty and mystery. It is also the realm of the dancing shadows on the wall of Plato's cave in *The Republic*. Rousseau, for his part, shows that he confronts the signifier when he writes in the *Confessions*:

> My natural inclination is to be frightened of shadows: I have fear and loathing of their dark appearance, and their mystery worries me to the point of foolishness. The most hideous aspect of a monster would frighten me little, it seems to me, but if at night I caught a glimpse of a figure under a white sheet, I would be terrified.[19]

With Rousseau, we are reminded that the veil covering a figure, so that it is impossible to discern exactly what kind of figure it is, produces the signifier. The latter's 'mystery' comes from the potential to link up with a multiplicity of signifiers. To become lost in the defiles of the 'pure' signifier, therefore, is to become cut off from meaning. The mask, like the veil, hides, but it reveals that it is hiding. Consequently the mask, too, is a source of mystery, and thus a problem for Rousseau. Every experience of the veil, every experience of the mask — every experience of mystery — is, in Lacanian terms, an experience of castration. Castration is equivalent to what gives the phallus its status as a pure signifier: its detachability. By analogy, then, language is essentially a collection of detachable entities. Context is the attachment of utterances to signifieds — this attachment producing meaning and thus (self-)certainty. For Rousseau, as we saw, real fear has its source in uncertainty as such, not in the certainty that comes from confronting a monster — that is, from confronting certain death.

The relationship between meaning and context in language was first theorised in an extensive way by Émile Benveniste.[20] Benveniste showed that the subject in language cannot be reduced to the subject of the *énoncé* — or completed utterance — but emerges in the fullest sense in the *énonciation*: the existential enactment of language – a speech act – the enactment of language being tied to context. This enactment, or instance, of discourse is essentially unique, being the product of a moment in time; it therefore challenges the representational power of the symbolic order. It is a clear sign of the subject divided in and by language as discussed by Kristeva in her chapter 'Name of Death or of Life' (see Section Two below). Language in its execution – as enacted – would, on this reading, be of equal importance with the formal structure of language: language as a system. Similarly, would not the *act* of writing be as much constitutive of writing, as such, as its concealed form in literature? In effect, what the poststructural era offers us is the open text, one actually constituted through the act of interpretation. This is not to say that a text is nothing but its interpretation (see Eco). None the less, it is to say that the act of writing is inextricably linked to the act of interpretation. The latter is also seen by Kristeva in 'Name of Death or of Life' as the level of metalanguage, or – in the terms of Michel Bréal, the nineteenth-century semanticist cited by Kristeva – meaning (interpretation) is the 'impresario' level of language, the level which allows for the intervention of the subject in his or another's language act, as it allows for a certain degree of objectification. The subject here is both 'actor and impresario', and is thus divided along the axis which distinguishes these two linguistic dimensions.

For applied psychoanalysis, writing would be viewed exclusively in terms of the 'impresario' pole – the metalinguistic pole – of language. Applied psychoanalysis thus tends to be an objectifier of texts, an interpreter ready to restore the hitherto lost, or hidden, meaning of a text as this relates to the person of the author. Has psychoanalysis ever really given up its applied orientation? Does it not always want to explain writing, to see it as the result of some rational, law-like process? And if this is the case, does not the desire to explain everything always put psychoanalysis on the trail of an origin of some kind? Does it not make it 'tree-like' in structure – as Deleuze and Guattari have argued – rather than open to chance: the epitome of the other as entirely unpredictable, and so not subject to existing 'laws'? Can writing be chance-like in return, and so leave psychoanalysis in the lurch? Mallarmé's wager was that writing (poetry) is a 'throw of the dice' (see 'Un Coup de dés'[21]); and shortly after him Joyce produces in *Finnegans Wake* writing which is almost a symptom (a *sinthome*, according to Lacan[22]); it is almost the sign of mental illness.

What can psychoanalysis do in the light of writing as chance? The answer – as always – depends largely on where one stands. Because there is no fixed psychoanalytic doctrine (however much the various psychoanalytic associations throughout the world might wish that there were) psychoanalytic discourse appears susceptible to modification in the light of new material – at least at some point in the institutional edifice. Certainly, this is Julia Kristeva's position. But Jeffrey Mehlman's chapter in this collection (see Section One below) shows that Freud himself was not in control of the institution he had inaugurated. Thus, in Mehlman's reading, Freudian theory emerges out of an interplay of various texts – one text intervening in the other without Freud (but not only him) having complete knowledge of this process. The real significance, and a good deal of the force of Freud's own discourse, is therefore made available only through the auspices of a third party. Indeed, Mehlman's view is that Freud, as much as anybody, was subject to the same psychic phenomena (e.g. repression) that he had done so much to theorise. And why should we be surprised at this? Does it not show another instance of the structure of language when the meta-, objective level competes with the active, poetic – or even psychotic – level, the level which comes to the fore when one has the sensation of drowning in language with words becoming things, as in a dream? A dream 'is a psychosis', said Freud.[23] Derrida, as is known,[24] has argued that dream in Freud's text is a form of writing – that it has the structure of writing because meaning emerges only through the differential play of the elements of the dream.

The Debt Psychoanalysis Owes to Literature – to Writing

Let us say, then, that the active, poetic side of language is the writing effect. Literature is the consolidation of this effect as a symbolic phenomenon. Without writing (poetry), there is no literature. No doubt the reverse is at least partially true: without the institution of literature, there would be nothing for writing to challenge or build upon. Do we also need to contemplate the possibility that without psychoanalysis, there would be no psyche? In a post-Romantic epoch, the question is hardly challenging any more. In trying to answer it, however, we may come closer to understanding the very intimate relationship between psychoanalysis and writing.

To state the issue clearly at the outset: if writing is what psychoanalysis has to give a meaning in order that it be saved from madness (or mental illness, as we say today) – if psychoanalysis were uniquely the 'body of *knowledge*, whose competence is called upon to *interpret*',[25] it would not be very different from any other objectifying discourse in the social sciences or the humanities. The point made above is that reflexivity is an essential aspect of psychoanalysis, in that it is a discourse which attempts to account for the mode of formation of subjectivity – the unconscious, we could say. Philosophy, by contrast, is an essentially objectifying discourse in the sense that its focus is on the objective status of subjectivity – or desire – not on its effects. Through Heidegger, philosophy is right to warn against reducing all of language, art, and so on, to the effects of subjectivity. Through Heidegger, we are alerted to the fact that subjectivity is not everything. This is his anti-humanist warning. But in acknowledging this, it is important to recognise that subjectivity is not nothing, either. There is a question of desire, and this – very plausibly – belongs to psychoanalysis. If psychoanalysis were only an objectifying discourse, it would be unable to provide the insights it does into subjectivity and desire.

If, in relation to writing, psychoanalysis is not essentially an objectifying discourse geared to explaining what a text really means, how does it relate to writing? For Shoshana Felman, it is via the notion of transference. Thus in a post-medical model, analysis engages with a text – not as if it were an object, but as if it were a subject: as if the analyst could learn something from it, not just the reverse. Historically, psychoanalysis has taken its key concepts from literary sources (Oedipus complex, narcissism, sadism), and clearly, Freud himself continually garnered ideas and scenarios from literary sources. The analyst, in short, learns from literature and from all forms of writing, just as in the analytic situation both analyst and analysand are changed by the unfolding of the analysis.

In this context, it is fair to say that few analysts have engaged with literary texts as literary texts, and have nevertheless been able to see the analytic effects involved. Julia Kristeva is a rare analyst in this regard. Not only is the analysand's creative product important for her in the analysis; in addition, only through writing can psychoanalytic scenarios be developed, only through the semiotic (the rhythm of language) can a self be forged. Only within the realm of art within which fiction is located can a true engagement with otherness take place. This engagement with otherness (not its control or elimination) is specific to the analytic project. To take an example: to engage with Proust's text as a body of writing (not as an illustration of psychoanalytic concepts or doctrine) is to become aware of a specifically Proustian perception of things, and of confronting a Proustian theory of perception. A discovery such as this can, potentially, transform the psyche because, as Kristeva sees it, the psyche is essentially an 'open system'. An encounter with otherness is therefore fundamental to the psyche's continued viability.[26] All this is a far cry from the notion that the psychoanalytic concepts and framework can be applied to – or foisted upon – literary works. As Kristeva says, it is a question of the constitution or dissolution of meaning, of finding or not finding a meaning – of being or not being. The very act of reading a truly innovative – or disturbing – piece of writing therefore relates to the very formation of an ego – of a self; and this self is subject to change and modification through its encounter with other, different texts. Of significance here, then, is that the writing itself, in its autonomy, is crucial – not a blueprint for self-development.

With Kristeva – and certainly with Derrida – the issue to be addressed is always that of knowing where psychoanalysis stands in relation to what it analyses. Previously, in more positivistic days, psychoanalysis aimed to speak the truth of its object. Now, the reflexive capacity of psychoanalysis – demonstrated in the ability to change – has led to the discovery of the subject status of the object – of writing, for example. Psychoanalysis is informed – and, therefore, formed – by what it analyses (or attempts to analyse). Its discovery, in short, is that the other is a subject – not a pure object.

Consequently, when Jeffrey Mehlman reads Freud on jokes through an astonishing juxtaposition of texts, he begins to show that Freud discovered a process which revealed the illusion behind the notion of pure mastery where the other would be essentially an object. In the light of this discovery, psychoanalysis is not a science in the positivist sense; for – to reiterate – its other (nature) is not an object. This tends to be the view running through the majority of texts chosen for this collection.

The other as subject: such a position undermines the Hegelian-inspired dialectic. The other as subject is the point at which all would-be masters

find their match. The other as subject is a limit which cannot be tran-
scended. To acknowledge — albeit symptomatically — the other as subject
is also to break out of the imaginary register and the trap of a specular
oscillation between self and other.

It has often been remarked that Lacan's formative period — like that of
a number of key French intellectuals — was marked by the experience of
Alexandre Kojève's reading of Hegel's Master–Slave dialectic. The Master
is undermined in his mastery by the recognition of the Slave's subjectivity. But does this mean that the Slave then becomes Master? Were this
the case, the result would be a (potentially infinite) specular oscillation
which, structurally speaking, leaves the positions of Master and Slave virtually untouched. Lacan's reading of Poe's 'The Purloined Letter' is an
exploration of intersubjectivity indebted to a Hegelian point of departure.
The schoolboy's game of 'even and odd', the King's blindness as to how
his power can be undermined (because the Queen is indeed a 'subject'),
the Minister's misplaced sense of invulnerability after stealing the letter,
the Dupin's *coup de grâce*, which consists in repeating the Minister's strategy for 'hiding' the letter — all these aspects raise the question of the nature
of the structure of intersubjectivity, a structure which Lacan analyses in
terms of the way the protagonists are influenced and even transformed by
the other, instead of being able to force the other to conform to the desire
of His Majesty, the ego. In short, Lacan discovers in Freud a point beyond
the specular oscillation of intersubjective rivalry — a purely symbolic point
— and this, we can safely assume, is the point of departure for all the modern, post-Freudian contributors to this collection.

The Reading Effect

To read in the light of psychoanalysis is to recognise that certain texts
already incorporate a 'reading effect' or commentary position. Ignoring this,
as Shoshana Felman has shown, has often resulted in critics repeating a
scenario set up by the text that is supposedly being analysed. Thus, in
James's 'The Turn of the Screw' the fact that the narrative is third-hand is
significant. 'Let me say here distinctly, to have done with it, that this narrative, from an exact transcript of my own made much later, is what I shall
presently give.'[27] The narrator's own narrative is in fact a transcription of
the story as written down by Douglas, one of the protagonists in James's
tale. When, as a result, the reader reads, making an actual or imaginary
transcript of the story, he or she is thus repeating a gesture already anticipated in the story itself.

Similarly, there has over the decades been a lively debate about
whether or not the governess in the story hallucinates the danger which
supposedly threatens the children, or whether the danger is real. Such
speculation, aimed at eliminating the ambiguity, forgets that the latter is
not at all external, but internal to James's narrative. The reader engaging
in such speculation repeats the issues already of concern to the story's
characters. Nothing is added, least of all insight. This, then, is not an analytic position. The analytic position consists in acknowledging that the

ambiguity and subtlety of the writing – the play of the signifier – is intrinsic to the text. It is what *possesses* the reader; for it is what the reader (or rather, an ego) wants to deny. The reader wants certainty, and so denies being possessed by uncertainty.

Sylvia Plath's poetry, as Jacqueline Rose demonstrates (see Section Four below), has within it a reading effect of which the reader should be aware. Rose's use of the psychoanalytic concepts of 'projection' and 'transference'[28] make it possible to gain some insight into this reading effect.

With 'The Purloined Letter', too, the reader does not know the contents of the letter, but in this he or she is in exactly the same situation as most of the story's protagonists. To speculate about the letter's contents, therefore, is to be caught up in the imaginary register that the Police and the Minister illustrate so well.

Rameau's Nephew is composed of a dialogue between *Moi* (Me) and *Lui* (Him). For 'Me', it is 'Him' who is a mystery. If a reader demands that the Me character tell us who the Him, or *Lui*, character is, he or she simply repeats the scenario of the story itself. For this is exactly the question that *Moi* also wants to answer. However, his task is made all the more difficult because 'nothing is less similar to Him than Him himself'. This is partly because 'Him' is simultaneously a composite of reason and unreason. This composite figure, as analysed by Foucault, still embodies a madness (or unreason) that is the necessary underside of reason. The Nephew, in effect, is the figure of madness prior to its being pathologised by nineteenth-century psychiatry. (Nietzsche, Artaud, Roussel, Van Gogh, rejoin the Nephew in this respect. Their otherness – to the point of delirium – is tragically part of themselves.) Instead of repeating the text, psychoanalytic reflexivity theorises the reader's place in relation to what is being read.

Beyond the Imaginary

One of the early questions that Lacan's reinterpretation of Freud opened up, therefore, was: what lies beyond the imaginary specular oscillation of the dual intersubjective relation? In practice, this meant asking whether any interpretation of a text – or of a work of art – could be anything more than the interpreter's fantasy. Recognition that a text is a play of signifiers is part of the breakthrough here. For as we saw above, a pure signifier is recognisable when uncertainty exists as to its signified. As a play of signifiers, the text begins to take on a life of its own, and cannot be seen simply as a reader's plaything – unsettling as this might be. This is how 'The Purloined Letter' (both as story and as the letter as an element in the story) comes to stand for the nature of all 'pure' signifiers. Derrida's basic reservation regarding Lacan's reading is whether it is possible to claim that the story itself – the fiction – illustrates the points Lacan wishes to make. For if the floating signifier – the letter – illustrates the nature of all signifiers, is this not equivalent to attributing to it a signified – in short, a meaning. In effect the story would show how an encounter with a pure signifier 'transcends the subjects in their intersubjectivity'. This is why, in the well-known debate, Derrida claims that Lacan in fact falls back into the position of the analyst telling the truth of the text.

But as Barbara Johnson's reading of this debate shows, it is difficult for Derrida (as accuser) not to repeat the very faults Lacan commits. Indeed, it is in the nature of the signifier (which is a structure, not a content) to bring about repetitions of this sort. And so, just as the Minister in Poe's story repeats the Queen's strategy for 'hiding' the letter, and just as the Dupin repeats the Minister's strategy for stealing it, so Derrida, Johnson shows, is caught up in repeating Lacan's claims about the real meaning of the letter — that it suggests the structure of castration, a uniquely psychoanalytic notion. The sense of loss specific to castration is not simply a psychoanalytic insight. It can also be linked to a literary source, just like Oedipus. Any mystery story is founded upon, and makes explicit, the structure of loss that an enigma evokes. The Oedipus myth also embodies this structure (Oedipus has to answer the Sphinx's riddle, and his own origin is a mystery); while, latterly, the writings of Kafka and Bataille have made loss in the sense of mystery and the expenditure of energy without return the productive principle of their art.

The Real Contribution of Psychoanalysis

In the light of these reflections, the reader may well wonder what contribution psychoanalysis can really make to (the interpretation of) writing. He or she may indeed feel that we have 'castrated' psychoanalysis, as it were — that is, we have left it no space of its own where it could truly contribute to the interpretation of writing. In order that it not be reductive, psychoanalysis has ceased to be productive. This is partly explained by the fact that 'The analyst is *involved* (through transference) in the very "object" of his analysis.'[29]

It is not because psychoanalysis does or does not propose a meaning for writing that it can take up a place close to it. Rather, because the destiny of psychoanalysis is to explore the workings of the signifier — or, in Kristeva's theory, the 'semiotic' — it can begin to mark out the (non-) space of writing and of literature. Psychoanalysis does not provide an essential meaning to literature because its concepts (Oedipus, repression, unconscious, repetition) are not to be understood literally, as empirically verifiable entities, but as general structures that indeed promote the literary/writing effect. The task of a psychoanalytically informed approach to writing, therefore, is to demonstrate the latter's (relative) autonomy and to question any reductive interpretations (e.g. that Gide's homosexuality is visible between the lines of *The Immoralist*). Psychoanalysis does not offer an essential meaning to literature or to writing; it is sensitive to the writing effect. But neither, I suggest, does it refuse the hermeneutic moment. A rush to judgement is one thing; a refusal of the responsibility implied in interpretation is quite another. To refuse metalanguage, meaning — and thus the Father principle embodied in the role of the impresario who can intervene in what is said, and is thus outside the text — is to run the risk of madness. Kristeva brings this to us particularly well in her writing. For her, we must come to terms with the following paradox: meaning is arbitrary – words are only words – yet we must believe in them; for meaning is what holds us back from the abyss of madness. Indeed:

> Signs are arbitrary because language starts with a *negation* (*Verneinung*) of loss, along with the depression occasioned by mourning. 'I have lost an essential object that happens to be, in the final analysis, my mother,' is what the speaking being seems to be saying. 'But no, I have found her again in signs, or rather since I consent to lose her I have not lost her (that is the negation), I can recover her in language.'[30]

Summarised in this passage is the principle around which this collection turns: the principle that psychoanalysis is linked to writing in the same way as is the subject in language, namely, ambivalently, unconsciously – as actor and impresario, as the subject experiencing loss, and as the subject whose loss is erased through signs of the lost object. Such a scenario implies that contemporary psychoanalysis alerts us to issues which it is unable to control. Rather than a master, the analyst is an almost knowing victim of the signifier.

Given that psychoanalysis (as a discourse) undermines self-certainty founded on the *cogito*, what does it mean to read in the light of it? Given that we know something about its theoretical foundations, what now is a psychoanalytic approach to writing? Here we can spell out a number of key points quite visible in the pieces in this collection:

1. Because psychoanalysis introduces the reader to the play of the signifier more than to the signified – because it shows that the reader, rather than possessing the signifier (as one possesses knowledge), is possessed by the signifier – there is no doctrine that any piece of writing, any literary text, could communicate unambiguously. Thus the signifier, as a continually displaced object, opens the way to a dialogical, polyphonic text, where meaning is never exhausted. Following the principle Freud enunciated – without knowing what to do with it – in *Beyond the Pleasure Principle*, the complete reduction of writing to the signified would bring it to an end – just as complete satisfaction in life would bring death.
2. Through the concept of identification, psychoanalysis breaks the rule of self-identity: through identification, I am an other; through identification, I can appreciate a hitherto heterogeneous text. But through identification, too, I am involved in a process of idealisation and the formation of identity. In this way, psychoanalysis brings fluidity to the reader–text relation without thereby allowing this fluidity to become an incommunicable delirium (hence the idealisations). Through identification, too, psychoanalysis breaks down the rigidity of the subject–object relation and reveals that the subject is better understood as an 'open system'.
3. After Lacan, psychoanalysis is not limited to the articulation of a pathology. In the light of this, the question arises as to whether there is any fixed doctrine: any symptom of illness, and so forth. Doctrine, as postmodern experience has shown, depends on an origin and a hierarchy of concepts. To all appearances, Oedipus is that origin for psychoanalysis. Signifer–signified, subject–object, conscious–unconscious, presence–absence, repressed–manifest, self–other, feminine–masculine,

active–passive, metaphor–metonymy, and so on, are some of the concepts of the hierarchy. In Deleuze and Guattari's conceptual framework, most of these conceptual doubles result in the privileging of the 'tree' (vertical axis) over the 'rhizome' (horizontal axis). For Eco, who is inspired by Deleuze and Guattari, the dictionary (vertical axis) is privileged over the encyclopaedia (horizontal axis). For certain feminists, it is a question of phallocentrism (privileging, among other things, the vertical axis). Be this as it may, it is impossible to show here whether or not psychoanalysis comes armed with its clinical, therapeutic gaze when it approaches writing. What the reader of this collection can appreciate, in the light of psychoanalytic insights, is that a crucial issue in the reading of texts involves the opposition between meaning and the loss, or breakdown, of meaning. Literary texts, too, from Mallarmé to Joyce and Artaud, have explored this opposition. Modern writing in the artistic sphere, like psychoanalysis in the therapeutic sphere, has confronted meaning and its loss – or should we not say: loss *tout court*? Consequently, the hypothesis that the reader could keep in mind as he or she approaches the pieces in this collection is that psychoanalysis and writing have, in the end, the same object: the formation and dissolution of meaning. The formation of meaning would be linked to identification – and thus to identity – while the dissolution of meaning would be linked to the otherness characteristic of the poetic word. If, for the reader, this also implies a movement to a new experience of language and subjectivity, the collection has succeeded.

Notes

1. See Niclas Luhmann, *Love as Passion: The Codification of Intimacy*, trans. Jeremy Gaines and Doris L. Jones, Cambridge: Polity Press, 1986.
2. Jacques Lacan, 'Seminar on "The Purloined Letter"', trans. Jeffrey Mehlman, *Yale French Studies* (French Freud), no. 48 (1972), pp. 38–72.
3. Jacques Derrida, 'Le Facteur de la vérité', in *La Carte postale: de Socrate à Freud et au-delà*, Paris: Aubier-Flammarion, 1980, p. 441. In English as 'Le Facteur de la vérité', in *The Postcard: From Socrates to Freud and Beyond*, trans. Alan Bass, Chicago and London: University of Chicago Press, 1987, p. 413. As Bass advises, *se trouver* can also mean 'to find oneself'. Psychoanalysis would thus find, or establish, itself.
4. Martin Heidegger, 'The Word of Nietzsche', in *The Question Concerning Technology and Other Essays*, trans. William Lovitt, New York: Harper Torchbooks, 1977, p. 88.
5. Friedrich Nietzsche, *The Will to Power*, trans. Walter Kaufmann and R. J. Hollingdale, New York: Vintage Books, 1968, sect. 853.
6. Sigmund Freud, *Delusions and Dreams in Jensen's 'Gradiva'*, in *Freud, Art and Literature*, Pelican Freud Library, vol. 14, Harmondsworth: Penguin, 1985, p. 40.
7. Michel Foucault, *The Order of Things*, trans. from the French, London: Tavistock, reprinted 1982.
8. For an explanation of Kristeva's use of 'semiotic' and 'symbolic' in a psychoanalytic framework, see John Lechte, *Julia Kristeva*, London: Routledge, 1990, esp. ch. 5.
9. Julia Kristeva, 'Joyce the Gracehoper or the Return of Orpheus', in Bernard

Benstock, ed., *James Joyce: The Augmented Ninth* (Proceedings of the Ninth International James Joyce Symposium), Syracuse, NY: Syracuse University Press, 1988, pp. 167–80.

10. Trans: 'My dream at the moment is to wear a short-sleeved red blouse, a red headscarf, high boots and to be a member of a Chinese secret society in Australia which has no goal.' Jacques Vaché, 'Lettres de Jacques Vaché', *Littérature* (first series), no. 5, July 1919, p. 3.

11. Elisabeth Roudinesco, *Jacques Lacan & Co.: A History of Psychoanalysis in France, 1925–1985*, trans. Jeffrey Mehlman, Chicago: University of Chicago Press, 1990, p. 26.

12. See André Breton and Philippe Soupault, *Magnetic Fields*, trans. David Gascoyne, London: Atlas Press, 1985.

13. Roudinesco, *Jacques Lacan & Co.*, p. 112.

14. See Jacques Lacan, *De la psychose paranoïaque dans ses rapports avec la personnalité* [On Paranoid Psychosis in its Relations with the Personality], Paris: Seuil, [1932] 1975, p. 177.

15. Umberto Eco, *Interpretation and Overinterpretation*, ed. Stefan Collini, Cambridge: Cambridge University Press, 1992, p. 48.

16. Freud, *Delusions and Dreams in Jensen's 'Gradiva'*, p. 35.

17. Philippe Sollers, 'Dostoevsky, Freud, la roulette', in *Théorie des exceptions*, Paris: Gallimard, 1984, p. 63. Unpublished English translation by David Buxton.

18. Marie Bonaparte, 'Selections from *The Life and Works of Edgar Allan Poe: A Psycho-analytic Interpretation*', in John P. Muller and William J. Richardson, eds, *The Purloined Poe: Lacan, Derrida & Psychoanalytic Reading*, Baltimore, MD and London: Johns Hopkins University Press, 1988, pp. 101–32.

19. Jean-Jacques Rousseau, *Confessions*, in *Œuvres complètes*, I, Paris: Gallimard, Bibliothèque de la Pléiade, 1959, p. 566.

20. See Émile Benveniste, *Problems in General Linguistics*, trans. Mary Elizabeth Meek, Coral Gables, FL: University of Miami Press, 'Miami Linguistics Series No. 8', 1971, p. 218. See also the entry for Benveniste in John Lechte, *Fifty Key Contemporary Thinkers: From Structuralism to Postmodernity*, London: Routledge, 1994.

21. Stéphane Mallarmé, 'Un coup de dés', in *Œuvres complètes*, Paris: Gallimard, 'Bibliothéque de la Pléiade', 1945, pp. 57–60.

22. A translation of a paper by Lacan on Joyce – 'Joyce le symptôme I' ('Joyce, The Symptom I') – would have been included in this collection had Jacques-Alain Miller agreed.

23. See Sigmund Freud, *An Outline of Psycho-Analysis*, trans. James Strachey, London: Hogarth Press and Institute of Psycho-Analysis, revised edition, 1969, p. 29.

24. Jacques Derrida, 'Freud and the Scene of Writing', in *Writing and Difference*, trans. Alan Bass, Chicago: University of Chicago Press, 1978, pp. 196–231, esp. 206–15.

25. Shoshana Felman, 'To Open the Question', in Shoshana Felman, ed., *Literature and Psychoanalysis: The Question of Reading: Otherwise*, Baltimore, MD and London: Johns Hopkins University Press, 1982, p. 5.

26. See Julia Kristeva, 'Is Sensation a Language?', ch. 12 in this volume. See also Kristeva, 'Joyce the Gracehoper'.

27. Henry James, 'The Turn of the Screw', in *The Turn of the Screw and Other Stories*, ed. T. J. Lustig, Oxford and New York: Oxford University Press, 'The World's Classics' series, 1992, p. 119.

28. For an explanation of 'projection' and 'transference', see Jacqueline Rose, 'She', ch. 11 in this volume, and Editor's Introduction to Rose's chapter.

29. Barbara Johnson, 'The Frame of Reference: Poe, Lacan, Derrida', in Shoshana

Felman, ed., *Literature and Psychoanalysis*, p. 502.
30. Julia Kristeva, *Black Sun*, trans. Leon S. Roudiez, New York: Columbia University Press, 1989, p. 43.

SECTION ONE

On Psychoanalysis and Writing

1

Gilles Deleuze, 'Repetition for Itself', in *Difference and Repetition.*

Trans. Paul Patton, London: Athlone, New York: Columbia University Press, 1994, pp. 96–116.

Editor's Introduction

Although this is a testing piece of writing, the reader may gain greater understanding of it if he or she recalls Freud's notion of 'displacement' and works through the implications stemming from it.

Deleuze, then, argues that repetition in itself – which exists in one series of events – is not secondary to what is repeated, and is always displaced; the real – which exists in another series of events – is never entirely primary, and is always disguised. Furthermore – and this is particularly pertinent to writing – repetition is always the repetition of a partial object – equivalent to Lacan's *objet petit a* (which is, for Lacan's reading of Freud, ultimately a sumbolic substitute for the mother the child has lost through separation). This makes it into a virtual object, by which Deleuze means that it is not identical with itself: it is there when it is not there, is not there when it is there, and is found only as lost. It ignores the law of contradiction. It is a purloined letter, with the emphasis on 'purloined'. Where is a letter that is essentially purloined to be found? Once found, it is no longer purloined. Like *objet petit a*, a virtual object has no identity of its own. It is what it is entirely through its displacements. The repressed, which can never appear directly in language (for language is symbolic, and the repressed is the real), always takes on a mask-like quality. The mask, as a virtual object, is also always displaced. The repressed, unable to appear directly in symbolic form, therefore becomes a mask. In Lacan's theory, this means that it becomes a signifier in the symbolic. Repetition is linked to Lacan's notion of the symbolic, and the phallus as its major signifier.

Even if it is claimed that, ultimately, the phallus (which is symbolic) must evoke the penis (which is real), this, for Deleuze, is not at all certain, because the symbolic (in its displacements) and the real (in its disguises) always interpenetrate. Crucially, then, the commonly accepted view that the real and the symbolic are two quite separate domains is here overturned. For part of the non-identity of the symbolic, and thus of repetition, is that it is not essentially symbolic: its non-identity has to do with the fact that it is penetrated by the real.

In developing his theory, Deleuze has in his sights the determinist readings of Freud on such subjects as: pleasure, drives, ego, repression, memory, unconscious, life and death, and so on, where a biologistic reading has often reduced these to physical forces, or chemical reactions, or both. However, the philosopher of difference looks at these phenonena within their symbolic (the 'place' of repetition) and their material base. Thus: pleasure, which is supposedly immediate, is also a 'principle', and so already foreshadows the renunciation inherent in the reality principle; the drives (as Freud's 'Project for a Scientific Psychology' [1895']¹ showed) are a form of 'bound' — or organised — energy, and contrast with the unbound energy to which they allude; the ego is dualistic, both real (linked to biological need) and symbolic (anxious to form links with others): it cannot simply be reduced to an egocentrism — even in the child; for the other (or otherness) is equally important in the formation of the self. Dominating the analysis here are the real series and the virtual (symbolic) series. Deleuze's basic point is that the two series cannot be separated from one another because of their very nature.

With regard to memory, Deleuze refers to Bergson's schema of 'perception-images' and 'memory-images'. The former are on the side of the real, the latter on the side of the virtual. Memory proper has to be understood as the interpenetration of perception (real) and memory (virtual). However, it is no more true that memory would be impossible without the real than it is that the real would be impossible without memory. Memory is a kind of purloined letter: to remember an event is to recall the perception of it and, thereby, possess it as an event; however, memory is forged in its difference from the event through what is lost from the perception; memory, in this sense, is the loss of the object. Memory is thus founded on what cannot be recalled — on what cannot be possessed. Hypothetically real objects are entirely present, while symbolic objects are characterised by a sense of loss or absence. Real objects are knowable only through the symbolic — through loss. We thus return to the interpenetration of the two series that Deleuze elaborates so painstakingly, if somewhat abstractly.

'We do not repeat because we repress, we repress because we repeat,' says Deleuze. Like the phallus which is symbolic because it is missing from its place (is displaced), no primacy can be given to the repressed by comparison to repetition. Repetition and repression interpenetrate; they confirm the bizarre, odd, enigmatic, or funny (but certainly noticeable) logic of virtuality and the symbolic.

We have learnt that the real is always disguised, always hidden, and is never missing from its place (Lacan). The virtual (symbolic) object is always circulating, and is never in its place. What, then, is the connection between disguise and displacement? The answer seems to be that the disguised object is a masked object, and a mask is an instance of a virtual object. The unconscious, on this basis, is masked, and the source of problems and enigmas which lead to questioning. The situation of Oedipus in the myth would be an exemplary instance of the interpenetration of the unconscious–real, symbolic–virtual series. In other words, it is impossible to keep the real series of the unconscious separate from the virtual series of the phallus. Something truly unconscious, however, would not be perceptible at all; something essentially symbolic would be totally vacuous – like a purloined letter which is always in the process of being stolen, and so is never read at all. Deleuze prompts us to consider that, through Freud and Lacan, writing as a whole is a virtual object. In order that this be so, however, it would have to be connected to the series of the real. The literary text, then – whether this be the myth of Oedipus, or Proust's exploration of time – is simultaneously symbolic and real, a product of the imagination and a disguised reality.

Note

1. Sigmund Freud, 'Project for a Scientific Psychology' [1895], in James Strachey, trans. and ed., *The Standard Edition of the Complete Psychological Works of Sigmund Freud* (24 vols), London: Hogarth Press and Institute of Psycho-Analysis, vol. 1, 1966, pp. 283–343.

Repetition for Itself

Biopsychical life implies a field of individuation in which differences in intensity are distributed here and there in the form of excitations. The quantitative and qualitative process of the resolution of such differences is what we call pleasure. A totality of this kind – a mobile distribution of differences and local resolutions within an intensive field – corresponds to what Freud called the Id, or at least the primary layer of the Id. The word 'id' [*Ça*] in this sense is not only a pronoun referring to some formidable unknown, but also an adverb referring to a mobile place, a 'here and there' [*Ça et là*] of excitations and resolutions. It is here that Freud's problem begins: it is a question of knowing how pleasure ceases to be a process in order to become a principle, how it ceases to be a local process in order to assume the value of an empirical principle which tends to organise biopsychical life in the Id. Obviously pleasure is pleasing, but this is not a reason for assuming a systematic value according to which it is what we seek 'in principle'. This is the primary concern of *Beyond the Pleasure Principle*: not the exceptions to this principle, but rather the determination of the conditions under which pleasure effectively becomes a principle. The Freudian answer is that excitation in the form of free difference must, in some sense, be 'invested', 'tied' or bound in such a manner that its resolution becomes systematically possible. This binding or investment of difference is what makes possible in general, not pleasure itself, but the value taken on by pleasure as a principle: we thereby pass from a state of scattered resolution to a state of integration, which constitutes the second layer of the Id and the beginnings of an organisation.

This binding is a genuine reproductive synthesis, a Habitus. An animal forms an eye for itself by causing scattered and diffuse luminous excitations to be reproduced on a privileged surface of its body. The eye binds light, it is itself a bound light. This example is enough to show the complexity of this synthesis. For there is indeed an activity of reproduction which takes as its object the difference to be bound; but there is more profoundly a passion of repetition, from which emerges a new difference (the formed eye or the seeing subject). Excitation as a difference was *already* the contraction of an elementary repetition. To the extent that the excitation becomes in turn the element of a repetition, the contracting synthesis is raised to a second power, one precisely represented by this binding or investment. Investments, bindings or integrations are passive syntheses or contemplations–contractions in the second degree. Drives are nothing more than bound excitations. At the level of each binding, an ego is formed in the Id; a passive, partial, larval, contemplative and contracting ego. The Id is populated by local egos which constitute the time peculiar to the Id, the time of the living present there where the binding integrations are carried out. The fact that these egos should be immediately narcissistic is readily explained if we consider narcissism to be not a contemplation of oneself but the fulfilment of a self-image through the contemplation of something else: the eye or the seeing ego is filled with an image of itself in contemplating the excitation that it binds. It produces itself or 'draws itself' from what it contemplates (and from what it contracts and invests by contemplation). This is why the satisfaction which flows from binding is necessarily a 'hallucinatory' satisfaction of the ego itself, even though hallucination here in no way contradicts the effectivity of the binding. In all these senses, binding represents a pure passive synthesis, a Habitus which confers on pleasure the value of being a principle of satisfaction in general. Habit underlies the organisation of the Id.

The problem of habit is therefore badly framed so long as it is subordinated to pleasure. On the one hand, the repetition involved in habit is supposed to be explained by the desire to reproduce a pleasure obtained; on the other hand, it is supposed to concern tensions which are disagreeable in themselves, but may be mastered with a view to obtaining pleasure. Clearly, both hypotheses already presuppose the pleasure principle: the *idea* of pleasure obtained and the *idea* of pleasure to be obtained act only under this principle to form the two applications, past and future. On the contrary, habit, in the form of a passive binding synthesis, precedes the pleasure principle and renders it possible. The idea of pleasure follows from it in the same way that, as we have seen, past and future follow from the synthesis of the living present. The effect of binding is to install the pleasure principle; it cannot have as its object something which presupposes that principle. When pleasure acquires the dignity of a principle, then and only then does the idea of pleasure act in accordance with that principle, in memory or in projects. Pleasure then exceeds its own instantaneity in order to assume the allure of satisfaction in general (the attempts to substitute 'objective' concepts for the instance of pleasure considered too subjective, such as those of achievement or success, only bear witness to this extension conferred by the principle, here under conditions such that the idea of pleasure is merely transposed into the mind of the experimenter). Occasionally we may empirically experience repetition as subordinated to a pleasure obtained or to be obtained, but in the order of conditions the relation is reversed. Binding synthesis cannot be explained by the intention or the effort to *master* an excitation, even though it may have that effect.[1] Once again, we must beware of confusing the activity of reproduction with the passion for repetition which underlies it. The repetition of an excitation has as its true object the elevation of the passive synthesis to a power which implies the pleasure principle along with its future and past applications. Repetition in habit or the passive synthesis of binding is thus 'beyond' the principle.

This first beyond already constitutes a kind of Transcendental Aesthetic. If this aesthetic appears more profound to us than that of Kant, it is for the following reasons: Kant defines the passive self in terms of simple receptivity, thereby assuming sensations already formed, then merely relating these to the a priori forms of their representation which are determined as space and time. In this manner, not only does he unify the passive self by ruling out the possibility of composing space step by step, not only does he deprive this passive self of all power of synthesis (synthesis being reserved for activity), but moreover he cuts the Aesthetic into two parts: the objective element of sensation guaranteed by space and the subjective element which is incarnate in pleasure and pain. The aim of the preceding analyses, on the contrary, has been to show that receptivity must be defined in terms of the formation of local selves or egos, in terms of the passive syntheses of contemplation or contraction, thereby accounting simultaneously for the possibility of experiencing sensations, the power of reproducing them and the value that pleasure assumes as a principle.

On the basis of passive synthesis, however, a twofold development appears, in two very different directions. On the one hand, an active synthesis is established upon the foundation of the passive syntheses: this consists in relating the bound excitation to an object supposed to be both real and the end of our actions (synthesis of recognition, supported by the passive synthesis of reproduction). Active synthesis is defined by the test of reality in an 'objectal' relation, and it is precisely according to the reality principle that the Ego tends to be 'activated', to be actively unified, to unite all its small composing and contemplative passive egos, and to be topologically distinguished from the Id. The passive egos were already integrations, but only local integrations, as mathematicians say; whereas the active self is an attempt at global integration. It would be completely wrong to consider the positing of reality to be an effect induced by the external world, or even the result of failures encountered by passive syntheses. On the contrary, the test of reality mobilises, drives and inspires all the activity of the ego: not so much in the form of a negative judgement, but in moving beyond the binding in the direction of a 'substantive' which serves as a support for the connection. It would also be wrong to suppose that the reality principle is opposed to the pleasure principle, limiting it and imposing renunciations upon it. The two principles are on the same track, even though one goes further than the other. The renunciations of immediate pleasure are already implicit in the role of principle which pleasure assumes, in the role that the idea of pleasure assumes in relation to a past and a future. A principle is not without duties. Reality and the renunciations that it inspires within us only populate the margins, they work only within the extensions acquired by the pleasure principle; and the reality principle determines an active synthesis only in so far as it is founded upon the preceding passive syntheses.

However, the real objects, the objects proposed as reality or as support for the connection, are not the only objects of the ego, any more than they exhaust the totality of so-called objectal relations. We can distinguish two simultaneous dimensions in such a way that there is no movement beyond the passive synthesis towards an active synthesis without the former also being extended in another direction, one in which it utilises the bound excitation in order to attain something else – albeit in a manner different from the reality principle – even while it remains a passive and contemplative synthesis. Moreover, it seems that active syntheses would never be erected on the basis of passive syntheses unless these persisted simultaneously, unless they did not develop on their own account at the same time, finding new formulae at once both dissymmetrical and complementary with the activity. A child who begins to walk does not only bind excitations in a passive synthesis, even supposing that these were endogenous excitations born of its own movements. No one ever walked endogenously. On the one hand, the child goes beyond the bound excitations towards the supposition or the intentionality of an object, such as the mother, as the goal of an effort, the end to be actively reached 'in reality' and in relation to which success and failure may be measured. But *on the other hand and at the same time*, the child constructs for itself another object, a quite different kind of object which is a *virtual* object or centre and which then governs and compensates for the progresses and failures of its real activity: it puts several fingers in its mouth, wraps the other arm around this virtual centre, and appraises the whole situation from the point of view of this virtual mother. The fact that the child's glance may be directed at the real mother and that the virtual object may be the goal of an apparent activity (for example, sucking) may inspire an erroneous judgement on the part of the observer. Sucking occurs only in order to provide a virtual object to contemplate in the context of extending the passive synthesis; conversely, the real mother is contemplated only in order to provide a goal for the activity, and a criterion by which to evaluate the activity, in the context of an active synthesis. There is no need to speak of an egocentrism on the part of the child. The child who begins to handle a book by imitation, without being able to read, invariably holds it back to front. It is as though the book were being held out to the other, the real end of the activity, even though the child seizing the book back to front is the virtual centre of its passion, of its own extended contemplation. Widely diverse phenomena, such as left-handedness, mirror-writing, certain forms of stuttering, certain stereotypes, may be explained on the basis of this duality of centres in the infant world. What is important, however, is that neither one of these two centres is the ego. The same lack of understanding leads to the interpretation of the child's behaviour as stemming from a supposed 'egocentrism' and to the interpretation of infantile narcissism as excluding the contemplation of other things. In fact the child is constructed within a double series: on the basis of the passive synthesis of connection and on the basis of the bound excitations. Both series are objectal: one series comprises real objects which serve as correlates of active synthesis; the other virtual objects which serve as correlates of an extension of passive synthesis. The extended passive ego fulfils itself with a narcissistic image in contemplating the virtual centres. One series would not exist without the other, yet they do not resemble one another. For this reason, Henri Maldiney is correct to say, in analysing children's movement, that the infantile world is in no way circular or egocentric but elliptical; that it has two centres and that these differ in kind, both nevertheless being objective or objectal.[2] In virtue of their dissimilarity, perhaps a crossing, a twist, a helix or a figure 8 is even formed between the two centres. What, then, would be the ego, where would it be, given its topological distinction from the Id, if not at the crossing of the 8, at the point of connection between these two intersecting asymmetrical circles, the circle of real objects and that of the virtual objects or centres?

The differentiation between self-preservative and sexual drives must be related to this duality between two correlative series. The self-preservative drives are, after all, inseparable from the constitution of the reality principle, from the foundation of active synthesis and the active global ego, and from the relations with the real object perceived as satisfying or menacing. The sexual drives are no less inseparable from the constitution of virtual centres, or the extension of passive syntheses and the passive egos which correspond to them: in pre-genital sexuality, actions are always observations or contemplations, but it is always the virtual which is contemplated or observed. The fact that the two series cannot exist without each other indicates not only that they are complementary, but that by virtue of their dissimilarity and their difference in kind they borrow from and feed into one another. We see both that the virtuals are deducted from the series of reals and that they are incorporated in the series of reals. This derivation implies, first, an isolation or suspension which freezes the real in order to extract a pose, an aspect or a part. This isolation, however, is qualitative: it does not consist simply in subtracting a part of the real object, since the subtracted part acquires a new nature in functioning as a virtual object. The virtual object is a *partial* object – not simply because it lacks a part which remains in the real, but in itself and for itself because it is cleaved or doubled into two virtual parts, one of which is always missing from the other. In short, the virtual is never subject to the global character which affects real objects. It is – not only by its origin but by its own nature – a fragment, a shred or a remainder. It lacks its own identity. The good and the bad mother – or, in terms of the paternal duality, the serious and the playful father – are not two partial objects but the same object in so far as it has lost its identity in the double. Whereas active synthesis points beyond passive synthesis towards global integrations and the supposition of identical totalisable objects, passive synthesis, as it develops, points beyond itself towards the contemplation of partial objects which remain non-totalisable. These partial or virtual objects are encountered under various names, such as Melanie Klein's good *and* bad object, and the 'transitional' object, the fetish-object, and above all Lacan's object *a*. Freud definitively showed how pregenital sexuality consisted of partial drives deducted from the exercise of self-preservative drives; such a derivation presupposes the constitution of objects which are themselves partial and which function as so many virtual centres, so many poles always doubled with sexuality.

Conversely, these virtual objects are incorporated in the real objects. In this sense they can correspond to parts of the subject's body, to another person, or even to very special objects such as toys or fetishes. This incorporation is in no way an identification, or even an introjection, since it exceeds the limits of the subject. Far from opposing itself to the process of isolation, it complements it. Whatever the reality in which the virtual object is incorporated, it does not become integrated: it remains planted or stuck there, and does not find in the real object the half which completes it, but rather testifies to the other virtual half which the real continues to lack. When Melanie Klein shows how many virtual objects the maternal body contains, it must not be thought that it totalises or englobes them, or possesses them, but rather that they are planted in it like trees from another world, like Gogol's nose or Deucalion's stones. Incorporation nevertheless remains the condition under which the self-preservative drives and the active synthesis which corresponds to them can – in turn, and with their own resources – fold sexuality back on to the series of real objects and, from without, integrate it into the domain ruled by the reality principle.

Virtual objects belong essentially to the past. In *Matter and Memory*, Bergson proposed the schema of a world with two centres, one real and the other virtual, from which emanate on the one hand a series of 'perception-images', and on the other a series of 'memory-images', the two series collaborating in an endless circuit. The virtual object is not a former present, since the quality of the present and the modality of its passing here affect exclusively the series of the real as this is constituted by active synthesis. However, the pure past as it was defined above does qualify the virtual object; that is, the past as contemporaneous with its own present, as pre-existing the passing present and as that which causes the present to pass. Virtual objects are shreds of pure past. It is from the height of my contemplation of virtual centres that I am present at and preside over my passing present, along with the succession of real objects in which those centres are incorporated. The reason for this may be found in the nature of these centres. Although it is deducted from the present real object, the virtual object differs from it in kind: not only does it lack something in relation to the real object from which it is subtracted, it lacks something in itself, since it is always half of itself, the other half being different as well as absent. This absence, as we shall see, is the opposite of a negative. Eternal half of itself, it is where it is only on condition that it is not where it should be. It is where we find it only on condition that we search for it where it is not. It is at once not possessed by those who have it and had by those who do not possess it. *It is always a 'was'.* In this sense, Lacan's pages assimilating the virtual object to Edgar Allan Poe's purloined letter seem to us exemplary. Lacan shows that real objects are subjected to the law of being *or* not being somewhere, by virtue of the reality principle; whereas virtual objects, by contrast, have the property of being *and* not being where they are, wherever they go:

> what is hidden is never but what is *missing from its place*, as the call slip puts it when speaking of a volume lost in the library. And even if the book be on an adjacent shelf or in the next slot, it would be hidden there, however visibly it may appear. For it can *literally* be said that something is missing from its place only of

what can change it: the symbolic. For the real, whatever upheaval we subject it to, is always in its place; it carries it glued to its heel, ignorant of what might exile it from it.[3]

The passing present which bears itself away has never been better opposed to the pure past which perpetually differs from itself and whose universal mobility and universal ubiquity cause the present to pass. The virtual object is never past in relation to a new present, any more than it is past in relation to a present which it was. It is past as the contemporary of the present which it is, in a frozen present; as though lacking, on the one hand, the part which, on the other hand, it is at the same time; as though displaced while still in place. This is why virtual objects exist only as fragments of themselves: they are found only as lost; they exist only as recovered. Loss or forgetting here are not determinations which must be overcome; rather, they refer to the objective nature of that which we recover, as lost, at the heart of forgetting. Contemporaneous with itself as present, being itself its own past, pre-existing every present which passes in the real series, the virtual object belongs to the pure past. It is pure fragment and fragment of itself. As in a physical experiment, however, the incorporation of this pure fragment changes the quality and causes the present to pass into the series of real objects.

This is the link between Eros and Mnemosyne. Eros tears virtual objects out of the pure past and gives them to us in order that they may be lived. Lacan discovers the 'phallus', understood as a symbolic organ, behind all these virtual or partial objects. He is able to give this extension to the concept of the phallus (such that it subsumes all the virtual objects) because the concept effectively comprises the preceding characteristics: testifying to its own absence and to itself as past, being essentially displaced in relation to itself, being found only as lost, being possessed of an always fragmentary identity which loses its identity in the double; since it may be searched for and discovered only on the side of the mother, and since it has the paradoxical property of changing its place, not being possessed by those who have a 'penis', yet being *possessed* by those who do not have one, as the theme of castration shows. The symbolic phallus signifies no less the erotic mode of the pure past than the immemorial of sexuality. The symbol is the always-displaced fragment, standing for a past which was never present: the object = x. But what is the meaning of this idea that virtual objects refer, in the last instance, to an element which is itself symbolic?

Undoubtedly, the whole psychoanalytic – or, in other words, amorous – game of repetition is at issue here. The question is whether repetition may be understood as operating from one present to another in the real series, from a present to a former present. In this case, the former present would play the role of a complex point, like an ultimate or original term which would remain in place and exercise a power of attraction: it would be the one which provides the *thing* that is to be repeated, the one which conditions the whole process of repetition, and in this sense would remain independent of it. The concepts of fixation and regression, along with trauma and the primal scene, express this first element. As a consequence, repetition would in principle conform to the model of a material, bare and brute repetition, understood as the repetition of the same: the idea of an 'automatism' in this context expresses the modality of a fixated drive, or, rather, of repetition conditioned by fixation or regression. And if this material model is in fact perturbed and covered over with all kinds of disguises, with a thousand and one forms of disguise or displacement, then these are only secondary even if they are necessary: the distortion in the majority of cases does not belong to the fixation, or even to the repetition, but is added or superimposed on to these; it necessarily clothes them, but from without, and may be explained by the repression which translates the conflict (without the repetition) between the repeater and what is repeated. The three very different concepts of fixation, automatic repetition and repression testify to this distribution between a supposed last or first term in relation to repetition, a repetition which is supposed to be bare underneath the disguises which cover it, and the disguises which are necessarily added by the force of a conflict. Even – and above all – the Freudian conception of the death instinct, understood as a return to inanimate matter, remains inseparable from the positing of an ultimate term, the model of a material and bare repetition and the conflictual dualism between life and death. It matters little whether or not the former present acts in its objective reality, or, rather, in the form in which it was lived or imagined. For imagination intervenes here only in order to gather up the resonances and ensure the disguises between the two presents in the series of the real as lived reality. Imagination gathers the traces of the former present and models the new present upon the old. The traditional theory of the compulsion to repeat in psychoanalysis remains essentially realist, materialist and subjective or individualist. It is realist because everything 'happens' between presents. It is materialist because the model of a brute, automatic repetition is presupposed. It is individualist, subjective, solipsistic or monadic because both the former present – in other words, the repeated or disguised element – and the new present – in other words, the present terms of the disguised repetition – are considered to be only the conscious or unconscious, latent or manifest, repressed or repressing *representations* of the subject. The whole theory of repetition is thereby subordinated to the requirements of simple representation, from the standpoint of its realism, materialism and subjectivism. Repetition is subjected to a principle of identity in the former present and a rule of resemblance in the present one. Nor do we believe that the Freudian discovery of a phylogenesis or the Jungian discovery of archetypes can correct the weaknesses of such a conception. Even if the rights of the imaginary as a whole are opposed to the facts of reality, it remains a question of a 'psychic' reality considered to be ultimate or original; even if we oppose spirit and matter, it remains a question of a bare, uncovered spirit resting upon its own identity and supported by its derived analogies; even if we oppose a collective or cosmic unconscious to the individual unconscious, the former can act only through its power to inspire representations in a solipsistic subject, whether this be the subject of a culture or a world.

The difficulties of conceptualising the process of repetition have often been emphasised. Consider the two presents, the two scenes of the two events (infantile and adult) in their reality, separated by time: how can the former present act at a distance upon the present one? How can it provide a model for it, when all its effectiveness is retrospectively received from the

later present? Furthermore, if we invoke the indispensable imaginary operations required to fill the temporal space, how could these operations fail
ultimately to absorb the entire reality of the two presents, leaving the repeti-
tition to subsist only as the illusion of a solipsistic subject? However, while
it may seem that the two presents are successive, at a variable distance apart
in the series of reals, in fact they form, rather, *two real series which coexist
in relation to a virtual object of another kind*, one which constantly circulates and is displaced in them (even if the characters, the subjects which give
rise to the positions, the terms and the relations of each series, remain, for
their part, temporally distinct). Repetition is constituted not from one present to another, but between the two coexistent series that these presents
form in function of the virtual object (object = *x*). It is because this object
constantly circulates, always displaced in relation to itself, that it determines
transformations of terms and modifications of imaginary relations within the
two real series in which it appears, and therefore between the two presents.
The displacement of the virtual object is not, therefore, one disguise among
others, but the principle from which, in reality, repetition follows in the form
of disguised repetition. Repetition is constituted only with and through the
disguises which affect the terms and relations of the real series, but it is so
because it depends upon the virtual object as an immanent instance which
operates above all by *displacement*. In consequence, we cannot suppose that
disguise may be explained by repression. On the contrary, it is because repetition is necessarily disguised, by virtue of the characteristic displacement
of its determinant principle, that repression occurs in the form of a consequence in regard to the representation of presents. Freud, no doubt, was
aware of this, since he did search for a more profound instance than that of
repression, even though he conceived of it in similar terms as a so-called
'primary' repression. We do not repeat because we repress, we repress
because we repeat. Moreover – which amounts to the same thing – we do
not disguise because we repress, we repress because we disguise, and we disguise by virtue of the determinant centre of repetition. Repetition is no more
secondary in relation to a supposed ultimate or originary fixed term than
disguise is secondary in relation to repetition. For if the two presents, the
former and the present one, form two series which coexist in the function
of the virtual object which is displaced in them and in relation to itself, *neither of these two series can any longer be designated as the original or the
derived*. They put a variety of terms and subjects into play in a complex
intersubjectivity in which each subject owes its role and function in the series
to the timeless position that it occupies in relation to the virtual object.[4] As
for this object itself, it can no longer be treated as an ultimate or original
term: this would be to assign it a fixed place and an identity repugnant to
its whole nature. If it can be 'identified' with the phallus, this is only to the
extent that the latter, in Lacan's terms, is always missing from its place, from
its own identity and from its representation. In short, there is no ultimate
term – our loves do not refer back to the mother; it is simply that the mother
occupies a certain place in relation to the virtual object in the series which
constitutes our present, a place which is necessarily filled by another character in the series which constitutes the present of another subjectivity,
always taking into account the displacements of that object = *x*. In some-

what the same manner, by loving his mother the hero of *In Search of Lost Time* repeats Swann's love for Odette. The parental characters are not the ultimate terms of individual subjecthood but the middle terms of an inter-subjectivity, forms of communication and disguise from one series to another for different subjects, to the extent that these forms are determined by the displacement of the virtual object. Behind the masks, therefore, are further masks, and even the most hidden is still a hiding place, and so on to infinity. The only illusion is that of unmasking something or someone. The symbolic organ of repetition, the phallus, is no less a mask than it is itself hidden. For the mask has two senses. 'Give me, please, give me ... what then? another mask.' In the first place, the mask means the *disguise* which has an imaginary effect on the terms and relations of the two real series which properly coexist. More profoundly, however, it signifies the *displacement* which essentially affects the virtual symbolic object, both in its series and in the real series in which it endlessly circulates. (Thus, the displacement which makes the eyes of the bearer correspond with the mouth of the mask, or shows the face of the bearer only as a headless body, allowing that a head may none the less, in turn, appear upon that body.)

Repetition is thus in essence symbolic, spiritual, and intersubjective or monadological. A final consequence follows with regard to the nature of the unconscious. The phenomena of the unconscious cannot be understood in the overly simple form of opposition or conflict. For Freud, it is not only the theory of repression but the dualism in the theory of drives which encourages the primacy of a conflictual model. However, the conflicts are the result of more subtle differential mechanisms (displacements and disguises). And if the *forces* naturally enter into relations of opposition, this is on the basis of differential elements which express a more profound instance. The negative, under its double aspect of limitation and opposition, seemed to us in general secondary in relation to the instance of problems and questions: in other words, the negative expresses only within consciousness the shadow of fundamentally unconscious questions and problems, and owes its apparent power to the inevitable place of the 'false' in the natural positing of these problems and questions. It is true that the unconscious desires, and only desires. However, just as desire finds the principle of its difference from need in the virtual object, so it appears neither as a power of negation nor as an element of an opposition, but rather as a questioning, problematising and searching force which operates in a different domain from that of desire and satisfaction. Questions and problems are not speculative acts, and as such completely provisional and indicative of the momentary ignorance of an empirical subject. On the contrary, they are the living acts of the unconscious, investing special objectivities and destined to survive in the provisional and partial state characteristic of answers and solutions. The problems 'correspond' to the reciprocal disguise of the terms and relations which constitute the reality series. The questions or sources of problems correspond to the displacement of the virtual object which causes the series to develop. The phallus as virtual object is always located by enigmas and riddles in a place where it is not, because it is indistinguishable from the space in which it is displaced. Even Oedipus's conflicts depend upon the Sphinx's question. Birth and death, and the difference between the sexes, are the complex themes of problems before they are the simple terms of an opposition. (Before the opposition between the sexes, determined by the possession or lack of the penis, there is the 'question' of the phallus which determines the differential position of sexed characters in each series.) It may be that there is necessarily something mad in every question and every problem, as there is in their transcendence in relation to answers, in their insistence through solutions and the manner in which they maintain their own openness.[5]

It is enough that the question be posed with sufficient force, as it is by Dostoevsky or Shevstov, in order to quell rather than incite any response. It is here that it discovers its properly ontological import, the (non)-being of the question which cannot be reduced to the non-being of the negative. There are no ultimate or original responses or solutions, there are only problem–questions, in the guise of a mask behind every mask and a displacement behind every place. It would be naïve to think that the problems of life and death, love and the difference between the sexes are amenable to their scientific solutions and positings, even though such positings and solutions necessarily arise without warning, even though they must necessarily emerge at a certain moment in the unfolding process of the development of these problems. The problems concern the eternal disguise; questions, the eternal displacement. Neuropaths and psychopaths perhaps explore this original ultimate ground, at the cost of their suffering, the former asking *how to shift the problem*, the latter *where to pose the question*. Precisely their suffering, their pathos, is the only response to a question which in itself is endlessly shifted, to a problem which in itself is endlessly disguised. It is not what they say or what they think but their life which is exemplary, and is larger than they are. They bear witness to that transcendence, and to the most extraordinary play of the true and the false which occurs not at the level of answers and solutions but at the level of the problems themselves, in the questions themselves – in other words, in conditions under which the false becomes the mode of exploration of the true, the very space of its essential disguises or its fundamental displacement: the *pseudos* here becomes the pathos of the True. The power of the questions always comes from somewhere other than the answers, and benefits from a free depth which cannot be resolved. The insistence, the transcendence and the ontological bearing of questions and problems is expressed not in the form of the finality of a sufficient reason (to what end? why?) but in the discrete form of difference and repetition: what difference is there? and 'repeat a little'. There is never any difference – not because it comes down to the same in the answer, but because it is never anywhere but in the question, and in the repetition of the question, which ensures its movement and its disguise. Problems and questions thus belong to the unconscious but as a result the unconscious is differential and iterative by nature; it is serial, problematic and questioning. To ask whether the unconscious is ultimately oppositional or differential, an unconscious of great forces in conflict or one of little elements in series, one of opposing great representations or differentiated little perceptions, appears to resuscitate earlier hesitations and earlier polemics between the Leibnizian tradition and the Kantian tradition. However, if Freud was completely on the side of a Hegelian post-Kantianism – in other words, of an unconscious of opposition – why did he pay so much

homage to the Leibnizian Fechner and to his 'symptomologist's' differential
finesse? In truth, it is not at all a question of knowing whether the unconscious implies a non-being of logical limitation or a non-being of real opposition. Both these two forms of non-being are, in any case, figures of the
negative. The unconscious is neither an unconscious of degradation nor an
unconscious of contradiction; it involves neither limitation nor opposition;
it concerns, rather, problems and questions in their difference in kind from
answers–solutions: the (non-)being of the problematic which rejects equally
the two forms of negative non-being which govern only propositions of consciousness. The celebrated phrase 'the unconscious knows no negative' must
be taken literally. Partial objects are the elements of little perceptions. The
unconscious is differential, involving little perceptions, and as such it is different in kind from consciousness. It concerns problems and questions which
can never be reduced to the great oppositions or the overall effects that are
felt in consciousness (we shall see that Leibnizian theory already indicated
this path).

We have thus encountered a second beyond the pleasure principle, a second synthesis of time in the unconscious itself. The first passive synthesis, that
of Habitus, presented repetition as a binding, in the constantly renewed form
of a living present. It ensured the foundation of the pleasure principle in two
complementary senses, since it led both to the general value of pleasure as
an instance to which psychic life was henceforth subordinated in the Id, and
to the particular hallucinatory satisfaction which filled each passive ego with
a narcissistic image of itself. The second synthesis, that of Eros–Mnemosyne,
posits repetition as *displacement* and *disguise*, and functions as the ground of
the pleasure principle: in effect, it is then a question of knowing how this
principle applies to what it governs, under what conditions of use and at the
cost of what limitations and what extensions. The answer is given in two directions: one is that of a general law of reality, according to which the first synthesis points beyond itself in the direction of an active synthesis and ego; in
the other direction, by contrast, the first synthesis is extended in the form of
a second passive synthesis which gathers up the particular narcissistic satisfaction and relates it to the contemplation of virtual objects. The pleasure
principle here receives new conditions, as much in regard to a produced reality as to a constituted sexuality. Drives, which are defined only as bound excitation, now appear in differenciated form: as self-preservative drives following
the active line of reality, as sexual drives in this new passive extension. If the
first passive synthesis constitutes an 'aesthetic', the second may properly be
defined as the equivalent of an 'analytic'. If the first passive synthesis concerns the present, the second concerns the past. If the first makes use of repetition in order to draw off a difference, the second passive synthesis includes
difference at the heart of repetition, since the two figures of difference, movement and disguise – the displacement which symbolically affects the virtual
object and the disguises which affect, in imaginary fashion, the real objects
in which it is incorporated – have become the elements of repetition itself.
This is why Freud experienced some difficulty in distributing difference and
repetition from the point of view of Eros, to the extent that he maintains the
opposition between these two factors and understands repetition on the material model of cancelled difference, while defining Eros by the introduction,

or even the production, of new differences.[6] In fact, Eros's force of repetition derives directly from a power of difference – one which Eros borrows from Mnemosyne, one which affects virtual objects like so many fragments of a pure past. As Janet in some ways suspected, it is not amnesia but rather a hypernesia which explains the role of erotic repetition and its combination with difference. The 'never-seen' which characterises an always displaced and disguised object is immersed in the 'already-seen' of the pure past in general, from which that object is extracted. We do not know *when* or *where* we have seen it, in accordance with the objective nature of the problematic; and ultimately, it is only the strange which is familiar and only difference which is repeated.

It is true that the synthesis of Eros and Mnemosyne still suffers from an ambiguity. In relation to the first passive synthesis of Habitus, the series of the real (or the presents which pass in the real) and the series of the virtual (or of a past which differs in kind from any present) form two divergent circular lines, two circles or even two arcs of the same circle. But in relation to the object $= x$ taken as the immanent limit of the series of virtuals, as the principle of the second passive synthesis, these are the successive presents of the reality which now forms coexistent series, circles or even arcs of the same circle. It is inevitable that the two references become confused, the pure past assuming thereby the status of a former present, albeit mythical, and reconstituting the illusion it was supposed to denounce, resuscitating the illusion of an original and a derived, of an identity in the origin and a resemblance in the derived. Moreover, Eros leads its life as a cycle, or as an element within a cycle, where the opposing element can only be Thanatos at the base of memory, the two combining like love and hate, construction and destruction, attraction and repulsion. Always the same ambiguity on the part of the ground: to represent itself in the circle that it imposes on what it grounds, to return as an element in the circuit of representation that it determines in principle.

The essentially lost character of virtual objects and the essentially disguised character of real objects are powerful motivations of narcissism. However, it is by interiorising the difference between the two lines and by experiencing itself as perpetually displaced in the one, perpetually disguised in the other, that the libido returns or flows back into the ego and the passive ego becomes entirely narcissistic. The narcissistic ego is inseparable not only from a constitutive wound but from the disguises and displacements which are woven from one side to the other, and constitute its modification. The ego is a mask for other masks, a disguise under other disguises. Indistinguishable from its own clowns, it walks with a limp on one green and one red leg. Nevertheless, the importance of the reorganisation which takes place at this level, in opposition to the preceding stage of the second synthesis, cannot be overstated. For while the passive ego becomes narcissistic, the activity must be *thought*. This can occur only in the form of an affection, in the form of the very modification that the narcissistic ego passively *experiences* on its own account. Thereafter, the narcissistic ego is related to the form of an I which operates upon it as an 'Other'. This active but fractured I is not only the basis of the superego but the correlate of the passive and wounded narcissistic ego, thereby forming a complex whole that

Paul Ricœur aptly named an 'aborted cogito'.[7] Moreover, there is only the aborted Cogito, only the larval subject. We saw above that the fracture of the I was no more than the pure and empty form of time, separated from its content. The narcissistic ego indeed appears in time, but does not constitute a temporal content: the narcissistic libido, the reflux of the libido into the ego, abstracts from all content. The narcissistic ego is, rather, the phenomenon which corresponds to the empty form of time without filling it, the spatial phenomenon of that form in general (it is this phenomenon of space which is presented in a different manner in neurotic castration and psychotic fragmentation). The form of time in the I determines an order, a whole and a series. The formal static order of before, during and after marks the division of the narcissistic ego in time, or the conditions of its contemplation. The whole of time is gathered in the image of the formidable action as this is simultaneously presented, forbidden and predicted by the superego: the action = x. The temporal series designates the confrontation of the divided narcissistic ego with the whole of time or the image of the action. The narcissistic ego repeats once in the form of the before or lack, in the form of the *Id* (this action is too big for me); a second time in the form of an infinite becoming equal appropriate to the *ego ideal*; a third time in the form of the after which realises the prediction of the *superego* (the id and the ego, the condition and the agent, will themselves be annihilated)! For the practical law itself signifies nothing other than that empty form of time.

When the narcissistic ego takes the place of the virtual and real objects, when it assumes the displacement of the former and the disguise of the latter, it does not replace one content of time with another. On the contrary, we enter into the third synthesis. It is as though time had abandoned all possible mnemic content, and in so doing had broken the circle into which it was lead by Eros. It is as though it had unrolled, straightened itself and assumed the ultimate shape of the labyrinth, the straight-line labyrinth which is, as Borges says, 'invisible, incessant'. Time empty and out of joint, with its rigorous formal and static order, its crushing unity and its irreversible series, is precisely the death instinct. The death instinct does not enter into a cycle with Eros, but testifies to a completely different synthesis. It is by no means the complement or antagonist of Eros, nor in any sense symmetrical with him. The correlation between Eros and Mnemosyne is replaced by that between a narcissistic ego without memory, a great amnesiac, and a death instinct desexualised and without love. The narcissistic ego has no more than a dead body, having lost the body at the same time as the objects. It is by means of the death instinct that it is reflected in the ego ideal and has a presentiment of its end in the superego, as though in two fragments of the fractured I. It is this relation between the narcissistic ego and the death instinct that Freud indicated so profoundly in saying that there is no reflux of the libido on to the ego without it becoming *desexualised* and forming a neutral *displaceable* energy, essentially capable of serving Thanatos.[8] Why, however, did Freud thus propose a death instinct existing prior to that desexualised energy, independent of it in principle? Undoubtedly for two reasons – one relating to the persistence of a dualistic and conflictual model which inspired the entire theory of drives; the other to the material model which presided over the theory of repetition. That is why Freud insisted on the one hand on the difference in kind between Eros and Thanatos, according to which Thanatos should be addressed in his own terms in opposition to Eros; and on the other hand on a difference in rhythm and amplitude, as though Thanatos had returned to the state of inanimate matter, thereby becoming identified with that power of bare or brute repetition that the vital differences arising from Eros are supposed only to cover or contradict. In any case, determined as the qualitative and quantitative return of the living to inanimate matter, death has only an extrinsic, scientific and objective definition. Freud strangely refused any other dimension to death, any prototype or any presentation of death in the unconscious, even though he conceded the existence of such prototypes for birth and castration.[9] This reduction of death to an objective determination of matter displays the same prejudice according to which repetition must find its ultimate principle in an undifferentiated material model, beyond the displacements and disguises of a secondary or opposed difference. In truth, the structure of the unconscious is not conflictual, oppositional or contradictory, but questioning and problematising. Nor is repetition a bare and brute power behind the disguises, the latter affecting it only secondarily, like so many variations: on the contrary, it is woven from disguise and displacement, without any existence apart from these constitutive elements. Death does not appear in the objective model of an indifferent inanimate matter to which the living would 'return'; it is present in the living in the form of a subjective and differentiated experience endowed with its prototype. It is not a material state; on the contrary, having renounced all matter, it corresponds to a pure form – the empty form of time. (As a means of filling time, it makes no difference whether repetition is subordinated to the extrinsic identity of a dead matter or to the intrinsic identity of an immortal soul.) For death cannot be reduced to negation, neither to the negative opposition nor to the negative of limitation. It is neither the limitation imposed by matter upon mortal life, nor the opposition between matter and immortal life, which furnishes death with its prototype. Death is, rather, the last form of the problematic, the source of problems and questions, the sign of their persistence over and above every response, the 'Where?' and 'When?' which designate this (non-)being where every affirmation is nourished.

Blanchot rightly suggests that death has two aspects. One is personal, concerning the I or the ego, something which I can confront in a struggle or meet at a limit, or in any case encounter in a present which causes everything to pass. The other is strangely impersonal, with no relation to 'me', neither present nor past but always coming, the source of an incessant multiple adventure in a persistent question:

> It is the fact of dying that includes a radical reversal, through which the death that was the extreme form of my power not only becomes what loosens my hold upon myself by casting me out of my power to begin and even to finish, but also becomes that which is without any relation to me, without power over me – that which is stripped of all possibility – the unreality of the indefinite. I cannot represent this reversal to myself, I cannot even conceive of it as definitive. It is not the irreversible step beyond which there would be no return, for it is that which is not accomplished, the interminable and the incessant.... It is inevitable but inaccessible death; it is the abyss of the present, time without a present, with which

I have no relationships; it is that toward which I cannot go forth, for in it *I* do not die, I have fallen from the power to die. In it *they* die; they do not cease, and they do not finish dying ... not the term, but the interminable, not proper but featureless death, and not true death but, as Kafka says, 'the sneer of its capital error'.[10]

In confronting these two aspects, it is apparent that even suicide does not make them coincide with one another or become equivalent. The first signifies the personal disappearance of the person, the annihilation of *this* difference represented by the I or the ego. This is a difference which existed only in order to die, and the disappearance of which can be objectively represented by a return to inanimate matter, as though calculated by a kind of entropy. Despite appearances, this death always comes from without, even at the moment when it constitutes the most personal possibility, and from the past, even at the moment when it is most present. The other death, however, the other face or aspect of death, refers to the state of free differences when they are no longer subject to the form imposed upon them by an I or an ego, when they assume a shape which excludes *my* own coherence no less than that of any identity whatsoever. There is always a 'one dies' more profound than 'I die', and it is not only the gods who die endlessly and in a variety of ways; as though there appeared worlds in which the individual was no longer imprisoned within the personal form of the I and the ego, nor the singular imprisoned within the limits of the individual – in short, the insubordinate multiple, which cannot be 'recognised' in the first aspect. The Freudian conception refers to this first aspect, and for that reason fails to discover the death instinct, along with the corresponding experience and prototype.

We see no reason to propose a death instinct which would be distinguishable from Eros, either by a difference in kind between two forces, or by a difference in rhythm or amplitude between two movements. In both cases, the difference would already be given and Thanatos would be independent as a result. It seems to us, on the contrary, that Thanatos is completely indistinguishable from the desexualisation of Eros, with the resultant formation of that neutral and displaceable energy of which Freud speaks. This energy does not serve Thanatos, it constitutes him: there is no analytic difference between Eros and Thanatos, no already-given difference such that the two would be combined or made to alternate within the same 'synthesis'. It is not that the difference is any less. On the contrary, being synthetic, it is greater precisely because Thanatos stands for a synthesis of time quite unlike that of Eros; all the more exclusive because it is drawn from him, constructed upon his remains. It is all in the same movement that there is a reflux of Eros on to the ego, that the ego takes upon itself the disguises and displacements which characterise the objects in order to construct its own fatal affection, that the libido loses all mnemic content and Time loses its circular shape in order to assume a merciless and straight form, and that the death instinct appears, indistinguishable from that pure form, the desexualised energy *of* that narcissistic libido. The complementarity between the narcissistic libido and the death instinct defines the third synthesis as much as Eros and Mnemosyne defined the second. Moreover, when Freud says that perhaps the process of *thought* in general should be attached to that desexualised energy which is the correlative of the libido become narcissistic, we should understand that, contrary to the old dilemma, it is no longer a question of knowing whether thought is innate or acquired. It is neither innate nor acquired but genital – *in other words*, desexualised and drawn from that reflux which opens us on to empty time. In order to indicate this genesis of thought in an always fractured I, Artaud said: 'I am an innate genital', meaning equally thereby a 'desexualised acquisition'. It is not a question of acquiring thought, nor of exercising it as though it were innate, but of engendering the act of thinking within thought itself, perhaps under the influence of a violence which causes the reflux of libido on to the narcissistic ego, and in the same movement both extracting Thanatos from Eros and abstracting time from all content in order to separate out the pure form. There is an experience of death which corresponds to this third synthesis.

Freud supposes the unconscious to be ignorant of three important things: Death, Time and No. Yet it is a question only of time, death and no in the unconscious. Does this mean merely that they are acted [*agis*] without being represented? Furthermore, the unconscious is ignorant of no because it lives off the (non-)being of problems and questions, rather than the non-being of the negative which affects only consciousness and its representations. It is ignorant of death because every representation of death concerns its inadequate aspect, whereas the unconscious discovers and seizes upon the other side, the other face. It is ignorant of time because it is never subordinated to the empirical contents of a present which passes in representation, but rather carries out the passive syntheses of an original time. *It is these three syntheses which must be understood as constitutive of the unconscious.* They correspond to the figures of repetition which appear in the work of a great novelist: the binding, the ever renewed fine cord; the ever displaced stain on the wall; the ever erased eraser. The repetition–binding, the repetition–stain, the repetition–eraser: the three beyonds of the pleasure principle. The first synthesis expresses the foundation of time upon the basis of a living present, a foundation which endows pleasure with its value as a general empirical principle to which is subject the content of the psychic life in the Id. The second synthesis expresses the manner in which time is grounded in a pure past, a ground which conditions the application of the pleasure principle to the contents of the Ego. The third synthesis, however, refers to the absence of ground into which we are precipitated by the ground itself: Thanatos appears in third place as this groundlessness, beyond the ground of Eros and the foundation of Habitus. He therefore has a disturbing kind of relation with the pleasure principle which is often expressed in the unfathomable paradoxes of a pleasure linked to pain (when in fact it is a question of something else altogether: the desexualisation which operates in this third synthesis, in so far as it inhibits the application of the pleasure principle as the prior directive idea in order then to proceed to a resexualisation in which pleasure is invested only in a pure, cold, apathetic and frozen thought, as we see in the cases of sadism and masochism). In one sense the third synthesis unites all the dimensions of time, past, present and future, and causes them to be played out in the pure form. In another sense it involves their reorganisation, since the past is treated in function of a totality of time as the condition by default which characterises the Id, while the present is defined by the metamorphosis of the agent in the ego ideal. In a third sense, finally, the ultimate synthesis concerns only the future, since it announces in the superego the destruction of the Id and the ego, of the past as well as the present, of the condition and the agent. At this extreme point the straight line of time forms a circle again, a singularly tortuous one; or alternatively, the death instinct reveals an unconditional truth hidden in its 'other' face – namely, the eternal return in so far as this does not cause everything to come back but, on the contrary, affects a world which has rid itself of the default of the condition and the equality of the agent in order to affirm only the excessive and the unequal, the interminable and the incessant, the formless as the product of the most extreme formality. This is how the story of time ends: by undoing its too-well-centred natural or physical circle and forming a straight line which then, led by its own length, reconstitutes an eternally decentred circle.

The eternal return is a force of affirmation, but it affirms everything of the multiple, everything of the different, everything of chance *except* what subordinates them to the One, to the Same, to necessity, everything *except* the One, the Same and the Necessary. It is said that the One subjugated the multiple once and for all. But is this not the face of death? And does not the other face cause to die in turn, once and for all, everything which operates once and for all? If there is an essential relation between eternal return and death, it is because it promises and implies 'once and for all' the death of that which is one. If there is an essential relation with the future, it is because the future is the deployment and explication of the multiple, of the different and of the fortuitous, for themselves and 'for all times'. Repetition in the eternal return excludes two determinations: the Same or the identity of a subordinating concept, and the negative of the condition which would relate the repeated to the same, and thereby ensure the subordination. Repetition in the eternal return excludes both the becoming equal or the becoming similar in the concept, and being conditioned by lack of such a becoming. It concerns instead excessive systems which link the different with the different, the multiple with the multiple, the fortuitous with the fortuitous, in a complex of affirmations always coextensive with the questions posed and the decisions taken. It is claimed that man does not know how to *play*: this is because, even when he is given a situation of chance or multiplicity, he understands his affirmations as destined to impose limits upon it, his decisions as destined to ward off its effects, his reproductions as destined to bring about the return of the same, given a winning hypothesis. This is precisely a losing game, one in which we risk losing as much as winning because we do not affirm the *all* of chance: the pre-established character of the rule which fragments has as its correlate the condition by default in the player, who never knows which fragment will emerge. The system of the future, by contrast, must be called a divine game, since there is no pre-existing rule, since the game bears already upon its own rules and since the child player can only win, all of chance being affirmed each time and for all times. Not restrictive or limiting affirmations, but affirmations coextensive with the questions posed and with the decisions from which these emanate: such a game entails the repetition of the necessarily winning move, since it wins by embracing all possible combinations and rules in the system of its own return. On this question of the game of repetition and difference as governed by the death instinct, no one has gone further than Borges, throughout his astonishing work:

> if the lottery is an intensification of chance, a periodic infusion of chaos into the cosmos, would it not be desirable for chance to intervene at all stages of the lottery and not merely in the drawing? Is it not ridiculous for chance to dictate the death of someone, while the circumstances of his death – its silent reserve or publicity, the time limit of one hour or one century – should remain immune to hazard? ... The ignorant suppose that an infinite number of drawings require an infinite amount of time; in reality, it is quite enough that time be infinitely subdivisible. ... In all fiction, when a man is faced with alternatives he chooses one at the expense of the others. In the almost unfathomable Ts'ui Pên, he chooses – simultaneously – all of them. He thus *creates* various futures, various times which start others that will in their turn branch out and bifurcate in other times. This is the cause of the contradictions in the novel. 'Fang, let us say, has a secret. A stranger knocks at his door. Fang makes up his mind to kill him. Naturally there are various possible outcomes. Fang can kill the intruder, the intruder can kill Fang, both can be saved, both can die and so on and so on. In Ts'ui Pên's work, all the possible solutions occur, each one being the point of departure for other bifurcations.'[11]

Notes

1. Daniel Lagache has examined the possibility of applying the psychological concept of habit to the unconscious and to repetition in the unconscious (but it seems that that repetition is here considered only from the perspective of a mastery of tensions): 'Le Problème du transfert', *Revue française de psychanalyse*, January 1952, pp. 84–97.

2. Henri Maldiney, *Le Moi*, course summary, Bulletin Faculté de Lyon, 1967.

3. Jacques Lacan, 'Seminar on *The Purloined Letter*', trans. Jeffrey Mehlman, *Yale French Studies*, no. 48, 1972, p. 55. This text is undoubtedly the one in which Lacan most profoundly develops his conception of repetition. Certain disciples of Lacan have strongly insisted upon this theme of the 'non-identical' and on the relation between difference and repetition which follows from it: J.-A. Miller, 'La Suture' (trans. 'Suture (elements of the logic of the signifier)', *Screen*, vol. xviii, no. 4, 1977/8, pp. 24–34); J.-C. Milner, 'Le Point du signifiant'; S. Leclaire, 'Les Éléments en jeu dans une psychanalyse', *Cahiers pour l'analyse*, nos 1, 3 and 5 respectively, 1966.

4. Lacan discloses the existence of series in two very important texts: 'The Seminar on *The Purloined Letter*', cited above (first series: 'king–queen–minister', second series: 'police–minister–Dupin'); and in a commentary on 'the rat man', 'Le Mythe individual du nevrose', C.D.U. ('The Neurotic's Individual Myth', trans. Martha Noel Evans, *The Psychoanalytic Quarterly*, 48, 1979, pp. 405–25) (here the two series, one paternal and one filial, put into play in different situations the debt, the friend, the poor woman and the rich woman). The elements and relations in each series are determined by their position in relation to the always displaced virtual object – the letter in the first example; the debt in the second: 'it is not only the subject, but the subjects, grasped in their intersubjectivity, who line up ... The displacement of the signifier determines the subjects in their acts, in their destiny, in their refusals, in their blindnesses, in their end and in their fate, their innate gifts and social acquisitions notwithstanding, without regard for character or sex ...' *Yale French Studies*, no. 48, 1972, p. 60. In this manner, an intersubjective unconscious is defined which reduces

neither to an individual unconscious nor to a collective unconscious, and in relation to which one can no longer describe one series as original and the other as derived (even though Lacan continues to use these terms – for ease of expression, it seems).

5. Serge Leclaire has outlined a theory of neuroses and psychoses in terms of the notion of the question as the fundamental category of the unconscious. In this connection he distinguishes between the hysteric's mode of questioning ('Am I a man or a woman?') and that of the obsessive ('Am I dead or alive?'); he also distinguishes the respective positions of the neurotic and the psychotic in relation to this instance of the question: 'La Mort dans la vie de l'obsédé', *La Psychanalyse*, no. 2, 1956 ('Jerome, or Death in the Life of the Obsessional', *Returning to Freud: Clinical Psychoanalysis in the School of Lacan*, ed. and trans. Stuart Schneiderman, New Haven, CT and London: Yale University Press, 1980, pp. 94–113); 'A la recherche des principes d'une psychothérapie des psychoses', *Évolution psychiatrique*, II, 1958. This research on the form and content of the questions lived by patients seems to us of enormous importance, implying a revision of the role of the negative and of conflict in the unconscious in general. Here again, they have their origin in some remarks by Lacan: on the kinds of question in hysteria and obsessions, see *Écrits, A Selection*, trans. Alan Sheridan, London: Tavistock/Routledge, 1989: 'The function and field of speech and language in psychoanalysis', pp. 89–90; on desire, its difference from need and its relation with 'enquiry' and with the 'question', see ibid., 'The direction of the treatment and the principles of its power', pp. 263–5; 'The signification of the phallus', pp. 285–8.

Was not one of the most important points of Jung's theory already to be found here: the force of 'questioning' in the unconscious, the conception of the unconscious as an unconscious of 'problems' and 'tasks'? Drawing out the consequences of this led Jung to the discovery of a process of differentiation more profound than the resulting oppositions (see *The Ego and the Unconscious*). Freud, it is true, violently criticised this point of view, notably in 'The Wolf Man', s. 5, where he maintains that the child does not question but desires, and that rather than being confronted with tasks it is confronted with emotions governed by opposition; and also in 'Dora', s. 2, where he shows that the kernel of the dream can only be a desire engaged in a corresponding conflict. Nevertheless, the discussion between Jung and Freud is perhaps not well situated, since it is a question of knowing whether or not the unconscious can do anything other than desire. In truth, should it not be asked whether desire is only an oppositional force rather than a force completely founded in the power [*puissance*] of the question? Even Dora's dream, which Freud invokes, can be interpreted only from the perspective of a problem (with the two series father–mother, Herr K.–Frau K.) which develops a hysterical question (with the jewel box playing the role of the object = x).

6. Even though Eros implies the union of two cellular bodies, thereby introducing new 'vital differences', 'we still feel our line of thought appreciably hampered by the fact that we cannot ascribe to the sexual instinct the characteristic of a compulsion to repeat which first put us on the track of the death instincts'. Freud, *Beyond the Pleasure Principle*, 1920, *Standard Edition*, vol. 18, p. 56.

7. See Paul Ricœur, *De l'interprétation*, Paris: Éditions du Seuil, 1965, pp. 413–14, trans. Denis Savage as *Freud and Philosophy: An Essay on Interpretation*, New Haven, CT and London: Yale University Press, 1970.

8. Freud, *The Ego and the Id*, 1923, *Standard Edition*, vol. 19, pp. 43–7.

9. Freud, *Inhibitions, Symptoms and Anxiety*, 1926 [1925], *Standard Edition*, vol. 20, pp. 138 ff. It is all the more strange that Freud reproaches Rank for having a too objective conception of birth.

10. Maurice Blanchot, *The Space of Literature*, trans. Ann Smock, Lincoln and London: University of Nebraska Press, 1982, pp. 106, 154–5.

11. Jorge Luis Borges, *Ficciones*, New York: Grove Press, 1962, 'The Babylon Lottery', pp. 69–70; 'The Garden of Forking Paths', p. 98.

2

Jeffrey Mehlman, 'How to Read Freud on Jokes: The Critic as *Schadchen*'.

New Literary History, vol. VI, no. 2 (Winter 1975), pp. 439–61.

Editor's Introduction

As a preliminary, the reader should note that Mehlman is working on (at least) two fronts: first, he is concerned to counter American ego psychology's version of the ego as centred and identical with itself − the kind of ego that 'knows what it likes' even if it cannot always obtain satisfaction. In doing this, our author's reading of Freud shows that sexuality, being inextricably linked to the unconscious, is originally − and not just secondarily − repressed. Original repression decentres pleasure, renders it disguised and the product of unconscious repetition.

Second, Mehlman makes his case through engaging in a particular type of reading (a reading that he made famous in the 1970s): the superimposition of texts. The method is encapsulated in the German term *Schadchen* (featured in the present text), or 'marriage-broker'. The point about the image of 'broker' is that it well captures Mehlman's intention to read one text through the prism of another − to 'marry' one text to another. Mehlman's wager, then, is that a flawed, applied psychoanalytic approach (and also an applied literary approach) can be avoided if one reads one (Freudian) text through the prism of another. And if it turns out that a marginal text illuminates a key text of a thinker like Freud, so much the better.

Freud's marginal text on jokes (or Freud's text on a marginal topic) thus comes to illuminate the supposedly more central writings on sexuality − such as *Three Essays on the Theory of Sexuality.* Here, to begin with, the two texts are brought into proximity because Mehlman wants to analyse sexual pleasure. And he notes in particular that the joke has a ternary structure (in contrast to the comic, which illustrates the dilemma of ego psychology), because its main feature derives from the fact that a sexual relation with a woman cannot be consummated by the man telling the joke to a third (Oedipal) party (the one who ensures that no actual sexual relation will eventuate). What is left is a 'pleasure in signs' (the joke). This pleasure, however, is fundamentally decentred (because it is indirect and unexpected) − one that was not ostensibly aimed for, says Freud.

Mehlman detects a similar structure in Freud's theory of child sexuality. In fact, he proposes that if we read this Freudian theory through the prism of the work on jokes, we will come to appreciate that sexual pleasure − and ultimately sexuality itself, due to repression − is 'another kind of pleasure', and thus far from being an essential biological urge. For just as the woman fled from the joke scene, and just as the third party to whom the joke is told ensures that the joke leads to another kind of pleasure, so too the child at the mother's breast finds a pleasure in excess of biological need. This is what Mehlman calls, after Freud, 'anaclitic' or auto-erotic pleasure. It is perverse in the sense that it is pleasure that has become detached from the satisfaction of a need. Anaclitic pleasure is thus a masked repetition of the pleasure from signs characteristic of the joke.

As anaclitic pleasure is essentially supplementary to the thing aimed at, it is never possible to take it immediately into account. For Mehlman, sexual pleasure recalls the North American potlatch spoken of by Mauss and Lévi-Strauss. There, the focus of celebration and the functionalist exchange of wedding gifts gives way to pseudo-weddings which allow the ostensibly secondary business of exchange to continue. Potlatch thus imitates − structurally speaking − the perverse pleasure of jokes.

Finally, it should be noted that Mehlman draws attention to the importance of the example of the case of Emma, featured in the 'Project for a Scientific Psychology of 1895'. This early case study, Mehlman shows, throws light on the relation between 'innocent' and 'perverse' pleasure. As we shall see, all of the above has fundamental implications for a theory of the ego.

How to Read Freud on Jokes: The Critic as *Schadchen*

> Ni roi, ni valet, mais *joker*.
>
> (Jacques Derrida)

I

In the sixth chapter of *Der Witz*, Freud, in the course of a didactic exposition of the 'dream-work,' writes: 'The newly-created common elements of condensation enter the manifest content of the dream as representatives of the dream-thoughts, so that an element in the dream corresponds to a nodal point [*Knotenpunkt*] or junction in the dream thoughts. . . .'[1] The allusion to the *Knotenpunkt* reminds the reader of that perspective in Freud more concerned with discovering a latent organization of the manifest content than a hidden meaning behind it. To locate the dream element in which the various associative strands of the dream converge is no doubt to isolate the 'other center' of dreams and consequently to come to terms with the strange 'syntax' regulating the transformations of the dream-work. This for Freud constituted the analytic task *par excellence*: to bring into relief the structural function – even more than the meaning(s) – of a 'nodal term.' It is for this reason that the reader may he surprised to find the following statement, toward the end of the same chapter, in the course of the author's comments on his own procedure: '[one] rightly refuses to regard the relation of the hypothesis to the material from which it was inferred as a "proof" of it. It can only be regarded as "proved" if it is reached by another path as well and if it can be shown to be the *nodal point* of still other connections'

(p. 202; our emphasis). This second reference to the *Knotenpunkt*, by requiring the same kind of coherence in Freud's own writing as he finds in dreams, undermines the metalinguistic distance between fantasy and theory. Might the proper reading of Freud then be similar to Freud's own readings of dreams and jokes? Such a reading would no doubt be an apprenticeship in a new style of obliqueness, constructing 'artificial and transient' links from fragment to fragment, decentering texts in an intertextual circuit as rigorous as it may appear superficial. It is such an exercise in perverse reading that we would undertake here, in the conviction that *Der Witz* will reveal its import only to him who is prepared to see in it the allusive structure .. . of a joke. It is for that reason that we would place these pages under the sign of the critic as *Schadchen*, the shrewdly perverse marriage-broker who at times seems the protagonist of Freud's volume. For as we marry text to text, proliferate 'ingenious interlacements,' and eventually establish the 'nodality' of this marginal work, our efforts will be seen to converge with those of Freud's joker *par excellence* (p. 40). And it is through the series of displacements from *Schadchen* to Freud to critic, in that circuit of exchange, that the distance we will take from Freud's apparent intention will assume the form of a journey toward the core of his text, were not the role of the *Schadchen* – at once subject and commentator of Freud's text, within and without *Der Witz*, no longer *presiding* at what is less a marriage than his own divorce *from himself* – incompatible with the very idea of a center.

If *Der Witz* is in a sense a joke (*ein Witz*), it is one which has been monumentally missed by American ego psychology. Which is not to say that Ernst Kris, in an essay whose prestige these pages would call into question, has not made 'comic' use of the text. (We shall eventually have to delineate how the 'comic,' in the sense in which we have just used it, functions in *Der Witz*.) For at a crucial moment in the introductory, programmatic chapter of *Psychoanalytic Explorations in Art*, he will seek confirmation of his argument in Freud's study.[2] Kris concludes that chapter by formulating the following thesis: 'The shifts in cathexis of mental energy which the work of art elicits or facilitates are, we believe, pleasurable in themselves. . . . All these processes, however, are controlled by the ego, and the degree of completeness of neutralization (of various types of energy discharge) indicates the degree of ego autonomy.'[3] We recognize the ego psychologist's position as part of a general effort to affirm psychoanalysis' right to contend in the literary-critical arena. The thrust of Kris's position is that there is an analytic stance every bit as humane as – indeed, barely distinguishable from – that of the New Critic. Whereby Freud becomes a respectable – and, alas, eminently 'safe' – colleague in the academy. If we begin with this reference to Kris, it is because he immediately seeks to consolidate his position through a symptomatic allusion to *Der Witz*, whose untenability we shall undertake to demonstrate: 'In assuming that the control of the ego over the discharge of energy is pleasurable in itself, we adopted one of the earliest, and frequently neglected, thoughts of Freud in this area: the suggestion that under certain conditions man may attempt to gain pleasure from the very activity of the psychic apparatus.'[4] Art then, for Kris, is to be regarded as a form of psychic gymnastics. Freed from the utilitarian constraints imposed by 'reality,' the mind is at liberty to commune with itself, to engage in an exemplary exercise in spiritual 'health.'

Now the passage in *Der Witz* Kris alludes to occurs in the context of the elaboration of the distinction between 'innocent' and 'tendentious' jokes. It will be recalled that the opposition is homologous with that between the aesthetic and the practical, and ultimately between form and substance. In the course of defining the 'innocent' variety, Freud imports a notion from the 'philosophers,' according to whom an aesthetic idea may be defined by the condition that 'in it we are not trying to get anything from things or do anything with them, that we are not needing things in order to satisfy one of our major vital needs, but that we are content with contemplating them and with the enjoyment of the idea' (p. 103). This notion in turn is cast in analytic terms in the sentence to which Kris clearly refers: 'If we do not require our mental apparatus for supplying one of our indispensable satis-factions, we allow it itself to work in the direction of pleasure and we seek to derive pleasure from its own activity' (p. 104). Having transposed the philosopher's notion into his own jargon, Freud then narrows its extension to the field of jokes and affirms that 'it [joking] is an activity which aims at deriving pleasure from mental processes, whether intellectual or otherwise' (p. 104).

It is clear from this initial exposition of the letter of Freud's text that Kris has proceeded in a direction precisely opposite to Freud's. However unen-lightening the original text's move from a commonplace of aesthetics to its restricted application to jokes may appear at this stage, there can be no doubt that the later text's move has been from that restricted application to what is at bottom a reaffirmation of the commonplace. Thus it is that many a move 'beyond Freud' is simply a regression to a pre-Freudian position. But what of our own 'Freudian' reading of the text? We shall pursue two lines of inquiry. On the one hand, we shall demonstrate that the author's incorporation of the commonplace is not the end but the beginning of his intellectual labor, that the notion he has introduced will undergo a series of transformations Freud himself is far from mastering, and whose net result is to undermine his own distinction between the 'innocent' and the 'ten-dentious.' (The collapse of that dualism, moreover, will entail the under-mining of a series of other other oppositions: e.g. self/other, fiction/reality.) On the other hand, we were struck by the fact that the transformation we refer to parallels, and indeed *repeats*, the most potently idiosyncratic ele-ments in the text that Freud was working on simultaneously with *Der Witz*: *Three Essays on the Theory of Sexuality*.[5] Ernest Jones writes that the author kept the two manuscripts on adjoining tables and added to the one or the other according to his mood.[6] Our effort to intertwine these two texts is therefore anything but arbitrary. Our purpose in so doing is twofold: (1) by demonstrating the 'nodality' of *Der Witz* to reveal in it a type of validity quite different from that which might attach to an empirical study of jokes; (2) to lend confirmation to a radically important reinterpretation of the *Three Essays* and, in fact, of the entirety of Freud's work. We refer to Jean Laplanche's *Vie et mort en psychanalyse*, to which these pages are in many ways an extended footnote.[7] Our effort will thus be in part an exposition, in part a continuation, of that 'return to Freud' which the French, under the aegis of Jacques Lacan, have been pursuing in the last decade.[8]

The passages from *Der Witz* which we have already transcribed are from the chapter entitled 'The Purposes [*Tendenzen*] of Jokes.' But, as we have already indicated, they are part of a delineation of what may only be called the 'purpose' of 'innocent' as opposed to 'tendentious' jokes. The 'innocent' is thus the nontendentious, the nonpurposeful within the purposeful. And in the description of 'innocent' jokes, we have come across a term used to designate this pseudo-teleological instance. It occurs in the phrase 'joking... is an activity which aims [*abzielt*] at deriving pleasure from mental processes, whether intellectual or otherwise.' Thus the *aim* masks the erosion of purpose (*Tendenz*) in opposition to which it is constituted. At the same time this *aim* is presented in diacritical opposition to another term: 'the major vital needs' which tend toward 'satisfaction.' Indeed, were we to ask what the 'innocent' joke – and specifically the marginal pleasure, *aiming* only to perpetuate or repeat itself – is 'innocent' of, our answer would be: subservience to 'the major vital needs.'

But it is here that we would introduce a series of passages from the *Three Essays*, on which, it will be recalled, Freud was working simultaneously. For – to anticipate our argument – it may be demonstrated that Freud, in that work, was busy defining just such 'innocence' (of subservience to 'vital need' or 'function') as *perversion*. We shall defer that demonstration until we approach Freud's analysis of tendentious jokes. For the moment, it is necessary only (a) to show that the terms of *Der Witz* are masked repetitions of those of the *Three Essays*; (b) to set forth those crucial terms in the *Three Essays* which will pursue a complex, subterranean existence in the rest of Freud's work. Already, the term *aim* (*Ziel*), for instance, is implicated in the theory of sexual drives (*Triebe*), and specifically in the determination of their characteristics (aim, impetus, source, object). In fact, a transformation of the very sentence in which the word aim appears (in *Der Witz*) may be found in the *Three Essays*. For: 'joking...is an activity which aims at deriving pleasure from mental processes, whether intellectual or otherwise...' finds its masked repetition in: '...there are present in the organism contrivances which bring it about that in the case of a great number of internal processes sexual excitation arises as a concomitant effect [*Nebenwirkung*], as soon as the intensity passes beyond certain quantitative limits' (p. 106). Clearly the 'derived,' supplementary joking pleasure, in excess of the utilitarian satisfaction brought about by a 'process,' may be superimposed on the 'concomitant effect' through which sexual excitement is generated. And what of the 'process' in excess of which the supplementary pleasure occurs? In the case of joking, we saw it to be the satisfaction of a 'major vital need.' In the case of the genesis of infantile sexuality – for that is what is under discussion – we read:

> Our study of thumb-sucking or sensual sucking (taken as a model of oral sexuality) has already given us the three essential characteristics of an infantile sexual manifestation. At its origin it *attaches itself to* [*entsteht in Anlehnung an*] a *bodily function which is very important for life* [*eine der lebenswichtige Körperfunktionen*]; it has as yet no sexual object, and is thus *auto-erotic*; and its sexual aim is dominated by an erotogenic zone. (p. 83)

Thus the 'major vital need' of *Der Witz* may be superimposed on the 'bodily function which is very important for life' of the *Three Essays*. Moreover, it should be noted that the distinction between 'marginal pleasure' and 'need' or 'function' may by no means be assimilated to the mind/body dichotomy. For if need, in the case of the *Three Essays*, is the eminently bodily one of ingesting mother's milk, in the case of *Der Witz*, explicit reference is made to 'mental processes, intellectual or otherwise.' Thus the mind/body dualism is subsumed by one of the terms of the dichotomy operative in Freud's two texts ('need').

In the process of demonstrating the interdependence of those texts, we have italicized – specifically, in our last quotation from the *Three Essays* – two terms which will take on increasing importance in our analysis. The first – (*in*) *Anlehnung* (*an*) – is rendered verbally as 'attaches itself to' in the translation. It is thus not at all a marked term in Strachey's English. And yet it is clear that it is situated at the critical moment of 'derivation' (*Der Witz*) of the marginal excitation from 'need.' Nine years later, *Anlehnung* will surface as part of Freud's official jargon in 'On Narcissism: An Introduction' (1914). At that time it will be opposed, as 'anaclitic [*Anlehnungstypus*] object choice,' to 'narcissistic object choice.' Our later comments will bear on the relation of that distinction to our discussion. But in what follows our focus will be on *Anlehnung* when it is not yet recognized as a critical term by the translators, no doubt not fully mastered by Freud himself. The second term we have italicized is as well one with a bifurcating destiny in Freud's work: *auto-erotic*. Later it will be part of the genetic groundplan of psychoanalytic ego psychology. But in 1905, as we shall see, it – and its derivative in *Der Witz*: *Selbstzweck* (having an end in itself) – are inseparable from the notion of *Anlehnung*, part of a conceptual scheme totally at odds with that groundplan. Whereupon we return to the passage in *Der Witz* under analysis.

In writing of innocent jokes, then, Freud had somehow deviated from his subject: the *purposes* of jokes. For the 'aim' of the innocent joke, entirely in itself, is but the shadow of a purpose, an apparent perversion of the *Tendenz*. Which is why the author interrupts what may have seemed almost a digression and broaches the *substance* of his subject: tendentious jokes, serving 'real' purposes.

In his delineation of the genesis of tendentious jokes, Freud presents a primal scene or scenario: the utterance of 'smut [*Zote*].' The phenomenon is defined as the 'intentional bringing into prominence of sexual facts and relations by speech' (p. 105). In fact, we are told, this primal scene is a seduction attempt (*Verführungsversuch*). By aggressively broaching sexual subjects, the man attempts to excite the object of his desire sexually and ultimately to consummate that desire. 'If the woman's readiness emerges quickly the obscene speech has a short life; it yields at once to a sexual action.' Despite the intervention of language in this example, it is clear that we are dealing here with a hypothetical case wherein a 'sexual' *need* or *function*, almost biological in nature, is satisfied or extinguished. As such it parallels the 'bodily function which is very important for life' (*Three Essays*) or the 'major vital need' (*Der Witz*). But, as though the earlier digression on 'innocent' jokes were anything but accidental, Freud immediately interferes with that satisfaction, focuses on a domain extrinsic to the functional. For what if the woman, we read, were to resist the attempt at seduction? 'In that case, the sexually exciting speech becomes an aim in itself [*Selbstzweck*] in the shape of smut' (p. 108). Previously, in an effort to differentiate the innocent from the tendentious, Freud had written: 'where a joke is not an aim in itself [*Selbstzweck*] – that is, where it is not an innocent one ...' (p. 105). The reader is thus led to wonder what it is that deflects the 'purpose' of the joke into this perverse – i.e. 'innocent' – form, why, in what purports to be a conceptual *distinction* (innocent/tendentious), we are above all struck by the insistence of a *repetition*. Freud continues, nuancing this deviation from purpose: 'Since the sexual aggressiveness is held up [*aufgehalten ist*] in its advance toward the act, it pauses [*verweilt sie*] at the evocation of the excitement [*Erregung*] and derives pleasure from the signs of it [*zieht Lust aus den Anzeichen derselben*] in the woman. In so doing the aggressiveness is no doubt altering its character as well [*ändert dabei wohl auch ihr Charakter*]' (p. 108). Were we to pinpoint this change in character, we would define it as the transition from the satisfaction of a need through a gratifying object to the satisfaction occasioned by the production of signs as ends in themselves (*Selbstzweck*). And these signs, which are 'innocent' of utilitarian function, are sexual through and through. We would even claim that they constitute the domain of the sexual *par excellence*. For such is the import of the parallelism between the passage we have just quoted and the following one from the *Three Essays*, which we too will *pause* to graft into our text:

> It is also easy to guess the occasions on which the child had his first experiences of the pleasure which he is now striving to renew. [Freud's focus is once more the paradigmatic case of oral eroticism.] It was the child's first and most vital activity, his sucking at his mother's breast, or at substitutes for it, that must have familiarized him with this pleasure. The child's lips, in our view, behave like an erotogenic zone, and no doubt excitement [*Reizung*] by the warm flow of milk is the cause of the pleasurable sensation. The satisfaction of the erotogenic zone is associated [*vergesellchaftet*], in the first instance with the satisfaction of the need for nourishment. To begin with, sexual activity attaches itself to [*lehnt sich zunächst an*] one of the functions aiming at preserving life and does not become independent of it until later. No one who has seen a baby sinking back satiated from the breast and falling asleep with flushed cheeks and a blissful smile can escape the reflection that this picture persists as a prototype of the expression of sexual satisfaction in later life. But soon the desire for repetition of the sexual gratification is separated from the desire for taking nourishment. (p. 82)

Thus the term *Anlehnung*, this time in verbal form, once more serves to designate the move by which the supplementary pleasure is derived from the functional activity. It will be noted that this 'anaclisis,' in the case of the *Three Essays*, takes place in *excess* of that activity, whereas, in *Der Witz*, the pleasure is generated in the *absence* of such satisfaction, which it *replaces*. We shall soon return to this vibration between excess and replacement (of a lack) and the obligation it imposes on us to problematize the 'origin' of sexuality in Freud. At present, our superimposition of texts calls for the following observations:

1. Although Freud eventually attributes the existence of the emerging joke to the 'proper' prudishness of women, it would be naïve to dismiss Freud or this text as *simply* a manifestation of a nineteenth-century ideology. For

the parallel case (in the *Three Essays*), whereby the 'need for nourishment' is gradually eliminated from the center of Freud's focus, suggests that the ideological statement is but the pretext for the repetition of something more fundamental, insistent in both, but reducible to neither.

2. What is being generated in place of (*Der Witz*), in addition to (*Three Essays*) the simple quenching of natural need, is 'sexual excitement' (*Three Essays*), a 'pleasure from signs' (*Der Witz*). Note that these are then not signs (symbolic) *of* the sexual but a variety of signs which are constituted *as* the sexual *per se*.

3. This 'pleasure from signs' may be superimposed on 'the desire for repetition of the sexual gratification' in the *Three Essays*. This confirms our second observation, for if the sign has its end in itself (*Selbstzweck*), its reactivation alone would constitute its 'gratification' or (wish-)fulfillment. With this pleasure in repetition (of signs), then, Freud's text(s) are already, in 1905, moving 'beyond the pleasure principle.' Earlier we had asked what it was that seemed insistent in our two texts: the first presenting a portrait of innocence (child at mother's breast), the second, an opposite image of perversity (a man attempting to excite and seduce a virtuous lady). We now have our answer: *das Bedürfnis nach Wiederholung*, a desire for masked repetition (as an end in) itself. Beyond the specular dualism *innocent/perverse*, Freud presents an instance which is one *and* the other, *differently*. The insistent 'innocence' of (even tendentious) jokes may be superimposed on that *anaclitic* movement whereby nature is displaced and *perverted* into the *signs* of 'sexual excitement.'

Our interpretation may be clarified and extended through consideration of the following remarkable passage in the *Three Essays*:

> At a time at which the first beginnings of sexual satisfaction are still linked with the taking of nourishment, the sexual instinct [*Sexualtrieb*] has a sexual object outside the infant's own body in the shape of his mother's breast. It is only later that he loses it, just at the time, perhaps, when he is able to form a total idea of the person to whom the organ that is giving him satisfaction belongs. As a rule the sexual instinct then becomes auto-erotic, and not until the period of latency has been passed through is the original relation restored. There are thus good reasons why a child sucking at his mother's breast has become the prototype of every love relation. The finding of an object is in fact a re-finding of it [*Wiederfindung*]. (p. 123)

The point of departure of this passage is clearly the anaclitic situation, in which the sexual impulse (*Trieb*) is about to achieve independence from an instinctual pattern. What is remarkable in the passage is that the term *auto-erotic*, in opposition to a later usage which would have it designate the original, solipsistic state of the 'psychic organism,' is here employed to describe not an initial stage, but a secondary one: the moment in which the natural object is lost. It would appear that sexuality becomes – is constituted as – *auto-erotic* exactly as smut, in the emerging joke, becomes 'an aim in itself' (*Selbstzweck*). This is the 'altering of [the aggression's] character' whereby the domain which Freud has access to – unconscious sexuality – comes into being. This loss of object harmonizes with the insistence on signs (*Anzeichen*) in *Der Witz*. But there is a hitch. For the passage we have just cited would appear to conclude with auto-erotic sexuality as the sign of the lost object. But our previous references to *Anlehnung* have shown that the lost object is different from the object of the sexual drive. For a displacement has occurred: if the object of the instinctual hunger is mother's milk, the object of the sign is a fantasized breast. The drive then will never be satisfied by refinding (*Wiederfindung*) the 'original' object because its object is different: whence the endless repetition (*Wiederholung*).

A step further. The pleasurable signs of *Der Witz* are in fact signs of signs. They occur not in the subject of the transaction but in the desired object: the woman. And what they signify or refer to is their relation to those other signs produced by the subject and whose end is to excite the production of the pleasurable signs themselves. Thus we are dealing with a symbolic circuit of exchange which exceeds the individual subject. It is for that reason that we would attach special weight to the clause in the *Three Essays*: 'just at the time, perhaps, when he is able to form a total idea of the person to whom the organ that is giving him satisfaction belongs.' It is as though Freud were suggesting that the moment of *Anlehnung*, of the constitution of the sexual fantasy, corresponded to the moment at which the subject becomes vulnerable to the fantasies of the other. And indeed one might suspect that the infant's fantasies of mother's breast are originally a function of her unconscious fantasies (and so on, indefinitely). Thus the signs or fantasies we have referred to are best conceived of as mobile, intersubjective scenarios. What should not be missed, however, is the havoc that such a formulation wreaks on the familiar, teleological notion of auto-eroticism. To state our conclusion most concisely: *unconscious fantasy is fundamentally auto-erotic, fundamentally intersubjective.*

II

Along with the hypothetical teller of smut, we have 'paused' long enough to observe the generation of a new pleasure in 'signs' and their repetition, to chart the intertextual repetitions through which that pleasure becomes manifest in Freud. It is time now to close the parenthesis of *Anlehnung*, or rather to observe the new complication through which Freud terminates it: 'The ideal case of a resistance of this kind on the woman's part occurs if another man is present at the same time – a third person – for in that case an immediate surrender by the woman is as good as out of the question' (p. 108). Our superimpositions of *Der Witz* and the *Three Essays* confirm our impression that this third party is the Oedipal father, he through whom a triangular situation comes about. And yet this third party does not alter the situation so much as he facilitates a process which is already underway and essentially independent of him: anaclisis. The real change comes with the deviation from brute satisfaction to a 'pleasure in signs,' and the third party's presence merely stabilizes or focuses that modification. From which it follows that Oedipal sexuality is fundamentally linked with the process of anaclisis and is therefore structural in nature. Consequently, the Oedipus complex is at the heart of a book like the *Three Essays* in which its manifest place is very small indeed. In the mother–child interaction discussed above the third element is the intersubjective fantasy generated in excess of the vital satisfaction: less than a particular structure the Oedipal reference concerns the fact of structure itself.

To return to *Der Witz*: the third person soon acquires 'the greatest importance' in the development of the smut. 'Gradually, in place of a woman, the onlooker, now the listener, becomes the person to whom the smut is addressed...' (p. 108). With the transition from a dual to a triangular configuration, the loss of the object is consolidated. The joke is consummated when the woman leaves the room. The center of gravity of the interaction has shifted from the second to the third (i.e. Oedipal) term. But that third term, we have seen, is less a term (a person) than a symbolic circuit, a structure of exchange which happens secondarily to find support or incarnation in an additional person. He embodies the 'sign' (system) as obstacle to the unmediated satisfaction of instinct. Freud calls him the *Instanz* to whom the emergent joke is now addressed, a word which Strachey translates 'person,' but which is as well the term Freud uses to designate one of the *sub-structures* of the psychic apparatus (English: 'agency'). In brief, the transaction we are describing resembles nothing so much as an Alaskan ritual described by Lévi-Strauss in *Les Structures élémentaires de la parenté*: 'In Alaska and British Columbia, the marriage of a girl is necessarily accompanied by a *potlatch*, to such an extent that the Comox aristocrats organize *pseudo-marriages with no bride*, for the sole purpose of acquiring rights in the course of the exchange rites.'[9] The absent Alaskan bride is like the offended lady whose departure permits the progress of the joke in Freud's model. Each is but a pretext for the reactivation and reaffirmation of a structure of exchange by which she – and the respective subjects of each transaction – are exceeded. It is in this light that we would read Freud's interest in the fact that 'it is not the person who makes the joke who laughs at it and who therefore enjoys its pleasurable effect, but the inactive listener [*der untätige Zuhörer*]' (p. 109). No doubt Freud, with his *apparently* hedonistic interpretation of the psychical apparatus, must have been struck by a complicated psychical process whose end seems to be the pleasure *of another*. But that *other's* pleasure, we have seen, is also *another* kind of pleasure: one whose end – or object – seems self-contained (*Selbstzweck, autoerotisch*), a pleasure in (the exchange of) signs (*Anzeichen*). The locus of this transaction, Freud writes, is: '[the] third in whom the joke's aim [*Absicht*] of producing pleasure is fulfilled [*erfüllt*].' Now (a derivative of) the word *erfüllt* occurs at the heart of *Die Traumdeutung* in the problematic notion of 'wish-fulfillment' (*Wunscherfüllung*). One of the implications of our inquiry would then be an oblique confirmation of the French in their effort to interpret wish-fulfillment (French: *accomplissement du désir*) as something radically different from the satisfaction of a need.[10] At the same time, we would restore the Oedipal problematic, relegated to a marginal subchapter in *Die Traumdeutung*, to the very center of that work: for the fulfillment (*Erfüllung*) of pleasure takes place in the strangely silent, almost indifferent *third* party.

III

If the sexuality we have seen Freud discover is fundamentally a semiotic affair (a 'pleasure from signs'), it remains for us to account for the specific rules of transformation governing those signs. We refer to that bizarre rhetoric of fantasy – displacement, condensation, etc. – which the analyst termed 'primary process thinking.' In the chapter of *Der Witz* we have considered, Freud is quick to come up with a thoroughly suspect explanation. If the joke is so trickily allusive, we are told it is because, among the upper classes, a direct reference to the intended 'sexual' aggression would be impermissible. This at bottom is the ultimate refinement of a process whose point of origin is 'in reality, nothing other than women's incapacity to tolerate undisguised sexuality [*das unverhüllte Sexuelle zu ertragen*]' (p. 110). More important than denouncing the all too obvious prejudices which motivate these explanations is to affirm that they are themselves incompatible with Freud's fundamental discoveries. For we would claim that the sexuality Freud had isolated was not accidentally but essentially *disguised*: insistent only in the uncontrolled *metaphoricity* of primary process thinking. In our own brief analyses, we have seen this distance of the 'sexual' from 'itself' in the *supplementary* pleasure of *Anlehnung*.[11] The 'origin' of sexuality is divided from itself, at once an excess (*Three Essays*) and a replacement (*Der Witz*). It is as though sexuality, which Freud saw as electively repressed, were as well originarily – as opposed (or in addition) to secondarily – repressed. It is to such primal repression (later to be called *Urverdrängung*), in its relation to sexuality, that we now shall turn. For it is through such an analysis that the striking 'nodality' of the brief section of *Der Witz* on which we have focused may best be brought into relief.

In coming to terms with this special link between repression and sexuality, we shall turn to the text in which Freud approaches that problem most directly: the *Project for a Scientific Psychology* of 1895.[12] We shall focus specifically on the case of Emma in the brief chapter entitled 'The Hysterical Proton Pseudos.' For it is there that the original nature of the displacement at the heart of human sexuality is most clear.

The facts of the case are as follows: Emma, a young lady, attributes her symptom – a fear of entering shops alone – to the following recollection (dating from the age of twelve): 'She went into a shop to buy something, saw the two shop assistants ... laughing together, and rushed out in some sort of *fright*. In this connection it was possible to elicit the idea that the two men had been laughing at her clothes and that one of them had attracted her sexually' (p. 433). Analytic investigation reveals that behind this scene there is an earlier, original scene (or memory) which has been forgotten. 'On two occasions when she was a child of eight, she had gone into a shop to buy some sweets and the shopkeeper had grabbed at her genitals through her clothes' (p. 433). Thus there are two scenes, separated by four years. The first is of a sexual attack. The second is of an insignificant occurrence, linked to the first by the most marginal of elements (the 'laughter' and the 'clothes'). Now the remarkable fact is that the formation of the symptom dates not from the brutal first scene but from the insignificant second one. Freud underscores the oddity of the situation: 'Here we have an instance of a memory exciting an affect which it had not excited as an experience' (p. 435). And he proposes the following explanation: 'in the meantime the changes produced by puberty had made possible a new understanding of what was remembered' (p. 435).

Such an analysis calls for a series of comments. In the first place, Freud's (posthumously published) text plays havoc with the commonplace notion of the traumatic event. Quite simply, the passages we have quoted split that event in two. What is in fact traumatic is not the event but the memory-trace. Or rather it is the oblique, metonymic relationship between the two. For the original scene in itself was not traumatic. Before 'puberty' the subject was incapable of understanding this violent incursion of an alien sexuality, of appreciating its violence. But in itself, of course, the second scene, in its triviality, is even less traumatic. Only the relationship between them is: a displacement through which the laughter and clothes shared by both scenes allow the second to symbolize and reactivate the first posthumously: 'This case is typical of repression in hysteria. We invariably find that a memory is repressed which has only become a trauma after the event [*nachträglich*]' (p. 435). For the subject what is traumatic is the activation of an *alien* element *from within*. But for the reader of Freud is not the true trauma the erosion of the very notion of an original, grounding event (or trauma)?

It will be objected that the entire section from which we have quoted is dependent on Freud's 'seduction theory,' which the author himself was the first to disavow. 'I no longer believe in my *neurotica*,' as he wrote to Fliess in a famous letter of 1897 (in which he denied the truth of the original seduction scenes 'remembered' by his patients). But we would respond briefly to this objection by two observations. First, the temporal scheme of retroactive efficacy will persist in Freud's writings long after the seduction theory is abandoned. Thus the analysis of the Wolf-Man will be dependent on the concept of *Nachträglichkeit*, a term which, like *Anlehnung*, has been partially obliterated in the translation of the Standard Edition. Second, the seduction theory itself will not be totally abandoned but will in fact find its final refuge in such passages as the following one from the *Three Essays*:

> A child's intercourse with anyone responsible for his care affords him an unending source of sexual excitation and satisfaction from his erotogenic zones. This is especially so since the person in charge of him, who, after all, is as a rule his mother, herself regards him with feelings that are derived from her own sexual life: she strokes him, kisses hims, rocks him and quite clearly treats him as a substitute for a complete sexual object. (p. 124)

Thus, if 'seduction' there be, it is no doubt in the subtle form of the implantation of parental fantasies into a child not yet prepared to integrate them. Whereby the problematic of *Nachträglichkeit* converges with that of *Anlehnung*.

But if we have discussed at some length this prototypal case of repression in Freud, it is because we sensed its profound connection with the genesis of the joke as described in *Der Witz*. In the first case we begin with a hypothetically 'primal' scene in which the shopkeeper attempts to violate the patient. In the second, the corresponding 'original [*ursprüngliche*] situation' is an 'attempt at seduction [*Verführungsversuch*].' This might be regarded as mere coincidence were it not for the similarities between the two subsequent scenes. In the flight of the offended girl from the two laughing shop assistants do we not find a repetition of the joke situation, in which the exchange of laughter between first and third parties (men) is rendered possible by the disappearance of the second (woman)? And what of the connection between the sequence of scenes? In *Der Witz*, we are told that the original scene is present in the second through displacement: 'that is, replacement by something small, something remotely connected, which the bearer reconstructs in his imagination into a complete and straightforward obscenity' (p. 109). In the *Project* we are told what the common element is, the girl's clothes. It would be tempting to see in the transition from the attempted rape *through* the girl's clothes to the liberation of laughter *at* those clothes themselves (as a condition of the effectiveness of the process) a first instance of what will be repeated in *Der Witz* as the generation of a new 'pleasure in signs.' For such a valorization of the garment itself as veil, mask, or sign is suggested by Freud's own diction: 'The whole complex was represented in consciousness by the one idea "clothes" – obviously its most innocent [*harmloseste*] element. At this point a repression accompanied by symbolization occurred' (p. 434). The garment is 'innocent' of that which it masks. But its 'innocence' is of the same sort as that of the 'innocent' joke: fundamentally perverse. Without 'clothes [*Kleider*],' the original episode would be without psychic effect; the 'undisguised' sexuality of *Der Witz* is but a myth.

After reading the text on the production of jokes as a masked repetition of the process of *Anlehnung* in the *Three Essays*, we have found equally detailed justification for viewing that same text as a displaced repetition of the temporality of *Nachträglichkeit* in the *Project*. Now whereas *Anlehnung* is the mode by which sexuality is generated in Freud, *Nachträglichkeit* designates the rhythm of sexuality's repression. Our thesis that sexuality in Freud is essentially divided from itself, involved originarily in figural transformations, is then at bottom no more (nor less) remarkable than the fact that the brief section of *Der Witz* which we have considered is in its structure a transformation of both the process by which human sexuality emerges and that by which it is repressed. With this 'textualization' of sex, we may note, has come the elimination of two symmetrical plenitudes, each of which is normally associated with Freud as read in America. On the one hand, the analysis of *Anlehnung* has shown that unconscious sexuality is generated not in continuity with biological nature (instinct, function) but in opposition to it: the Freudian wish (*Wunsch*) is far removed from natural need. On the other hand, the very notion of *Nachträglichkeit* subverts the idea of a traumatic *event*: the 'trauma' is suspended in the vibratory displacements between two temporally separate events. Our task will be complete when we indicate – briefly – how *Der Witz* contains an implicit critique of a third illusory plenitude, occasionally championed by Freud, but secretly eroded by an intertextual play we hope to bring into relief: the ego. It is to that final task that we now shall turn.

IV

Academic critics are understandably uncomfortable with *Der Witz*. For in this most elaborate effort at 'applied psychoanalysis,' Freud seems to have focused on the most marginal – indeed trivial – of genres: the joke. Might not Freud's analysis of jokes be turned to 'richer' domains, and specifically to comedy? Such will be the hypothesis, for instance, of Charles Mauron, whose *Psychocritique du genre comique* is based on the assumption that 'a well constructed comedy is but a vast and complex joke'.[13] And yet this tempting assimilation leaves the reader of Freud uneasy. For the comic, to which Freud devotes the final chapter of *Der Witz*, seems to have no other claim on the author's attention than its *diacritical opposition* to jokes. Freud explicitly rejects an exhaustive treatment of the comic and contents himself with 'throwing light on the problem of the comic *only so far as it contrasts clearly with the problem of jokes*' (p. 248; our emphasis). Repeatedly we are presented with the affirmation that 'jokes are from their nature to be distinguished from the comic...' (p. 237).

Our question then will be: wherein lies the mutual incompatibility of jokes and the comic? But it will be doubled by a second question: assuming the validity of our previous assimilation of the structure of the genesis of jokes to that of the emergence–repression of human sexuality, to what is such sexuality diacritically opposed? And what is the relation of that fourth term in our hypothetical proportion to the comic?

Our task will be facilitated if we begin by answering the second series of questions. In fact, it may be claimed that we have already presented a response in our analysis of *Anlehnung*. For the thrust of our comments was that unconscious sexuality is constituted in excess (or in place) of biological instinct. The Freudian wish (*Wunsch*) persists in opposition to its natural support; everything begins with this perversion or disqualification of 'nature.' And indeed we do find in Freud a model of psychical conflict which pits sexuality against the 'instincts of self-preservation.' The problem is that this abstract model *never* intervenes in clinical explanations. It is as though the 'instinct of self-preservation' were less one of the terms of psychical conflict than the very ground on which it takes place.[14]

What then is the second term opposed to sexuality in psychical conflict? Our difficulty begins with the apparently unequivocal answer Freud's texts dictate: the ego. For that term itself designates two different series of concepts:

1. The first is the 'ego' which will eventually flourish in ego psychology. The ego here is the progressively differentiated surface of the 'psychical organism.' Its functions are synthesis, integration, mastery of libidinal impulses, and adaptation. It exists in continuity with the more 'primitive' id and is teleologically oriented toward a 'reality' whose representative in the psyche the ego is. As our quotation from Kris at the beginning of this essay suggests, the ego is pre-eminently the hero – or humanist – of the intrapsychic drama. Freud himself is not beyond assimilating the opposition ego/id to that between 'reason' and 'passion.'

2. The second concept of the ego is presented most explicitly in the 1914 essay 'On Narcissism: An Introduction.' Here the ego comes into being through 'some new operation in the mind' and is no longer produced through a progressive differentiation from the id.[15] It is characterized as a *unified* object in relation to the anarchical sexuality of a preceding auto-

erotic phase. It may function as a love object cathected by unconscious sexuality, and although narcissism (without which the ego's constitution as a 'reservoir' of libido is unthinkable) is manifest in the object choice of homosexuals, Freud points out the important narcissistic component in all experiences of passionate love.[16]

Perhaps the clinical reality most aligned with this model is that of 'melancholia.'[17] For the concomitant phenomenon of 'identification with a lost love object' entails a profound modification of the patient's ego, reducing it to the status of intrasubjective vestige of an intersubjective relation. Indeed the transformation of the ego through identification with a lost object seems so thoroughgoing that it is tempting to infer that the ego was constituted originally as the introjected image of another. For such might be 'the new operation in the mind' through which the ego is constituted.[18] Now it is remarkable that we should find just such a model of the constitution of the ego implicit in Freud's *Project* of 1895.[19] The function of the ego in that text is primarily defensive or inhibitory. Its mode of existence is as a *stasis* of libidinal energy which prevents the excessively mobile discharge of unconscious energy. (The diacritical distinction between ego and unconscious here is that between two syntactical modes: 'secondary' and 'primary process' thinking.) Freud describes at length the *function* of this inhibitory presence within the 'subject' or 'psychical apparatus': to deprive the mad displacements and condensations of that apparatus – the chaotic, 'unbound' sexuality of what will later be called the 'auto-erotic' phase – of the attribute of consciousness. He describes the ego's *form* as well. Having distinguished between a stable core and an instable periphery of the ego, Freud writes, concerning the process of perception: 'Language later applies the term "judgment" to this process of analysis, and discovers the resemblance which exists between the nucleus of the ego and the constant portion of the perceptual complex on the one hand and between the changing cathexes in the pallium and the inconstant portion of the perceptual complex on the other' (p. 413). In the realm of perception, the first entity will be a 'thing' and the second its activity or attribute, its 'predicate.' Now in the following section of the *Project*, Freud claims that this process occurs in the case of the prototypal experience of learning, the perception of a fellow human being.

> Let us suppose that the object presented by the perception is similar to the (percipient) subject himself – that is to say a fellow human-being [*Nebenmensch*]. The theoretical interest taken in it is then further explained by the fact that an object *of a similar kind* was the subject's first satisfying object (and also his first hostile object) as well as being his sole assisting force. For this reason it is on his fellow-creatures that a human-being first learns to cognize. (p. 415)

Now this primary 'judgment,' the recognition of another as total form or object, takes place according to primary process thinking, in the absence of the ego. But its result is the establishment in (and rendering available to) perception of something possible only through its structural analogy to the ego. As a result we are led to infer a single psychical act whereby, simultaneously, the complete object *and* the ego would be constituted. Such, to close our seeming digression, would be the 'new operation in the mind' called for nineteen years later in the essay on narcissism.

We conclude these remarks on the narcissistic model of the ego, and specifically on the phenomenon of melancholia, by underscoring the ambivalence which characterizes narcissistic identifications. Indeed depression ('melancholia') was seen to be an intrasubjective attack in which one part of the ego persecutes another part (the introjected object): 'the ego debases itself and rages against itself.'[20] Moreover, this mechanism, for Freud, is at work as well through the quotient of narcissism in all passionate relations. The antithesis of the narcissistic obliteration of the other is not a 'genital' relation to the other in his 'reality' but a symmetrical, narcissistic obliteration *by* the other. The 'end-of-the-world' fantasy, Freud reminds us, is shared by the psychotic Dr. Schreber *and* the lover Tristan.

Having distinguished between two concepts of the ego, we are faced with the obligation of coming to terms with their articulation. For it would be intellectual cowardice *simply* to present the difference, affirming perhaps that – for reasons of 'national character' – the French have preferred the second model and the Americans the first. In the context of our own effort – a Freudian reading of Freud – we prefer to adopt the second position *because it contains a theory of the inadequacy of the first.*

More specifically, the ego of ego psychology corresponds to the *manic* phase of the 'melancholic' ego we have just seen Freud posit. By which we mean that the reintroduction of a *biological* model, on which ego – as progressively differentiated surface of the 'psychical *organism*' – is dependent, constitutes an obliteration of that *loss* of the biological which is at the heart of *anaclitic* sexuality. This reversion to vitalism entails quite simply the loss – or repression – of the concept of the unconscious (or repression). Our proof is that there are no theoretical obstacles which prevent the Freud of ego$_1$ from assimilating the opposition ego/id to the commonplace dualism reason/passion. And this obliteration of the originality of Freud's own thought is precisely what one would expect from an 'ego' constituted above all to defend against the reality of the unconscious. Ego psychology is then the subtlest ruse of narcissism; it is psychoanalysis written from the point of view of the agency whose existence is inseparable from the compulsion to blot out or domesticate the most virulent discoveries of psychoanalysis.

Our analysis of the status of the ego in Freud's thought was intended to aid in our understanding of the comic. It is with this end in mind that we shall demonstrate that the structure of the comic in *Der Witz* is quite simply *identical* to the structure of the narcissistically constituted ego. Whereas Freud assigns to comic phenomena the *attribute* of location in the (pre-)conscious, we would suggest that the analysis of the comic in *Der Witz* is in fact an unintended delineation of the *essence* of (the field of) consciousness – the ego – broached nine years later in the essay on narcissism. It is to this remarkable convergence that we now shall turn.

Freud's first distinction between jokes and the comic involves the social arrangement through which each operates. Jokes, we recall, require a triangular interaction, involving subject (the teller), object (the woman who disappears), and a third person to whom the joke is told. The comic, on the other hand, may be content with two persons: 'a first who finds what is comic and a second in whom it is found. The third person, to whom the comic thing is told, intensifies the comic process but adds nothing new to it' (p. 206). Thus, whereas the transition from 'smut' to 'jokes' was from a *dual* to a *triangular* relation, the passage from jokes to the comic is from a triangular to a dual one. And whereas the genesis of the jokes was dependent on a new 'pleasure from signs,' the linguistic dimension loses significance in the case of the comic. What then is the relation between smut and the comic? Precisely that between the 'instinct of self-preservation' and the ego. In the latter case, a careful superimposition of texts allowed us to define and motivate that relation. To transpose into Lévi-Straussian terms: the 'instinct' is the hypothetical Nature in opposition to which Freud thinks through his discovery of a bizarre region of Culture (unconscious sexuality), and the ego represents the emergence within Culture of a pseudo-Nature. In *Der Witz* we find the *form* of that entire transaction faithfully projected onto an entirely different domain, in which the same relationships may lack a comparable dialectical urgency. We are thus faced with the sheer *fact* of (masked) repetition, of the insistence of structure: the attribute *par excellence* of manifestations of the unconscious.

The relationship between the two parties in the comic is one of 'empathy' (*Einfühlung*). Regarding the prototypal case of laughter at a naïve comment, Freud writes: 'Thus we take the producing person's psychical state into consideration, put ourselves into it and try to understand it by comparing it with our own. It is these processes of empathy and comparison that result in the economy in expenditure which we discharge by laughing' (p. 212). Such will be the mechanism of the comic in *Der Witz*: a temporary identification with the other allows me better to affirm - in a spasm of laughter - my difference from (superiority to) him. Thus there are two simultaneous processes: (1) 'I behave exactly as though I were putting myself in the place of the person I am observing' (p. 221); (2) 'I disregard the person whom I am observing and behave as though I wanted to reach the aim of the movement' (p. 221). The reader senses that we are facing here an aesthetic projection of the 'circular insanity' of 'Mourning and Melancholia.' The condition of my being comically superior to my other is a willing assumption of his inferiority: the mastery of the 'master' is entirely dependent on the slave's recognition of it ... which renders the master ultimately subservient to the slave.

The pleasure of the comic is then one whose source is power: 'our laughter expresses a pleasurable sense of the superiority which we feel to him (the other)' (p. 223). Jokes, on the other hand, involve a strange lack of power: one never quite controls the unconscious process through which a joke is made. Perhaps this distinction between jokes and the comic is best revealed in the locus of pleasure. Whereas the comic gratifies the *first* person in the interaction, the joke, bizarrely enough, produces pleasure *elsewhere*: in the inactive (*untätige*) third party.

But is not this power which the ego affirms in comic laughter threatened from within? What if the subject were to lose control of the process of oscillation between self and other? This possibility is inscribed in the very theory of 'ideational mimetics [*Vorstellungsmimik*]' which grounds Freud's concept of the comic. According to this theory, to perceive a fellow human being perform an act is necessarily to imitate him mentally: 'An impulsion ... to imitation is undoubtedly present in perceptions of movements' (p. 218).

Moreover, this tendency would have a *quantitative* representation in expenditure of 'innervatory energy.' Now in perceiving a particularly clumsy individual, I marshal that energy (through mental mimesis) and simultaneously realize that, for *me* to perform a similar act, a much lesser expenditure of energy would be required. If it cannot be rechanneled elsewhere that *difference* in energy is spent in laughter. Now Freud prefaces this theory with the following comment: 'I have acquired the idea of a particular size by carrying the movement out myself *or by imitating it*, and through this action I have learnt a standard for this movement in my innervatory sensations' (p. 218; our emphasis). Thus we are faced with the possibility that the ego to whose capacities I triumphantly compare the actions which I imitate is itself the residue of imitations. And in that case, who will be laughing at whom? Our reading of the passage on 'ideational mimetics' thus converges with the earlier analysis of the role of the *Nebenmensch* in the *Project*: each text entertains the possibility of an ego which is alienated not secondarily but in its essence. And this comparison in turn parallels the one we have made between the comic situation in *Der Witz* and the 'circular insanity' of 'Mourning and Melancholia': the comic affirmation of the power of the ego, of a power or sense of wholeness no doubt inseparable from the very existence of the ego, is eroded from within by its simultaneous assumption of the inferiority of the other. The comic, like the ego, is in rivalry with itself.

V

Our *witzige* reading of *Der Witz* is now complete. In 'marrying' text to text, we have seen the book as a microcosm in whose structure the 'nodal' concepts of Freud's theory – *Anlehnung*, auto-erotism, *Nachträglichkeit*, narcissism – may be found in transformation, displaced. Which is to say that we have found transformed in this text the critical elements of a theory of intertextual transformation, displacement, repetition. No doubt the difficulty of *Der Witz* lies in the obliqueness with which that theory insists: for example, in the manner in which the text itself works to undermine the official distinction between the 'innocent' and the 'tendentious.' For we have attempted to focus on a level of his text which the author himself has not quite mastered and is capable of falling below. Whereas Freud, for instance, concludes that jokes 'make possible the satisfaction of an instinct ... in the face of an obstacle,' that they 'circumvent this obstacle and in that way draw pleasure from a source which the obstacle had made inaccessible,' we have demonstrated that it is an odd kind of 'instinct' indeed whose 'satisfaction' is dependent on the disappearance of its object, that the whole thrust of Freud's analysis is that the obstacle itself has now become the source (p. 110). To read Freud in the spirit we have suggested is to come to terms with such ruses and such lapses; it is to see the value of each text in terms of its 'nodality' or structural function in the overall economy of Freud's theory. It is a style of reading which no doubt entails a sacrifice. For it will be seen that the further we pursued our analysis of *Der Witz*, the more did the apparent object of Freud's analysis – jokes – disappear, like the woman – the second person – in Freud's paradigm of the joke. I confess that this homology between Freud's model and our own undertaking strikes me as sufficient consolation for that loss. Indeed I suspect that it is only when we stop seeing Freud as an empirical psychologist that we will learn how to read him.[21]

We began by referring to an ego psychologist's reading of *Der Witz*: an allegedly empirical reading of an alleged empiricist's text. If our own analyses are correct, we may now judge the magnitude of Kris's error. In passages from which we inferred a generalized *perversion* of the natural, Kris sees an apology for psychic gymnastics, a description of mental health. In a text which contains a subtle anticipation of the theory of narcissism, Kris finds a pretext for extolling the strengths of the ego. If we refer to such a reading as 'comic' (in Freud's sense), it is less because of the affirmation of the ego's power to which it leads than because of the hidden violence which the alleged act of critical 'empathy' hides. One identifies with the author's act – the complexities of his text – just long enough to 'disregard [*absehen*]' them and feel secure in reaffirming the values which the act of reading has, all along, been a pretext for celebrating. Such is the 'comedy' of ideological misreading. If our own reading may be distinguished from Kris's, it is in its effort to restore the third ('joking') term: the *fact* of intertextual structure, the medium of *exchange* between text and text, author and reader.

It is perhaps time to learn just *how* to laugh in reading Freud, to appreciate how *funny* (perversely allusive), how uncannily *uncomic* an author he is.

Notes

1. *Der Witz und seine Beziehung zum Unbewussten in Gesammelte Werke*, V (London, 1942) p. 186. Future page references to this edition are indicated in parentheses in the text. Translations are from James Strachey's version in the Standard Edition. See *Jokes and Their Relation to the Unconscious, S.E.*, 8.
2. E. Kris, *Psychoanalytic Explorations in Art* (New York, 1953).
3. *Ibid.*, p. 63.
4. *Ibid.*
5. *Drei Abhandlungen zur Sexualtheorie* in *Gesammelte Werke*, IV. Page references to this edition are indicated in parentheses in the text. Translations, occasionally modified, are from James Strachey's version in the Standard Edition. See *Three Essays on the Theory of Sexuality, S.E.*, 7.
6. E. Jones, *Sigmund Freud: Life and Work* (London, 1955), II, 13.
7. J. Laplanche, *Vie et mort en psychanalyse* (Paris, 1970). In English as *Life and Death in Psychoanalysis*, trans. Jeffrey Mehlman (Baltimore, MD, 1974).
8. See J. Lacan, *Écrits* (Paris, 1966).
9. C. Lévi-Strauss, *Elementary Kinship Structures*, ed. R. Needham (Boston, 1969), p. 63.
10. See Laplanche, *Vie et mort en psychanalyse*, p. 122: 'The dream does not *bring* the satisfaction of a wish; it is the fulfillment of a wish by its very existence.' This interpretation is solidary with a critique of the untenable notion of auto-erotism as the initial hallucinatory state of a biological monad.
11. We use the word *supplement* in a sense similar to Rousseau's. See J. Derrida, *De la grammatologie* (Paris, 1967). In English as *Of Grammatology*, trans. Gayatri Spivak (Baltimore, MD and London, 1976).
12. *Entwurf einer Psychologie* in *Aus den Anfängen der Psychoanalyse* (London, 1950). Subsequent page references to this edition are in parentheses in the text. The

translation is by E. Mosbacher and J. Strachey. In English as *The Origins of Psychoanalysis* (London and New York, 1954), and 'A Project for a Scientific Psychology' in S.E., 1.

13. C. Mauron, *Psychocritique du genre comique* (Paris, 1964), p. 18.

14. Our argument here follows that of Laplanche, Chs. 3, 4.

15. 'Zur Einführung des Narzissmus' in *Gesammelte Werke*, X, 142. See 'On Narcissim: An Introduction' in *S.E.*, 14.

16. See *Massenpsychologie und Ich-Analyse* in *Gesammelte Werke*, XIII. See *Group Psychology and the Analysis of the Ego* in *S.E.*, 18.

17. See 'Traure und Melancholie' in *Gesammelte Werke*, X. See 'Mourning and Melancholia' in *S.E.*, 14.

18. J. Lacan's *stade du miroir* (*Écrits*, pp. 93-100) is an attempt to formalize this model of the constitution of the ego.

19. The importance which we (with the French) attach to the *Project*, a text Freud chose not to publish, is symptomatic. We would not be averse to considering it the original and most eloquent 'Freudian slip'.

20. 'Trauer und Melancholie,' p. 146.

21. This is by no means to cut Freud's texts off from their grounding in clinical practice. It is rather a question of *reculer pour mieux sauter*: only by coming to terms with the structure of the contradictions in Freud's writings will we be able to understand the structure of the contradictory reality he discovered.

3

Jacques Derrida, 'My Chances/*Mes Chances*: A Rendezvous with Some Epicurean Stereophonies'.

Trans. Irene Harvey and Avital Ronell, in Joseph H. Smith and William Kerrigan, eds, *Taking Chances: Derrida, Psychoanalysis and Literature*, Baltimore, MD and London: The Johns Hopkins University Press, first published 1984, paperback 1988, pp. 1–32.

Editor's Introduction

The meaning of the title is obscure. It refers to 'chance' and 'fall' (as the text makes clear, the French '*mes chances*' evokes, by homophony, *échéance* – meaning 'expiry date', as when something (a subscription) falls due), as well as to the Epicurean and Lucretian theory of the *clinamen* – a small chance deviation in the trajectory, or fall, of an object. 'Stereophony' evokes the term 'stereotomy' (science of division) occurring in Poe's short story 'The Murders in the Rue Morgue'. 'Stereophony' plays on the homophony which divides things into insignificant pieces – the insignificant being what chance throws up, or what befalls us. The fact that references to Epicurus appear – by chance – in Poe and Freud, but hardly at all in Heidegger, where they could appropriately appear, governs (if this word can be used) much of Derrida's analysis.

Shortly after raising a number of questions about psychoanalysis and chance, Derrida poses the question of destination by saying that it is impossible for him to know precisely who his audience (*destinataire*) is (he does not know where his word will *fall*), or how his discourse is going to be received. The point is that there is no way of ensuring that perfect communication between sender and receiver can take place. The possibility always exists of a deviation from the 'true' discourse — hence the evocation of clinamen. A clinamen can be an infinitesimally small deviation from the true path, or norm. It is often so small as to be insignificant. This is the issue here, for Derrida connects the insignificant to writing and literature. The insignificant, then, is what characterises the mark and forms the basis of writing. It is also what characterises the letter. By itself, a letter is entirely insignificant — significance emerges only in relation to other letters or to other things. In this light, Derrida prefers the notion of 'mark' over the arbitrariness of the sign, as found in Saussure and Lacan. This is because the mark can be infinitely divided. It is essentially iterable, and so irreducible to any context. There is no assured destination. It is not subject to a horizon of anticipation, but is essentially an (unpredictable) event. By comparison to the mark as insignificance, the link between signifier and signified in the sign is only ever relatively arbitrary.

In an odd kind of way, though, radical insignificance becomes 'remarkable' and the source of an event. This event Derrida sees as literary when an *œuvre* is considered in terms of a proper name. Characteristic of the proper name is the fact that it has no meaning. In this sense, perhaps, it is radically insignificant. Only through the singularity of an *œuvre* does a proper name assume significance.

This singularity opens the way to chance. For the question is: can an *œuvre* — in literature, in art, etc. — be explained or predicted? Freud, of course, wrote on Michelangelo, Leonardo da Vinci and others, in order to explain how their childhood experience played a role in their artistic careers. Derrida takes up this theme, and asks whether psychoanalysis, in being unable to accept the chance that has no horizon of anticipation, is not beginning to resemble the paranoid patient who overinterprets. More exactly, Derrida notes that Freud, in some contexts, admits that psychoanalysis cannot explain art and that, indeed, poets and artists have discovered things that the analyst is only now beginning to understand. He thus shows us two Freuds: one who is torn between a 'compulsion' to interpret at all costs, and another who is humbled by artistic endeavour that cannot be explained.

As a different approach to Freud's dilemma, Derrida proposes a 'pragmatology' — a theoretical strategy which would take the marks of writing into account in the light of the problematic of randomness elaborated by various sciences. Pragmatology, we could say, is Derrida's way of bringing chance 'back in'.

My Chances/*Mes Chances*: A Rendezvous with Some Epicurean Stereophonies*

How should one go about calculating the age of psychoanalysis? Not everything under which psychoanalysis falls can be simply relegated to the manifestation of its name; but under this name it remains a rather young venture. One can contemplate its chances – those of yesterday and tomorrow.

You are perhaps wondering why I chose the theme of *la chance* when, according to the specific terms of our program or contract, I should speak to you about the relation of the one to the other, psychoanalysis to literature – that other thing of an incalculable age at once immemorial and altogether recent. Did I choose this theme haphazardly or by chance? Or, what is more likely, perhaps it was imposed upon me in that chance offered itself for the choosing as if I had fallen upon it, thus leaving me with the illusion of a free will. All this involves a very old story, which, however, I shall not endeavor to recount.

For the moment let us treat 'Psychoanalysis' and 'Literature' as presumably proper names. They name events or a series of events about which we can rightfully suppose the *singularity* of an irreversible process and a historical existence. On the basis of this singularity alone, their transaction with chance already gives us something to reflect upon.

If I may now make use of the apostrophe, let me tell you this much at once: I do not know to whom I am speaking. Whom is this discourse or lecture addressing here and now? I am delivering it to you, of course, but that doesn't change the situation much. You will understand why I say this. And once you find this intelligible, it becomes at least possible to demonstrate that, beginning with the first sentence, my lecture has not simply and purely missed its destination.

You understand very well why I am asking myself such questions as: to whom, in the final analysis, will this lecture have been destined? and, can one speak here of destination or aim? What are my chances of reaching my addressees if, on the one hand, I calculate and prepare a place of *encounter* or if, on the other, I hope, as we say in French, to *fall* upon them by accident?

Regarding those to whom I now speak, I do not know them, so to speak. Nor do I know you who hear me. I do not even know if, according to your declared interests or professional affiliations, the majority among you belong to the 'world' of psychiatry, as the title borne by this school tends to suggest, to the 'worlds' of psychoanalysis, to one and the other, to one or the other, or to the 'worlds' of science, literature, the arts, or the humanities. It is not certain that such 'worlds' exist. Their frontiers are those of 'contexts' and justificatory procedures currently undergoing rapid transformation. Even if I had at my disposition some information that might clarify this subject, it would still remain overly vague and general; I would have to make rough calculations and hold a lecture of loosely woven netting, counting on my chances in a way somewhat analogous to fishing or hunting. How indeed could I aim my argument at some singular destination, at one or another among you whose proper name I might for example know? And then, is knowing a proper name tantamount to knowing someone?

There. I have just *enumerated* the themes of my lecture. They are all presented in what was just said, including the theme of numbers, which has been added just now to the enumeration. This amounts to what I would like to discuss with you, but I shall have to do so in the dim light of a certain indetermination. I impart my words a bit haphazardly, trying my luck in front of you and others, yet what I say at this chance moment has more chance of reaching you than if I had delivered it to chance without speaking of this. Why? Well, at least because these effects of chance appear to be at once produced, multiplied, *and* limited by language.

Language, however, is only one among those systems of *marks* that claim this curious tendency as their property: they *simultaneously* incline toward increasing the reserves of random indetermination *as well as* the capacity for coding and overcoding or, in other words, for control and self-regulation. Such competition between randomness and code disrupts the very systematicity of the system while it also, however, regulates the restless, unstable interplay of the system. Whatever its singularity in this respect, the linguistic system of these traces or marks would merely be, it seems to me, just a particular example of the law of destabilization.

Even here, among us, the effects of chance are at once multiplied and limited (that is, relatively tempered or neutralized) by the multiplicity of languages and codes that, while they are engaged in intense translational activity, overlap at each instant. Such activity transforms not only words, a lexicon, or a syntax (for example, from French into English) but also non-linguistic marks, mobilizing thus the near totality of the present context and even that which might already exceed it. The text that I am now reading should be publishable; I was aware of this when writing this summer. It is destined in advance to addressees (*destinataires*) who are not easily determinable or who, as far as any possible calculation is concerned, in any case command a great reserve of indetermination. And this in turn involves, as I shall try to show, the most general structure of the mark. Running my chances over your heads, I therefore address myself to addressees unknown to you or me. But while waiting and in passing, this falls, as the French saying goes, upon you.

What do I or could I conceivably mean by declaring these addressees 'unknown' to you and me? What criteria would one use in order to arrive at a decision regarding them? Not necessarily the criteria of self-conscious knowledge. For I could be addressing myself to an unconscious and absolutely determined addressee, one rigorously localized in 'my' unconscious, or in yours, or in the machinery programming the partition of this event. Moreover, everything that comes to mind under the words 'consciousness' or 'unconscious' already presupposes the possibility of these marks in addition to all the possible disruptions connected with the destining of dispatches (*envois à destiner*). In any case, the fact that the proper name or the idiom of the other is a matter of ignorance to us does not mean that we know nothing about her or him. Despite the fact that I do not know you or can barely see you while addressing myself to you, and that you hardly know me, what I have been saying is, as of a moment ago, reaching you – regardless of the trajectories and translations of signs that we address to each other in this twilight. What I have been saying comes at you, to encounter and make contact with you. Up to a certain point it becomes intelligible to you.

The 'things' that I throw, eject, project, or cast (*lance*) in your direction to come across to you fall, often and well enough, upon you, at least upon certain of those among you. The things with which I am bombarding you are linguistic or nonlinguistic signs: words, sentences, sonorous and visual images, gestures, intonations, and hand signals. Within the range of our calculations we can count on certain probabilities. On the basis of numerous indices, we form, you and I, a certain schematic idea of one another and of the place where contact could be made. We certainly count on the calculating capacity of language, with its code and game, with what regulates its play and plays with its regulations. We count on that which is destined to random chance (*ce qui destine au hasard*), while at the same time reducing chance. Since the expression '*destiner au hasard*' can have two syntaxes and therefore can carry two meanings in French, it is at once of sufficient determination *and* indetermination to leave room for the chances to which it speaks in its course (*trajet*) and even in its 'throw' ('*jet*'). This depends, as they say, on the context; but a context is never determined enough to prohibit all possible random deviation. To speak in the manner of Epicurus or Lucretius, there is always a chance open to some *parenklisis* or *clinamen*. '*Destiner au hasard*' could mean resolutely 'to doom,' 'abandon,' 'yield,' or 'deliver' to chance itself. But it can also mean to destine something unwittingly, in a haphazard manner or at random. In the first of these cases, one destines to chance without involving chance, whereas in the second, one does not destine to chance but chance intervenes and diverts the destination. The same can be said for the expression 'to believe in chance': to believe in chance can just as well indicate that one believes in the existence of chance as that one does *not*, above all, believe in chance, since one looks for and finds a hidden meaning at all costs.

For a while now, I have been speaking to you about chance (*du hasard*), but I do not speak haphazardly (*au hasard*). Calculating my chances of reaching you through my speech (*parole*), I have above all spoken to you of speech. I thought that speaking to you about chance and language would give me the greatest chances of being pertinent, that is, of touching on my subject by touching you. This presupposes that, between us, there reigns a good number of contracts or conventions or what Lucretius would call explicit or implicit 'federations.' The organizers of this encounter have prescribed, for instance, that the dominant language here be English. And everything that I say should relate to something like the chances between psychoanalysis and literature, taking into account earlier works – among others, my own.

I shall cast out *two questions*, then. Once these questions are cast, imagine that suddenly (*d'un seul coup*) they become two dice. Afterward (*après coup*), when they have fallen, we shall try to see, if something still remains to be seen, at what sum they arrive between them: in other words, what their constellation means. And whether one can read my fortune (*mes chances*) or yours.

To Usher in the Fall

The first and preliminary question, as if thrown on the threshold, raises the issue of the downward movement. When chance or luck are under consideration, why do the words and concepts in the first place impose the particular signification, sense, and direction (*sens*) of a downward movement regardless of whether we are dealing with a throw or a fall? Why does this sense enjoy a privileged relation to the nonsense or insignificance which we find frequently associated with chance? What would such a movement of descent have to do with luck or chance (*la chance ou le hasard*)? From what viewpoint can these be related (and we shall see how precisely, in this place, vision comes to be missing)? Is our attention engaged by the ground or the abyss? As you know, the words 'chance' and 'case' descend, as it were, according to the same Latin filiation, from *cadere*, which - to indicate the sense of the fall – still resounds in 'cadence,' 'fall' (*choir*), 'to fall due' (*échoir*), 'expiry date' (*échéance*), as well as in 'accident' and 'incident.' But, apart from this linguistic family, the same case can be made for *Zufall* or *Zufälligkeit*, which in German means 'chance,' for *zufallen* (to fall due), *zufällig*, the accidental, fortuitous, contingent, occasional – and the word 'occasion' belongs to the same Latin descent. A *Fall* is a case; *Einfall*, an idea that suddenly comes to mind in an apparently unforeseeable manner. Now, I would say that the unforeseeable is precisely the case, involving as it does that which falls and is not seen in advance. Is not what befalls us or descends upon us, as it comes from above, like destiny or thunder, taking our faces and hands by surprise – is this not exactly what thwarts our expectation and disappoints our *anticipation*? Grasping everything in advance, anticipation (*antipare, ante-capere*) does not let itself be taken by surprise; there is no chance for it. Anticipation sees the *objectum* coming ahead, faces the object or *Gegenstand* that, in philosophical German, was preceded by the *Gegenwurf* in which the movement of the throw (*jet, werfen*) can once again be perceived. The *ob-jectum* (*ob-jet*) is kept under view or hand, within sight or *intuitus*, while it puts a handle on the hand or *conceptus*, the *Begreifen* or *Begriff*. And when something does not befall us 'by accident' ('*par hasard*'), as the saying or belief goes, then one can also fall oneself. One can fall well or badly, have a lucky or unlucky break – but always by dint of not having foreseen – of not having seen in advance and ahead of oneself. In such a case, when man or the subject falls, the fall affects his upright stance and vertical position by engraving in him the detour of a *clinamen*, whose effects are sometimes inescapable.[1]

For the time being, let us be content to take note of this law or coincidence, which in an odd way associates chance and luck with a descending movement, a finite throw (which is supposed therefore to fall vertically again), the fall, the incident, the accident, and, most certainly, coincidence. The attempt to submit chance to thought implies in the first place an interest in the *experience* (I emphasize this word) of that which happens unexpectedly (*ce qui arrive imprévisiblement*). Indeed, there are those of us who are inclined to think that unexpectability conditions the very structure of an event. Would an event that can be anticipated and therefore apprehended or comprehended, or one without an element of absolute encounter, actually be an event in the full sense of the word? There are those who lean toward the assumption that an event worthy of this name cannot be foretold. We are not supposed to see it coming. If what comes and then stands out horizontally on a horizon can be anticipated then there is no pure event. No horizon, then, for the event or encounter, but only verticality and the unforeseeable. The alterity of the other – that which does not reduce itself to the economy of our horizon – always comes to us from above, indeed, from the above.

This singular *experience* brings us into contact with what *falls* 'well' or 'badly,' as we would say in French (roughly meaning what falls opportunely or not), which, as such, constitutes fortune or luck (*une chance*). Depending on the context and cases, of which there are quite a few, such luck is a stroke of luck. This amounts to a pleonastic expression: to have luck is to have good luck. In other cases – the unfortunate ones – luck is *bad luck* (*une malchance*). What are the chances of my losing at a game or for the neutron bomb to be dropped? Bad luck (*malchance*) is when one is out of luck; having *no luck* (*pas de chance*); however, it is at the same time in a very significant way a phenomenon of luck or chance – an 'infelicity' as the Austinian theory of speech acts would have it – designating accidental or parasitical deviations in the production of performatives, promises, orders, or oaths – and, precisely, contracts.

Bad luck (*malchance*) is *méchance*. We could say that a spiteful person (*le méchant*) plays on bad luck (*malchance*) and on '*méschéance*,' which is an Old French word that associates being down on one's luck with spite and meanness (*méchanceté*). The mean, spiteful person falls short (*le méchant méchoit*), which is another way of saying that he is demeaned and loses his standing (*il déchoit*), first in the sense of mischance and then, if we shift the sense a bit, allowing it to deviate in turn, in the sense of that which brings him to do evil.

If I stress the multiplicity of languages, and if I play on it, you should not take this for a mere exercise or a gratuitous and fortuitous display. As I make my way from digression to deviation I wish to demonstrate a certain interfacing of necessity and chance, of significant and insignificant chance: the marriage, as the Greek would have it, of *Anankè*, of *Tukhè* and *Automatia*.

In any case, we can note the incidence in a system of coincidences of that which itself is prone to fall (well or badly) *with* something else, that is, at the same time or in the same place as something else. This is also the sense that the Greek gives to *symptôma*, a word meaning a sinking in or depression, a collapse but also a coincidence, a fortuitous event, an encounter or unfortunate event. Finally, we have the symptom as sign – a clinical one, for example. The clinic, let it be said in passing, names the integral space of the retiring or bedridden position, which is the position of illness par excellence, and thus, one invariably 'falls' ill.

The same semantic register supposes the idea of whatever falls (*ce qui est échu*) to someone's lot – that lottery said to be attributed, distributed, dispensed, and sent (*geschickt*) by the gods or destiny (*moira, nemein, nomos, Schicksal*), the fatal or fabulating word, the chance circumstances of heredity, the game of chromosomes – as if this gift and these givens obeyed, for better or for worse, the order of a throw coming down from above. We are in fact dealing with a logic and *topos* of the dispatch (*envoi*). Destiny and destination are dispatches whose descending trajectories or projections can meet with perturbation, which, in this case, means interruption or deviation. Within the same register we find (but can we speak in this case of a lucky find or a chance encounter?) the unforeseeable and inexplicable fall from grace into original sin or, in terms of the mythology of Plato's *Phaedrus*, we find the disseminating fall of the soul in a body, just as well as *lapsus* or 'slip' (which, as you know, means fall). The *lapsus*, when revealing its unconscious destination and manifesting thus its truth, becomes, for psychoanalytical interpretations, a symptom.

At this point we necessarily fall upon Democritus, Epicurus, and Lucretius again. In the course of their fall in the void, atoms are driven by a supplementary deviation, by the *parenklisis* or *clinamen* that, impelling an initial divergency, produce the 'concentration of material [*systrophè*] thus giving birth to the worlds and things they contain' (J. and M. Bollack, H. Wissmann, *La Lettre d'Epicure*, p. 182.3). The *clinamen* diverges from simple verticality, doing so, according to Lucretius, 'at an indeterminate moment' and 'in indeterminate places' (*incerto tempore ... incertisque locis*; *De rerum natura*, 2.218.9). Without this declension, 'nature would have never created anything' (224).

This deviation alone can change the course of an imperturbable destination and an inflexible order. Such erring (elsewhere I call it 'destinerring') can contravene in the laws of destiny, in conventions or contracts, in agreements of *fatum* (*fati foedera*, 2.254). I emphasize the word 'contract' for reasons that will soon become clear. But here I must ask you to allow me a brief digression toward a classical philological problem concerning the indeterminate reading of the word *voluptas* or *voluntas* (2.257). The mere difference of a letter introduces a *clinamen* precisely when Lucretius is at the point of explaining the extent to which the *clinamen* is the condition of the freedom and will or voluptuous pleasure that has been wrested from destiny (*fatis avolsa*). But in all cases the context leaves no doubt as to the link between *clinamen*, freedom, and pleasure. The *clinamen* of the elementary principle – notably, the atom, the law of the atom – would be the pleasure principle. The *clinamen* introduces the play of necessity and chance into what could be called, by anachronism, the determinism of the universe. Nonetheless, it does not imply a conscious freedom or will, even if for some of us the principle of indeterminism is what makes the conscious freedom of man fathomable.

When I have the names of Epicurus and Lucretius appear here, a kind of *systrophè* takes place in my discourse. For Epicurus, condensation or density – the systrophic relief - is in the first place a twisted entanglement and concentrated turn of atoms (mass, swarm, turbulence, downpour, troop) that produces the seed (*semence*) of things, the *spermata*, the seminal multiplicity (inseminal or disseminal). A number of elements are gathered up in the turbulent whirl of the *systrophè* that I bring to you. They ingather in their turn and follow several turns. Which ones? For what diverse and overlapping reasons might I have provoked this Epicurean downpour? They number at least three.

1. The atomic elements, the bodies that fall in the void, are often defined, particularly by Lucretius, as letters (*littera*). And inside their *systrophè* they are seeds (*spermata, semina*). The indivisible element, the *atomos* of the literal dissemination produced by the supplement of deviation, is the *stoikheion*, a word at once designating the graphic element as well as the mark, the letter, the trait, or the point. This theory of literal dissemination is also in turn a discourse on incidents and accidents as symptoms and even, among others, as 'symptoms of the soul.' And in order to account for the possibility of speaking of these psychic symptoms (*peri ten psuchen ta sumptômata*) Epicurus rejects the theories of the 'incorporeal' soul (*Letter to Herodotus*, 67.8–12).

2. In consideration of the principal movement in the literal scattering of seeds (*semences*), should one interpret verticality as a fall, as the displacements proceeding from up to down in view of man or a finite being – and, precisely, proceeding from his view, within his horizon? Epicurus seems to reject this perspective: 'In the infinite,' he proposes, 'one should not speak of up and down: we know that if what is above our heads were transferred to the infinite, it would never appear to us in the same way....' 'Now, the universe is infinite from two points of view; first, through the number of bodies it contains and then through the immensity of the void that it encompasses' (according to Diogenes Laertes). Let us retain at least this much: the sense of the fall in general (as symptom, lapsus, incident, accidentality, cadence, coincidence, expiration date (*échéance*), luck, good luck, and *méchance*) is conceivable solely in the situation and places or space of finitude, within the multiple relations to the multiplicity of elements, letters, or seeds (*semences*).

An admittedly violent condensation could precipitate the Epicurean interpretation of the disseminating dispersion into the Heideggerian analytic of *Dasein*. Apparently a fortuitous connection, this systrophic precipitation would, however, be that much more necessary given that *Dasein* as such does not reduce itself to the current and metaphysical characters of *human existence or experience* (that of man as subject, soul or body, ego, conscious or unconscious). In the case of *Dasein* Heidegger analyses the finitude of thrownness (*Geworfenheit, l'être-jeté*, thrownness into existence, into the 'there,' into a world, into uncanniness, into the possibility of death, into the 'nothing,' the thrown Being-with-one-another). This *Geworfenheit* or thrownness is not an empirical character among others, and it has an essential rapport to dispersion and dissemination (*Zerstreuung*) as the structure of *Dasein*. Originarily thrown (*jeté*), *Dasein* is not only a finite being (Kant's *intuitus derivativus*) that, as *subject* (*sujet*), would be passively subjected to the objects that it does not create and that are as if thrown ahead to encounter it. Neither *subjectum* nor *objectum* – and even before this opposition – *Dasein* is *itself thrown*, originarily abandoned to fall and decline or, we could say, to chance (*Verfallen*). *Dasein*'s chances are, in the first place and also, its falls. And they are always mine, *mes chances*, each time related to its relation to itself, to a *Jemeinigkeit*, a mineness (an 'in each case mine') that does not come down to a relation to an ego or an I (*Ich, moi*). Heidegger is certainly precise on this point (*Sein und Zeit*, sec. 38): the fall (*Verfallenheit, déchéance*) of *Dasein* should not be interpreted as the 'fall'

(*'Fall,' 'chute'*) from an original, purer, and more elevated state. We are surely not dealing with a question of the 'corruption of human nature.' Yet one is all the more struck by certain analogies with such a discourse. All the more so, given Heidegger's rather pronounced silence regarding Democritus, to whom he alludes only briefly when considering the relationship between Galileo and Democritus in *Die Frage nach dem Ding* (1935-62, pp. 61-2), and again - in a context that is, however, of greater interest to us – in 'Democritus and Plato' (p. 162) and to *rythmos* in '*Vom Wesen und Begriff der Physis*' (*Wegmarken*, p. 338). To my knowledge he cites Epicurus but once, when interpreting his *Lathè biôsas*, 'life in hiding,' in *Aletheia* (1943). We shall limit ourselves to this reference here. Even if the affinities were purely lexical and apparently fortuitous, should they be considered as insignificant, as accidental, or, in the same vein, as symptoms? Is it insignificant that Heidegger isolates three structures or types of movements in connection with the fall into inauthenticity (*Uneigentlichkeit*)? These comprise the suspension in the void (*den Modus eines bodenlosen Schwebens*), the fall as a catastrophic downward plunge (*Absturz: 'Wir nennen diese "Bewegtheit" des Daseins in seinem eigenen Sein den Absturz'*), and turbulence ('*die Bewegtheit des Verfallens als Wirbel*,' sec. 38, 'Falling and Thrownness').

That would be the first and far too schematically exposed reason for situating Heidegger's analytic here. The other concerns the place that has to be ceded to Heidegger in Lacanian theory. This is also a point that I tried to urge in my interpretation of Lacan's Seminar on Poe's 'Purloined Letter.' All this belongs to the context and contract of our encounter; the deviation of another systrophe will no doubt lead us here again.

3. Despite the difference or the shift in context, the indivisibility of letters plays a decisive role in the debate where, it seems to me, the most serious strategic stakes are being called. They are made in terms of a psychoanalytic problematic that addresses determinism, necessity or chance, writing, the signifier and the letter, the simulacrum, fiction or literature. Here I must refer you to 'The Purveyor of Truth,' where I introduced the term '*atomystique* of the letter' in order to place it in question: it sustains Lacan's entire interpretation of 'The Purloined Letter,' and particularly of its circular, ineluctable, and predetermined return to the point of departure despite all the apparently random incidents. The letter, Lacan claims, shows little tolerance for partition. I have tried to demonstrate that this axiom was dogmatic and inseparable from a whole philosophy of psychoanalysis. Indeed, it made the entire analytical interpretation possible while it also assured that interpretation of its hermeneutic power over the kind of writing we call literary. However, this power also argues a powerlessness and a lack of comprehension. Without returning to a published debate, I shall quickly indicate the point toward which my present aim is inclined. The phenomenon of chance as well as that of literary fiction, not to mention what I call writing or the trace in general, do not so much lead up to the indivisibility but to a certain divisibility or internal difference of the so-called ultimate element (*stoikheion*, trait, letter, seminal mark). I prefer to call this element – which, precisely, is no longer elementary and indivisible – a *mark* for reasons that I have explained elsewhere and to which I shall return again.

A diversion of atomism is at issue, then, if not one of an anti-atomism. Why would the Epicurean doctrine be shielded from the *clinamen*? – from this *clinamen* whose doctrine – a properly Epicurean one – was supposed to have rerouted, according to Marx, the tradition of Democritus? Why do we refrain from applying the *clinamen* to Epicurus's name, and in his name itself?

If I gave this lecture the title of *Mes chances*, it was in order to address the issue of my chances and luck. My chances are well known; they sum up the experience of 'my' work, as well as that of 'my' teaching and 'my' texts. To be in luck (*avoir de la chance*) is, according to the French idiom, often to fall upon or to fall as you are supposed to, to 'fall well,' at the opportune moment, to find something by chance, to chance upon the right encounter in step with the irresponsibility of making a good find. 'The Purveyor of Truth,' for instance, begins by repeating the expression '*si ça se trouve*' (if it is found) at least three times. In common French that means, 'if by chance...,' 'if by accident....' Now, the moment has come to present to you, with my chances, what I have just found or lucked upon.

First stroke of luck: Première chance. 'The Murders in the Rue Morgue' can also be read as a preface to 'The Purloined Letter.' After Dupin is presented by the narrator, the reference to the name of Epicurus and his theories is not long in coming. Is this pure chance? Is it insignificant? Dupin reminds the narrator how he had been *thrown* upon a pile of street stones ('a fruiterer ... thrust you'), and how he had 'stepped upon one of the loose fragments, slipped, slightly strained [his] ankle.' He adds: 'You kept your eyes upon the ground - glancing, with a petulant expression, at the holes and ruts in the pavement (so that I saw you were still thinking of the stones), until we reached the little alley ... which has been paved, by way of experiment, with the overlapping and riveted blocks. Here your countenance brightened up, and, perceiving your lips move, I could not doubt that you murmured the word "stereotomy" [science of the cut or division], a term very affectedly applied to this species of pavement. I knew that you could not say to yourself "stereotomy" without being brought to think of atomies, and thus of the theories of Epicurus; and since, when we discussed this subject not very long ago, I mentioned to you how singularly, yet with how little notice, the vague guesses of that noble Greek had met with confirmation....' I cut here in order to suggest that besides 'the late nebular cosmogony,' to quote Dupin, and besides the physical sciences, the above confirmation to which the old science gives rise could well be genetics, psychoanalysis, the 'theory' (*la pensée*) of writing or literature. Without wishing to engage a reading of Poe's text at this time, I shall stress an element of structure that seems important to me. The reference to atomism and to the name of Epicurus is itself only a minuscule atom, a detail of the text, an incident, a literal trait in the series of which it nevertheless seems to give a reading.

But the incident's inscription within the series is accompanied in a most significant manner. The narrator himself explains how Dupin, the creator and analyst, 'a Bi-Part Soul,' 'a double Dupin - the creative and the resolvent,' *divines* the narrator's mind. And he recounts that when the narrator believes the other to fathom his soul, he is in truth only analysing symptoms and saying *'peri ten psukhen ta sumptômata,'* to recall Epicurus's letter to Herodotus once again. Instead of divining – by intuition, luck, or chance – he enters calculations built upon the accidents in a story of a fall, and he symptomalizes contingency. You will remember that Dupin and the narrator err without a goal; they hang about aimlessly (*au hasard*). Then, all of a sudden, Dupin links his argument to the narrator's inner and silent reverie, as if transmission of thought or telepathy had come to pass. In the manner of an analyst, Dupin explains, however, that instead of divining he had actually calculated. Indeed, he had made calculations, but in a way that reckons with apparently random (*hasardeux*) incidents that are very small, minuscule, quasi-atomic particles and that, curiously, have an essential relationship to the throwing, ejecting, and trajecting movement of the fall. Dupin interprets these *cases* as symptoms. The narrator asks: ' "How was it possible you should know I was thinking of —?" Here I paused, to ascertain beyond a doubt whether he really knew of whom I thought.' Baudelaire translates 'to know' each time, rightly and wrongly, as 'to divine.' A little later, the narrator asks: 'Tell me, for Heaven's sake ... the method – if method there is – by which you have been able to fathom my soul in this matter' (which Baudelaire translates as *'dans le cas actuel,'* in this actual case). If we had the time to reconstitute the most minuscule grains of the systrophic and analytic calculation approved in Dupin's response, we would once again find evidence of the 'little,' the 'throw,' the 'fall.'

These issues arise with the 'diminutive figure' of a boy who made him 'unfitted for tragedy,' and with a man who has thrown himself at the narrator ('the man who ran up against you') and who in turn throws him on that pile of street stones that bring stereotomy to mind. 'The larger links of the chain run thus - Chantilly, Orion, Dr. Nichols, Epicurus, Stereotomy, the street stones, the fruiterer.' While the name of Epicurus forms just one link in the chain, his theory seems nonetheless secretly to command the entire deployment of symptomal analysis. I say 'analysis' deliberately, to evoke the solution and resolution that, taking a regressive path toward the elementary particles, disconnects the severed details or incidents. Dupin is presented not only as a 'resolvent' analyst but as that type of analyst for whom, according to Baudelaire's slightly deviant yet faithful translation, 'all is symptom and diagnostics.' This is Baudelaire's translation for 'indications' in 'all afford, to his apparently intuitive perception, indications of the true state of affairs.' Dupin exercises his 'analytical power' and 'calculating power' *par excellence* in gamelike situations, for 'it is in matters beyond the limits of mere rule that the skill of the analyst is evinced.' In such cases, his lucidity is not simply of a mathematical order, but shows itself capable of unmasking the thoughts of the other. The narrator notes as much when his focus shifts to a visibly transferential situation (unless it is countertransferential): Dupin 'examines the countenance of his partner ... counting trump by trump, and honor by honor, through the glances bestowed by their holders upon each. He notes every variation of face as the play progresses, gathering a fund of thought from the differences in the expression.... He recognizes what is played through feint, by the manner with which it is *thrown* upon the table' (emphasis added). We are dealing, then, with an expert at that very game that consists in throwing or falling: 'A casual or inadvertent word; the accidental dropping or turning of a card, with the accompanying anxiety or carelessness in regard to its concealment, the counting of the tricks, with the order of their arrangement... all afford, to his apparently intuitive perception, indications of the true state of affairs.' 'All for him is symptom and diagnostics,' Baudelaire translates. Nor does this prevent the narrator from saying of our Dupin-the-atomist: 'There was not a particle of *charlatanism* about Dupin,' which Baudelaire translates as 'there was not an atom of charlatanism in my friend Dupin.' A moment later, this atomist devoid of the smallest atom of charlatanism will say to the narrator as subject: 'I knew that you could not say to yourself "stereotomy" without being brought to think of atomies, and thus to the theories of Epicurus.'

Second stroke of luck: Deuxième chance. I shall not have the time to display all my chances. No luck. But if I do not stand much of a chance, it is mostly due to the calculation of a certain '*pas de chance*' (no chance, no luck, and the step of luck) that makes me fall upon the providentially necessary passages of Poe or Baudelaire. '*Méchance*' is not standing a chance, *pas de chance*. All Baudelaire's notes on Poe's life and works open with a meditation on the writing of 'not standing a chance':

> There are fatal destinies; there are in the literature of each country men who carry the words *rotten luck* [*guignon*, also 'jinxed'] written in mysterious characters on the sinuous folds of their foreheads. Some time ago, an unfortunate man was brought before the tribunals. On his forehead he had a singular tattoo: 'doesn't stand a chance' [*pas de chance*]. In this way he carried with him, as does a book its title, the label of his life – and when he took the stand, the cross-examination proved that his existence was in conformity with this sign. Analogous fortunes are to be found in literary history.... Is there then a diabolical Providence who prepares misfortune from the cradle? That man, whose somber and desolate talent frightens us, was *thrown* with premeditation into a milieu that was hostile to him. (emphasis added)

Four years later, Baudelaire writes another introduction to Poe. Here we find the same tattoo, 'Doesn't stand a chance!' ('*Pas de chance!*') and Providence who 'throws' angelic natures downward. And they try in vain to protect themselves, for instance, by blocking all the outlets, by 'padding' 'the windows against the projectiles of chance'! But 'the Devil will enter through the keyhole.' Projectiles of chance: this is a matter not only of projection, the throw and the send-off (*le lancer*), but of the missive or dispatch (*l'envoi*) as well, of all the missives in the world. In addition to the dispatch we have the sending back or adverting to (*renvoi*) and, indeed, the boost (*relance*). In poker, *relancer* means to *raise* the stakes, to make a higher bid. One raises or *relances* when one knows how to play with what falls and when, being keen on making it pick up again, one boosts it upward to defer the fall and to cut across the incidence of other bodies in the course of its ups and downs. All of this, of course, comes under the art of coincidence, the simulacra of atoms and the art of the juggler, which, according to Baudelaire, would be Poe's art. Though Poe would go even beyond juggling, Baudelaire uses the term in order 'to apply it,' he says, 'almost as an *éloge* to the noble poet.' His 'almost' is very subtle, but necessary: in itself juggling would imply too great a mastery in the art of coincidence, which must remain 'uncanny.' Of this noble poet who bounds and rebounds (*lance et*

relance), Baudelaire frequently observes that he 'throws himself' (for example, into the grotesque or the horrible), that he 'hurls challenges at difficulties,' or, exceeding this, that 'he has been thrown, like a defenseless child,
to the hazards of random life.'

I have just quoted my chances with regard to Poe's '*pas de chance,*' 'not
standing a chance,' because it comes to light as a preface or postface to 'The
Purveyor of Truth,' the idea (*pensée*) of the missive that it picks up again
(*relancée*), and to the haphazardness of missives and the missives of haphazard. You may think that I am juggling. For when chances increase
steadily, and too many throws of the dice come to fall well, does this not
abolish blind Chance (*le hasard*)? It would be possible to demonstrate that
there is nothing random in the concatenation of my findings. An implaca-
ble program takes shape through the contextual necessity that requires cutting solids into certain sequences (stereotomy), intersecting and adjusting
subsets, mingling voices and proper names, and accelerating a rhythm that
merely gives the *feeling* of randomness to those who do not know the pre-
scription – which, incidentally, is also my case.

From 'Literary' Ascendance

If, in addition to Democritus, who engendered Epicurus (via his disciple
Nausiphanes), who in turn engendered Lucretius, literature is also at the
place of rendezvous, is this by chance? This would be the *second question*
that I said a moment ago that I wanted to raise. It leads us again to Freud,
supposing that we had ever left him. His texts, when they deal with the question of chance, always revolve around the proper name, the number, and
the letter. And, almost fatally, they meet literature, a certain type of literature that uplifts them, each time raising their stakes and marking their limit.
Why is this so?

One could initially ask oneself what these elements have in common –
these *stoikheia* that include the letter or the trait, the number, and the
proper name – such that they are to be found thus associated in the same
series and such that their relation to chance would be analogous. That which
they have in common, I will claim, is their insignificance in marking
(*insignifiance marquante*). This insignificance marks. It belongs to the mark.
It is marked but above all re-markable. This re-markable insignificance destines them, makes them enter into the play of the destination, and therein
stamps the possible detour of a *clinamen*. That which I here call insignificance is this structure that establishes that a mark in itself is not necessarily linked, even in the form of the reference (*renvoi*), to a meaning or to a
thing. Take, for example, the case of the proper name. It has no meaning in
itself, at least insofar as it is a proper name. It does not refer (*renvoie*) to
anyone; it designates someone only in a given context, for example (and for
example only), because of an arbitrary convention. The French name Pierre
has no meaning in itself. It is untranslatable, and if in my language it is the
homonym of a common noun that not only has a possible referent but also
a stable signification (the *pierre* or stone that one can cut to make cobble-
stone streets) that can lead to confusion, contamination, lapsus, or symp-

toms, this can bring about a fall while leaving the two 'normal' functions of the mark without contact between each other. The proper name Pierre is insignificant because it does not name by means of a concept. It stands for only one person each time, and the multiplicity of Pierres in the world bears no relation to the multiplicity of stones (*pierres*) that form a class and possess enough common traits to establish a conceptual significance or a semantic generality. This will be equally evident in the relation between a numeral and a number and also in that between a number and a thing numbered. Between the meaning of the number 7 and the numerals 7 (Arabic or Roman numerals, the words *sept*, seven, *sieben*) there is no natural, necessary, or intrinsic affiliation. No natural bond, to use Saussurian terminology, between the signified and the signifier. Nor is there a natural bond between the signified (the general meaning of 7, the number 7) and all things (stones, horses, apples, stars or souls, men or women, for instance) that could be found together in groups of 7. One could say the same, *mutatis mutandis*, for all graphic marks, for all traits in general, phonic or not, linguistic or not. The paradox here is the following (I must state it in its broadest generality): to be a mark and to mark its marking effect, a mark must be capable of being *identified*, recognized as the same, being precisely *re-markable* from one context to another. It must be capable of being repeated, re-marked in its essential trait as the same. This accounts for the apparent solidity of its structure, of its type, its *stereotypy*. It is this that leads us here to speak of the atom, since one associates indestructibility with indivisibility. But more precisely, it is not simple since the identity of a mark is also its difference and its differential relation, varying each time according to context, to the network of other marks. The ideal iterability that forms the structure of all marks is that which undoubtedly allows them to be released from any context, to be freed from all determined bonds to its origin, its meaning, or its referent, to emigrate in order to play elsewhere, in whole or in part, another role. I say 'in whole or in part' because by means of this essential insignificance the ideality or ideal identity of each mark (which is only a differential function without an ontological basis) can continue to divide itself and to give rise to the proliferation of other ideal identities. This iterability is thus that which allows a mark to be used more than once. It is more than one. It multiplies and divides itself internally. This imprints the capacity for diversion within its very movement. In the destination (*Bestimmung*) there is thus a principle of indetermination, chance, luck, or of destinerring. There is no assured destination precisely because of the mark and the proper name; in other words, because of this insignificance.

If I speak of the mark or the trace rather than the signifier, letter, or word, and if I refer these to the Democritian or Epicurian *stoikheion* in its greatest generality, it is for two reasons. First of all, this generality extends the mark beyond the verbal sign and even beyond human language. Thus I hesitate to speak of the 'arbitrariness of the sign' in the manner of Hegel and Saussure. Then, within this very frame of reference, I prefer to diverge in turn from strict atomism and the atomistic interpretation of the *stoikheion*. My *clinamen*, my luck, or my chances (*mes chances*) are what lead me to think of the *clinamen* beginning with the divisibility of the mark.

Let me come back to literature, to the work of art, to the *œuvre* in gen-

eral or at least to that which one names as such in the tradition of our culture. Without the mark there is certainly no *œuvre*. Each *œuvre*, being
absolutely singular in some respect, must have and admit the proper name.
This is the condition of its iterability as such. From whence comes, perhaps,
the general form of the privilege that it retains for us in our experience inasmuch as it is the locus of luck and of chance. The *œuvre* provokes us to
think of the event. This in turn challenges our attempts to *understand* luck
and chance, to envisage them, to take them in hand, or to inscribe them
within an anticipatory horizon. It is at least because of this that they are
œuvres and that they create an event, thereby challenging any program of
reception. *Œuvres* befall us. They speak about or unveil that which befalls
in its befalling upon us. They overpower us inasmuch as they explain themselves with that which falls from above. The *œuvre* is vertical and slightly
leaning.

Freud often said that poets and artists – although he attempted to include
their lives and *œuvres* within the horizon of psychoanalytic knowledge (to
make them lie down horizontally in the clinic) – had always anticipated and
indeed overwhelmed the discourse of psychoanalysis. In the sense of filiation as well as authority, literature would be an ascendant akin to a house,
a family, or a lineage. But what, more precisely, is at issue in this play of
titles?

I will now take my chances with Freud's text. As you may already suspect, I am going to proceed somewhat by chance, without a horizon, as if
with my eyes closed.

Third stroke of luck. By chance, I fall initially upon an example. By definition, there are nothing but examples in this domain. Freud tries to *understand* the forgetting of a proper name. He wants, therefore, in understanding,
to efface the appearance of chance in the relation between a certain proper
name and its having been forgotten. Which proper name? As if by chance,
that of a disciple of Epicurus. In the third chapter of *The Psychopathology
of Everyday Life*, 'The Forgetting of Names and Sets of Words':

> Here is an example of name-forgetting[2] with yet another and very subtle moti-
> vation which its subject has explained himself: 'When I was examined in philos-
> ophy as a subsidiary subject I was questioned by the examiner about the teachings
> of Epicurus, and after that I was asked if I knew who had taken up his theories
> in later centuries. I answered with the name of Pierre Gassendi, whom I had heard
> described as a disciple of Epicurus while I was sitting in a café only a couple of
> days before. To the surprised question how I knew that, I boldly answered that I
> had long been interested in Gassendi. The result of this was a certificate *magna
> cum laude*, but also unfortunately a subsequent obstinate tendency to forget the
> name Gassendi. My guilty conscience is, I think, to blame for my inability to
> remember the name in spite of all efforts; for I really ought not to have known
> it on that occasion either.'

Now, Freud continues, to understand that, one must know that this subject
attached great value to the title of doctor (Freud does not say, as I do, to
the title of professor) 'and [for how] many other things it has to serve as a
substitute.'

The person who has forgotten the proper name of the disciple of Epicurus
is someone who is referring himself back to the time when he himself was

a disciple, a student appearing before his masters at the moment of an examination. Freud has only to cite, to reproduce the interpretation of this disciple forgetting the name of a disciple, in identifying himself purely and simply, without taking the slightest initiative in interpretation, with this disciple who explains why he does not by chance forget the name of a disciple of Epicurus. To exaggerate slightly, one could say that Freud simultaneously identifies and transfers a symptom that could be called: the disciple of Epicurus and the forgetting of his name. I leave it to you to explore further; but never forget that throughout the history of Occidental culture the Democritian tradition, in which the names of Epicurus and his disciples are recorded, has been submitted since its origin (and initially under the violent authority of Plato) to a powerful repression. One can now follow its symptomatology, which begins with the effacement of the name of Democritus in the writings of Plato, even though Plato was familiar with his doctrine. Plato probably feared that one would draw some conclusion with respect to the proximity, indeed to the filiation, of some of his philosophemes. I leave it to you to investigate further this path as well.

I have just named Democritus after having in fact only spoken of his disciples and of the disciples of his disciples: Epicurus, Lucretius, Gassendi. Now the *fourth stroke of luck*: here is the master in person in Freud's text, the father Democritus, as analyst and the one who deciphers symptoms. This is not the only reason that I will cite this passage at the end of chapter 9 of *Psychopathology* ('Symptomatic and Chance Actions'). In the same passage (is this by chance?) Freud also reminds us of the privilege of literature and the priority of the poet. The latter has already said everything that the psychoanalyst would like to say. The psychoanalyst therefore can only repeat and indebt himself within a filiation; in particular, on the subject of symptomal deciphering of seemingly insignificant accidents. The absolute precursor, the grandfather here, is the author of *Tristram Shandy*. I therefore cite Freud citing someone else citing Laurence Sterne (paragraph and citation that Freud added later as if to make amends for something previously forgotten in the earlier edition of 1920):

> In the field of symptomatic acts, too, psychoanalytic observation must concede priority to imaginative writers [*Dichter*]. It can only repeat what they have said long ago. Wilhelm Stross has drawn my attention to the following passage in Laurence Sterne's celebrated humorous novel, *Tristram Shandy*:
> '... And I am not at all surprised that *Gregory of Nazianzum*, upon observing the hasty and untoward gestures of *Julian*, should foretel he would one day become an apostate; – or that St. *Ambrose* should turn his *Amanuensis* out of doors, because of an indecent motion of his head, which bent backwards and forwards like a flail; – or that *Democritus* should conceive *Protagoras* to be a scholar, from seeing him bind up a faggot, and thrusting, as he did, the small twigs inwards.
> —There are a thousand unnoticed openings, continued my father, which let a penetrating eye at once into a man's soul; and maintain it, added he, that a man of sense does not lay down his hat in coming into a room, – or take it up in going out of it, but something escapes, which discovers him.'

In this sequence of citations taking us up to Democritus once again, the *descendance* will not have escaped you. Freud acknowledges the debt of the psychoanalyst, and this is also a filiation. This instance is exemplary since it engages Freud with respect to Sterne cited by Stross who in turn cites, from *Tristram Shandy*, the speech of a father. It is a father who speaks and whom he makes speak via the mouth of his son from a thousand unnoticed openings ('a thousand unnoticed openings, continued *my* father, which let a penetrating eye [*ein sharfes Auge*] at once into a man's soul'). By the mouth of his son, and by that of the poet, this father will have cited in turn the ancestor of ancestors in this matter – notably, Democritus – the prototype of the analyst who knew how to diagnose science itself, that is, 'scholarship,' and the *Gelehrtheit* of Protagoras, beginning with nothing, with mere twigs. Democritus did not identify just any symptom. In interpreting - an operation that consisted of *binding up* insignificant things, elementary bundles, in a certain way, of binding them evenly, and not in a haphazard fashion, by turning them inward – Democritus deciphered a symptom that is quite simply the symptom of knowledge, of the desire for knowledge, the *libido sciendi*, scholarship, the *skholè*: which is simultaneously that which tends toward laborious study and that which suspends ordinary activity, the everyday relation to praxis, for this end. Protagoras, a man of bonds and of disconnections, of the re-solution (*analuein*), is a type of analyst. That would be the diagnosis that the analyst 'Dupin' Democritus pronounces with regard to the symptom. Indeed, there are nothing but analysts. That is, those who are analysed in this textual abyss wherein each is ever more engendered, generated, indebted, affiliated, subjected, than the one before, all having descended or fallen from a series of proto-analysts in an eminently divisible chain of proper names and individuals: Freud, Stross, Sterne, the son and the father in *Tristram Shandy*, Protagoras, Democritus, etc. Each of them has simultaneously interpreted and reduced a random series. Each has passed it on to be read by the other before the other. This chain is heterogeneous; only the proper names, texts, and situations are different each time, yet all subjects are inscribed and implicated in the scene that they claim to interpret. This overall '*mise en scène*' certainly gives the impression of being predominantly literary. According to what Freud himself said, this would be *Tristram Shandy*. The great rendezvous could be the performative of the *œuvre*. It would seem necessary to explore elsewhere the theme of the 'rendezvous' (*Zusammentreffen*, *Zusammenkunft*) in the *Psychopathology*, notably in the last chapter.

The question I have just raised could be referred to as that of science and luck, or determinism and chance, and indeed this is the title of the last chapter of *Psychopathology* – 'Determinism, Belief in Chance and Superstition.' What happens to an interpretive science when its object is psychic and when it thus implicates in some respect the subject itself of that science? In this form, the question is rather classical. What happens when the 'savant' acknowledges his debt or his dependence with regard to apparently non-scientific statements such as, for example, poetic or literary ones? And when an analytic attitude itself becomes a symptom? When there is a tendency to interpret the incidents or accidents that befall us – opportunely or not – by means of the reintroduction of determinism, necessity, or signification, does this signify in turn an abnormal or pathological relation to the real? For example, what is the difference between superstition or paranoia on the one hand, and science on the other, if they all mark a compulsive tendency to interpret random signs in order to reconstitute a meaning, a necessity, or a destination?

Freud asks himself this in the same chapter, and he must do so in a quasi-autobiographical manner. Implicating himself in the situation, he tells us in sum (and here we could parody a Nietzschean title, a type of Freudian *Ecce Homo*): *Why I am a good analyst* or *Why I am above all not superstitious and even less paranoid*; why I am moderate in my desire to interpret, why this desire is simply normal. In other words, why I have a very good relation to chance and am lucky in my transactions with it. And so you see, Freud tells us, what my chances are.

What are his chances?

Let us allow him to tell us a story whose truth or falsity would be of little consequence. Remember that in 1897 he confided to Fliess his conviction that no 'index of reality' of any sort exists in the unconscious and that it is impossible to distinguish between truth and a fiction 'invested with affect.' But, as we shall examine shortly, Freud could only propose his work as scientific - in the classical sense - by reintroducing this limit between *Wahrheit* and *Dichtung*, so to speak.

Here is the exemplary story. It is not a story about vacations, as is the one of the *fort–da* with the mother, and yet it is the same. In this case, upon returning from vacation, we are between two types of *skholè*: leisure and study. When he returns from vacation Freud thinks of the patients that he will see again and initially of an elderly, ninety-year-old woman about whom he has already spoken and indeed whom he has already given several years of medical treatment. Each year he wonders how much time remains for the old woman. One particular day, Freud, being in a hurry, hires a coachman who, like everyone else in the neighborhood, knew the address of this patient. He knew the destination: all the problems that we are speaking about fall under the general category of the address, of forwarding, of the destination, and hence of the thrust (*jet*) or the project of the dispatch (*projet d'un envoi*). The fall, the accident, the case always arises to post the dispatch (*envoi*) from some interruption or detour that creates the symptom. (This is why I allow myself to record these modest reflections following more patiently elaborated work which is concerned with the relation between psychoanalysis, literature, and philosophy on the one hand, and the question of the dispatch (*envoi*) and of the destination on the other.) The coachman – who knows the address, the correct one – stops, however, in front of another house, which has the same number (always a question of number) but on a parallel street. Freud reproves the man, who then apologizes. Is this error concerning the address simply an accident or does it actually mean something? Freud's answer is clear and firm, at least in appearance: 'Certainly not to me, but if I were superstitious [*abergläubisch*], I should see an omen [*Vorzeichen*] in the incident, the finger of fate [*Fingerzeig des Schicksals*] announcing that this year would be the old lady's last.'

Along the way, two values of destination superimpose themselves upon each other: that of the address or place of destination and that of destiny (*Schicksal*), the dimensions and direction of that which is dispatched, sent, *geschickt*. (One of the meanings of the adresse in French, that is to say, skillfulness (*habilité*), translates the word *Geschick*.) One wonders, then, if the false address (and the apparent *maladresse* or blunder of the coachman) do not in advance point toward the true and correct destination – that is, the coming death of the old woman. Is it the case that the coachman did not actually go to the correct address, the one that is appropriate (*où ça tombe bien*), to speak of the accident that will not fail to occur? Bad luck (*malchance*) or wickedness (*méchance*) would invert its sign. This will be the chance for the truth to reveal itself. A lapsus is revealing in the sense that it gives another truth its chance. The limit between the conscious and unconscious, that is, between the unconscious 'I' and the other of consciousness, is perhaps this possibility for my fortune (*mes chances*) to be misfortune (*malchance*) and for my misfortune to be in truth fortunate (*une chance*).

Freud claims that he does not stop, in this case, at the revelation of *Schicksal* by the '*Adresse*' since he knows that he is not superstitious. He considers the incident (*Vorfall*) to be an accident or a contingency without further signification (*eine Zufälligkeit ohne weiteren Sinn*). It would have been otherwise, he continues, if he *himself* had been the origin of the error and if, by distraction and on foot, he had stopped at the wrong address. In that case, there would have been *Vergehen* – mistaken conduct calling for interpretation (*Deutung*). All of this without chance (*Zufall*) in the least. But this was not the case. It was the coachman who was mistaken and Freud is not superstitious. He stresses the point. If he were, he would have stopped at this interpretation. But he does not stop there. Well, not for a long time, since he found it necessary to raise such a question, which shows this hypothesis also to have crossed his mind. He only distinguishes himself from the superstitious person at the moment of concluding at the instant of judgment and not at all during the unfolding of the interpretation. But Freud does not recognize this at any point in the following paragraph since he explains to us everything that distinguishes him from a superstitious man. He will only go as far as admitting that the only thing he has in common with the superstitious man is the tendency, the 'compulsion' (*Zwang*), to interpret: 'not to let chance count as chance but to interpret it.' The hermeneutic compulsion – that is what superstition and 'normal' psychoanalysis have in common. Freud says it explicitly. He does not believe in chance any more than the superstitious do. What this means is that they both believe in chance if to believe in chance means that one believes that all chance means something and therefore that there is no chance. Thus we have the identity of non-chance and chance and of misfortune (*mé-chance*) and fortune (*la chance*).

Before examining the criteria proposed by Freud to distinguish between these two hermeneutic compulsions, we shall take a brief detour from this side of these fortunes, although I am less and less sure as to whether they are misfortunes, my fortunes, or those of Freud (*méchance, mes chances ou celles de Freud*). I reread as if for the first time the story of the address and the coachman. One should notice that he seems to have had neither of the two compulsions and not to have asked himself any such questions. Indeed, Freud seems immediately to exclude all communication between the coachman's unconscious and his own. Following my own compulsion again, I immediately said to myself: and what if the old woman were Freud's mother? Certainly you know very well how much he feared the death of his mother, but he was also afraid of dying before her – a double bind. For all kinds of reasons evident in the reading, this patient could not simply be his mother. She could nevertheless *represent* his mother and take her place. Now here is my stroke of luck, *the fifth*, I believe: Freud had already spoken of this old woman in a passage to which I hasten to return, for, according to his phantasm that he exhibits and interprets himself, she indeed is his mother. This entails, he tells us, the single example of a medical mistake in his experience as a doctor. Instead of administering two drops of eye lotion in the woman's eyes and giving her the usual injection of morphine, Freud does the opposite: he puts the morphine in her eyes. It is not a dream of injection, as in the case of Irma, but the reality of an instillation, and that of a liquid that he should have injected. Freud is frightened even though there is no real danger. A few drops of morphine at 2 per cent in the conjunctival sac would cause no great harm, but in analysing this disproportionate fear, which is a symptom, he falls upon the common expression '*sich an der Alten vergreifen*,' 'to do violence to the old woman,' *vergreifen* meaning both 'to make a blunder' and 'to commit an assault' (cf. Strachey). This puts him on the track of Oedipus and Jocasta. Freud develops this in greater detail in a passage to which I refer you (Chap. 8, '*Das Vergreifen*,' 'Bungled Actions'). Most of the symptoms in this chapter are found to be falls (*chutes*).

Let us now return to the inviolable frontiers that Freud wants to sustain at any price between the superstitious and himself. He does not propose a general distinction, however. Speaking in the first person, he uses all of his eloquence to convince us that he is certainly not superstitious: '*Ich unterscheide mich also von einem Abergläubischen in folgendem*, I am therefore different from a superstitious person in the following way. ...' All of his declarations are developed explicitly in the mode of 'I believe,' 'I do not believe,' I am not superstitious because '*Ich glaube dass*' or '*Ich glaube nicht dass*.' What does he not believe? That an event having nothing to do with his psychic life (the coachman's error, for example) could teach him anything about a future reality. But he believes that an apparently nonintentional manifestation of his psychic life unveils something hidden that belongs only to his psychic life. He summarizes this in the following: 'I believe in external (real) chance, it is true, but not in internal (psychical) accidental events. With the superstitious person it is the other way round.' A rather abrupt way of collecting things and marking limits. Freud forgets to formalize what he has just stated – the relation to the future. I must leave this issue aside. It relates to the laborious distinction that Freud attempts elsewhere between telepathy and thought transmission. I return here once again to the fragment detached from *La Carte postale*, entitled: 'Telepathy.'

'I believe [*Ich glaube*] in external (real) chance, it is true, but not in internal (psychical) chance. With the superstitious person it is the other way round [*Der Abergläubische umgekehrt*].' One must read this vocabulary of belief very carefully. While availing himself of the word 'belief' Freud seems in effect to oppose a normal attitude, that of scientific objectivity, to superstitious belief, that of the *Abergläubischer*, which he claims not to have. He opposes one belief to another, a belief to a credulity. He believes in determinism in the internal and psychic domain. This does not mean – and here one must be careful, I believe – that he does not believe in the occurrence of chance in the external world, nor does it mean that he would agree that the world is thrown to chance and to chaos. One could find a thousand declarations by Freud attesting a completely determinist conviction of the positivistic type prevalent in his day. He even hoped one day to see the science of the psyche united, in a certain way, with the biophysical sciences. And in this precise context, which we are analysing here, he is only interested in the type of *belief*, of attitude or subjective experience appropriate to the founding of scientific objectivity in the circumscribed domain of psychic events. One must not confuse the domains, he tells us, nor their proper causalities. For example, one must not confuse that which in the drive comes from the biophysical and organic with that which is represented in the world of the psyche. These are the limits that the superstitious person does not recognize in his or her disbelief in psychic determinism. Freud, however, does believe in it, and he thus affirms his project of founding psychoanalysis as a positive science. This tradition has been sustained. For example, Lacan follows Freud to the letter on this point, when he says that a letter always arrives at its destination. There is no chance in the unconscious. The apparent randomness must be placed in the service of an unavoidable necessity that in fact is never contradicted.

But we are speaking of chance. In this historical-theoretical conjuncture one might be tempted to calculate the probabilities of the appearance of the event named: psychoanalysis as a project of positive science. This is not my proposal, however.

I do not believe that Freud believes in *actual* chance in external things. For him, the *believing experience* that *finite* beings have of this external world, once the two series, worlds, or contexts are dissociated (inside/outside), is *normally* and *legitimately* the acceptance of chance, of a margin of chance or probability that it would not be normal or serious to want to reduce or exclude. One could then say, as with the classical determinist conception, that the *effects* of chance (empirically verified) appear in the interference of relatively independent series, of 'little worlds' that are not closed. The implicit question to which Freud is responding is thus not the larger one of chance (objective or subjective, in things or in us, mathematical or empirical). It is not this question in its modern or classical form. It is only that of the *believing attitude* before the effects of chance, given the two series of causality: psychic/physical, internal/external. Of course these two series or two contextual worlds are only distinguishable from within a culture (or a 'world') that therein forms the most general context. It is for us, in the Occident, the culture of common sense that is marked by a powerful scientifico-philosophic tradition, metaphysics, technics, the opposition of subject/object (*sujet/objet*), and precisely a certain organization of the throw (*jet*). Through several differentiated relays, this culture goes back at least to Plato, where the repression of Democritus perhaps leaves the trace of a very large symptom. Without being able to take this route today, I will locate only what I have called above a *mark*: in the construction of its concept none of the limits or oppositions that I have just invoked are considered absolutely pertinent or decisive, but rather as presuppositions to be deconstructed.

We also know that in other passages, in other problematic contexts, Freud carefully avoids ontologizing or substantializing the limit between outside and inside, between the biophysical and the psychic. But in the *Psychopathology* and elsewhere he requires this limit not only to protect this fragile, enigmatic, threatened defensive state that one calls 'normality' but also to circumscribe a solid context (once again stereotomy), the unity of a field of coherent and determinist interpretation, that which we so calmly call psychoanalysis *itself*. But he already had great difficulties with this in other places where he tackles such formidable issues as that of the drive ('a concept ... on the frontier between the mental and the physical,' *Three Essays, S.E.* 7: 168), of telepathy, or of the transmission of thought. At least to the extent that he circumscribes psychoanalysis, the science of the psyche, so as to separate it from the other sciences, Freud provisionally suspends all epistemological relations to the sciences or to the modern problems concerning chance. He wants, in short, to constitute a science of *experience* (conscious or unconscious) as the rapport of a finite being who is thrown (*jeté*) into the world. And this thrown being projects (*Cet être-jeté projette*).

Precisely at this point it is even more difficult for Freud to sustain this limit that separates him from the superstitious person since they both share the hermeneutic compulsion. If the superstitious person projects (*projette, projiziert*), if he throws (*jette*) toward the outside and ahead of himself the 'motivations' that Freud claims to be looking for on the inside, if he interprets chance from the standpoint of an external 'event' at the point where Freud reduces it or leads it back to a 'thought,' it is because essentially the superstitious person does not believe, any more than Freud, in the solidity of the spaces circumscribed by our Occidental stereotymy. He does not believe in the contextualizing and framing but not actual limits between the psychic and the physical, the inside and the outside, not to mention all of the other connected oppositions. More so than Freud, more so than this Freud here, the superstitious person is sensitive to the precariousness of the contextual circumscriptions of the epistemological frames, the *constructs* and the *artefacts* that enable us, for life's convenience and for the mastery of limited networks of knowledge and technics, to separate the psychic from the physical or the inside from the outside. The superstitious person simply has a different experience of this same finitude.

But let us not make the superstitious person into a thinker capable of deconstructing the limits or the oppositions that Freud himself sustained dogmatically here in order to circumscribe the field of a scientific psychoanalysis. Inversely, if I might be permitted to put this forward, some sensitivity to superstition is perhaps not a useless stimulation for the deconstructive desire. But in fact, in the eyes of Freud, the superstitious person, to the same extent as the religious one and the metaphysician, is not the one who places the limits in question in the name of science, of the enlightened, or even in that of deconstruction. It is someone who, respecting these limits, projects on the outside that which is inside and that in which he lives. Through this concept of *projection* (or throwing), the scheme of the *jet* again provides the essential mediation. In the following paragraph Freud describes superstition, modern religion, metaphysics itself as 'nothing but psychology projected [*projizierte*] into the external world.' (These projections evidently have a fictional structure and, as in the case of the unconscious, one does not distinguish here between reality and 'fiction invested with affect.') This paragraph multiplies the analogies, and Freud is overwhelmed by them. Such is always the case whenever he is forced to transgress the limits or the 'frames of reference' that are simultaneously convenient and without solidity. Not having the time for a more extensive development, I quote and emphasize the terms which situate the difficulty:

> The obscure recognition (the endopsychic perception, *as it were*) of psychical factors and relations in the unconscious *is mirrored* [*spiegelt sich – es ist schwer, es anders zu sagen*] – *it is difficult to express it in other terms, and here the analogy with paranoia must come to our aid* in the construction of a supernatural reality, which is *destined to be changed back once more by science into the psychology of the unconscious*. One could venture to explain in this way the myths of paradise and *the fall* of man, of God, of good and evil, of immortality and so on, *and to transform metaphysics into metapsychology*. The gap between the paranoiac's displacement and that of the superstitious person is less wide than it appears at first sight.... They [primitive human beings] behaved, therefore, just like paranoiacs, who draw conclusions from insignificant signs given them by other people, and just like all normal people, who quite rightly base their estimate of their neighbours' characters on their chance and unintentional actions.

This discourse is built on an impressive series of approximations and declared analogies. It does not only interpret the motif of the fall or decline, of the *méchance* of man as a superstitious projection – or even paranoiac, in any case, of a psychological order. It does not only suggest, as in *Totem and Taboo*, that there is a certain analogy between paranoid mania and a (deformed) philosophic system. It projects the reconversion into science or into metapsychology of the metaphysical discourse *from which it nonetheless obtains the concepts themselves for this project* and operation – notably the oppositional limits between the psychic and the physical, the inside and the outside, not to mention all those that depend on them. Playing fiction against fiction, projection against projection, this gesture could appear – depending on the case – naïve or audacious, dogmatic or hypercritical. I will not choose (*trancher*) between them, and indeed I wonder if there really is a choice.

Freud works by playing with the topologies and the conceptual limits of inherited discourses, be they philosophical or scientific. The provisional circumscription of an explanatory context – one might say of a field of knowledge – supposes something like the performative of a convention and a fiction each time, as well as the contract that serves to guarantee new performatives. Freud acknowledges that he does not believe in the substantial value of these limits nor in the definitive character of such circumscriptions. Having taken account of a certain state of the discourse, of discourses, and of many sciences at the same time, having taken account also of the necessity of constituting a theory and a practice, the assignment of such limits is indispensable. But it is indispensable to someone – Freud, for example – at a particular moment in a particular situation. Yet there is nothing relativist or empiricist in this claim. Elsewhere, I have tried to show how the inscription of a proper name, of a certain autobiography, and of a certain fictional projection might be constitutive for psychoanalytic discourse and indeed for the very structure of its occurrence (*événement*). The event of its occurrence thus raises within itself the questions of chance and literature. Not that all fiction and all inscriptions of proper names have had a literary dimension or a relation to the work of art as such; rather, they arise in the place where, between the movement of science (notably when it is concerned with random structure) and that of philosophy, of the arts – literary or not – the limits cannot be actual and static or *solid* but rather only the effects of contextual circumscription. Neither linear nor indivisible, they would arise instead from an analysis that I will call (with some circumspection) *pragrammatological*, at the intersection of a pragmatics and a grammatology. Open to a different sense of the dispatch (*envoi*) and of dispatches (*envois*), pragrammatology should always take the situation of the marks into account; in particular that of utterances, the place of senders and addressees, of framing and of the sociohistorical circumscription, and so forth. It should therefore take account of the problematics of randomness in all fields where it evolves: physics, biology, game theory, and the like. In this respect, the advent of psychoanalysis is a complex event not only in terms of its historical probability but in terms of a discourse that remains open and that attempts at each instant to regulate itself – yet affirming its originality – according to the scientific and artistic treatment of randomness, which in the course of this century has undergone continued transformation. This is where one can find overdetermined comings and goings (*allers et retours*), a game of advances and delays upon which I should renounce further speculation but that I wish to illustrate, in conclusion, by a citation. If I conclude with the conclusion of *Leonardo da Vinci and a Memory of His Childhood*, it is for three reasons. These do not exclude the randomness of the moment where, as my exposé is becoming much too long, *la chute* (in French one says *la chute* (the fall) or the *envoi* for the end of a lecture) makes me fall upon this text rather than another. This will be *my last chance*. It is the moment when suddenly (*d'un seul coup*) two dice come to a standstill and we must tally the score. We are thus touching upon the incalculable and the innumerable.

Freud concludes, as you will see, by an allusion to the incalculable and the innumerable. This is the first reason to cite him. But it is precisely a question of the incalculability and the innumerability of the reasons or the causes (*ragioni*, *causes*, *Ursachen*) that are in nature and that 'never enter experience.' Second reason: this allusion to nature as 'full of countless causes [*ragioni*] that never enter experience' is a quasi-citation and from an artist. Once again indebtedness and filiation. Freud cites Leonardo da Vinci, whom he had come to recognize as being out of the reach of analytical science by virtue of a certain random enigma. But Freud cites da Vinci approximately citing Shakespeare, or rather Hamlet the son: '*La natura è piena d'infinite ragioni che non furono mai in isperienza,*' in place of 'There are more things in heaven and earth, Horatio, / Than are dreamt of in your philosophy.' Extending across numerous mediators, the debt is once again acknowledged with respect to the poet or even to a dramatic character that one has so often wished to have lie down on the couch. Literature perhaps need not resist the clinic. To stay with our present argument, let us say that art, in particular the 'art of discourse' and literature, only represents a certain power of indeterminacy that sustains the capacity of *performatively* circumscribing its own context for its own event, that of the *œuvre*. It is perhaps a kind of freedom, a large margin in the play of this circumscription (*découpe*). This stereotomic margin is very large and perhaps even the largest of all at a certain time in history, but it is not infinite. The appearance of arbitrariness or chance (literature as the place of proper names, if you wish) has to do with this margin. But this is also the place of the greatest symptomatology. Giving the greatest chance to chance, it reappropriates chance itself into necessity or fatality. Literature plays nature for fortune – and art. ('Nature's above art in that respect' – *King Lear*.) Consequently, the third reason for this citation: it appeases the sense of remorse or misfortune ('How malicious is my fortune,' says the bastard Edmund in *King Lear*), the regret I feel in not having attempted with you, as I initially projected, an analysis of *King Lear* that would take us beyond Freud's observations in *The Theme of the Three Caskets* (1913). I would have followed the play of Nature and Fortune there, the words 'nature' and 'fortune,' and also the abundantly numerous 'letters' (for example, the 'thrown letter'), the 'wisdom of nature,' 'prediction' ('there's son against father: the king falls from bias of nature'), 'planetary influence' for 'a sectary astronomical,' of 'epicurism,' 'posts,' letters and lips to unseal, 'gentle wax' and the 'reason in madness' of Lear ('I am even / The natural fool of fortune'). And taking more time, but that will be for another time, I would have attempted to read with you together, between the lines of Shakespeare, Freud and Heidegger's reflections on *Moira* (in *The Theme of the Three Caskets* and in *Moira*). As a solution of compromise between the things I do and do not renounce here, I shall take my chances with the following citation of a citation of a citation. I shall cite Freud citing da Vinci citing Shakespeare. Notice in particular the play of limits and self-limitations that I stress in the passage. These are the strokes (*coups*) and the chances of psychoanalysis. I will be satisfied to propose a title in English for this citation:

Subliming Dissemination

Instincts and their transformations [*Die Triebe und ihre Umwandlungen*] are at the limit of what is discernible by psychoanalysis. From that point it gives place to biological research. We are obliged to look for the source of the tendency to repression and the capacity for sublimation in the organic foundations of character on which the mental structure is only afterwards erected. Since artistic talent and capacity are intimately connected with sublimation we must admit that the nature of artistic function is also inaccessible to us along psychoanalytic lines. The tendency of biological research today is to explain the chief features in a person's organic constitution as being the result of the blending of male and female dispositions, based on [chemical] substances. Leonardo's physical beauty and his left-handedness might be quoted in support of this view. *We will not, however, leave the ground of purely psychological research.*

Once again deliberate self-limitation gives psychoanalysis its only chance as a science. It circumscribes a context into which external randomness no longer penetrates. Biogenetics is not devoid of randomness and neither is the psyche, but the orders or the random sequences must not communicate or cross over into the same grouping, at least if one wants to distinguish between orders of calculable necessity. There must be no bastardy or hybridization, no accidental grafts between these two generalities, genres, or genealogies. But how is one to eliminate the throws of bastardy's dice?, one could ask the author of *Leonardo*. Is not the concept of sublimation, like that of the drive, precisely the concept of bastardy?

> Our aim remains that of demonstrating the connection along the path of instinc-
> tual activity between a person's external experiences and his reactions. Even if
> psychoanalysis does not throw light on the fact of Leonardo's artistic power, it at
> least renders its manifestations and its limitations intelligible to us. It seems at
> any rate as if only a man who had had Leonardo's childhood experiences could
> have painted the Mona Lisa and the St. Anne, have secured so melancholy a fate
> for his works and have embarked on such an astonishing career as a natural sci-
> entist, as if the key to all his achievements and *misfortunes* [emphasis added] lay
> hidden in the childhood phantasy of the vulture.
>
> But may one not take objection to the findings of an inquiry which ascribes to
> accidental circumstances [*Zufälligkeiten*] of his parental constellation so decisive
> an influence on a person's fate [*Schicksal*] – which, for example, makes Leonardo's
> fate depend on his illegitimate birth and on the barrenness of his first stepmother
> Donna Albiera? I think one has no right to do so. If one considers chance [*Zufall*]
> to be unworthy of determining our fate, it is simply a relapse into the pious view
> of the Universe which Leonardo himself was on the way of overcoming when he
> wrote that the sun does not move. We naturally feel hurt that a just God and a
> kindly providence do not protect us better from such influences during the most
> defenceless period of our lives. At the same time we are all too ready to forget
> that in fact every thing to do with our life is chance [*Zufall*], from our origin out
> of the meeting of spermatozoon and ovum onwards [this is also that which I name,
> in my language, dissemination – J.D.] – chance which nevertheless has a share in
> the law and necessity of nature, and which merely lacks any connection with our
> wishes and illusions. The apportioning of the determining factors of our life
> between the 'necessities' of our constitution and the 'chances' [*Zufälligkeiten*] of
> our childhood may still be uncertain in detail; but in general it is no longer pos-
> sible to doubt the importance precisely of the first years of our childhood. We all
> still show too little respect for Nature which (in the obscure words of Leonardo
> which recall Hamlet's lines) 'is full of countless causes ["*ragioni*"] that never enter
> experience.'
>
> Every one of us human beings corresponds to one of the countless experiments
> in which these '*ragioni*' of nature force their way into experience. (*S.E.* 11: 136–7)

Freud loves and looks after Nature.

Among the paths through which Nature erupts in our experience a mistake always remains possible – a *Vergreifen* or bastardy.

In looking after Nature Freud can still mistake the address or *pharmakon*,
he can replace the eye drops with morphine, the old woman could be his
mother or his mother-in-law, and the 'I' of the coachman is perhaps not an
other. He is perhaps not good. Maybe a bastard – maybe it is I rereading,
under the influence of some drug, the myth of the harnessing and fall of
souls in the *Phaedrus*. But Plato too, already, explained that coachmen are
always 'good' and composed 'of good elements' (*ex agatôn*), whereas for
other beings there is a mixture. It is true that when Plato makes Socrates
speak he cites *Stésichore* (244a) and that prior to the myth he reminds us:
'*ouk est' etymos logos ôs an ...*,' 'there is no true language if ...' I leave you

Notes

*The Edith Weigert Lecture, sponsored by the Forum on Psychiatry and the Humanities, Washington School of Psychiatry, 15 October 1982.

1. In a certain way this essay proposes an almost silent reading of the word '*tombe*' (tomb) or '*tomber*' (to fall) in *La Carte postale*. This is one of the most frequently used words in the *Envois*. Take for example the entry for 14 March 1979: 'Somebody else, whom I know well, would unbind himself to run in the other direction. I'll wager that he falls upon you again; I fell in well with you, so I'm staying.' On the following day: 'If you were insane you would have come to wait for me like a hallucinating woman. I would have run towards you along the platform, near the tracks, and I would have done everything not to fall.' If I quote this book, I do so because I find it included in the program of our encounter – it was in a certain sense inscribed in its charter. Don't accuse me, therefore, of being, as you say in English, 'self-centered.' In truth I always dreamt of writing a *self-centered* text; I never arrived at that point – I always fall upon the others. This will end up by being known.

2. The preceding passage in Freud was concerned with the substitution of the names of Nietzsche and Wilde, among others, for that of Jung, which a woman could not remember, associating Wilde and Nietzsche with the idea of 'mental illness.' 'You Freudians will go on looking for the causes of insanity till you're insane yourselves [*geisteskrank*].' Then: 'I can't bear Wilde and Nietzsche. I don't understand them. I hear they were both homosexuals.' Nietzsche is also a name that Freud would have very much liked to forget. He occasionally succeeded and he avows this. Concerning chance and chaos there would be a great deal to say at this point in the name of Nietzsche.

References

Baudelaire, C. *Edgar Allan Poe: Sa vie et ses ouvrages*, ed. W. T. Bandy, Toronto: University of Toronto Press, 1973.

Bollack, J. and M. and Wismann, H. *La Lettre d'Epicure*, Paris: Minuit, 1971.

Derrida, J. *La Carte postale*, Paris: Flammarion, 1980.

Epicurus. *Letters, Principal Doctrines, and Vatican Sayings*, trans. R. Geer, Indianapolis: Bobbs-Merrill, 1964.

Freud, S. *Standard Edition of the Complete Psychological Works*, London: Hogarth, 1953–74.

—— *The Psychopathology of Everyday Life* (1901), *S.E.*, vol. 6.

—— *Three Essays on the Theory of Sexuality* (1905), *S.E.*, vol. 7.

—— *Leonardo da Vinci and a Memory of His Childhood* (1910), *S.E.*, vol. 11.

—— 'The Theme of the Three Caskets' (1913), *S.E.*, vol. 12.

Heidegger, M. *Die Frage nach dem Ding* (1935–62), Tübingen: Niemeyer, 1962.

—— *Aletheia*, 1943.

—— *Wegmarken*, Frankfurt: Klostermann, 1967.

—— *Sein und Zeit*, Frankfurt: Niemeyer, 1977.

Lacan, J. 'The Seminar on "The Purloined Letter"', trans. Jeffrey Mehlman, *Yale French Studies*, 48 (1972), 39–72.

Lucretius. *De rerum natura*, Zurich: Hans Rohr, 1975.

Poe, E. A. 'The Murders in the Rue Morgue', in *Selected Writings of Edgar Allan Poe*, ed. D. Galloway, Harmondsworth: Penguin, repr. 1975.

—— 'The Purloined Letter', in *Selected Writings of Edgar Allan Poe*, ed. D. Galloway, Harmondsworth: Penguin, repr. 1975.

Sterne, L. *Tristram Shandy*, New York: Norton, 1979.

SECTION TWO

Writing and Madness

4

Michel Foucault, 'On Madness in *Rameau's Nephew*', in *Histoire de la folie à l'âge classique.*

Paris: Gallimard, Collection 'TEL', 1972, pp. 363–72.

Editor's Introduction

Focusing closely on Diderot's dialogical short story *Rameau's Nephew*, Foucault endeavours to show how, almost anachronistically, the figure of the Nephew both harks back to the unity of reason and unreason found in the Middle Ages, and presages a similar kind of unity in modern figures of madness like Nerval, Nietzsche, Van Gogh, Roussel, and Artaud. If the Nephew recalls the odd unity of reason and unreason in the middle of the eighteenth century, this also has the effect of signalling their separation in the nineteenth. What Foucault asks, with true poetic brilliance, is: why has the separation of reason and unreason come about? Why is it that unreason has moved to be on the side of the pathological and become quite foreign to reason, when once it was what gave reason its very identity? As Foucault writes: 'Unreason becomes the reason of reason – even to the extent that reason recognises itself only in the mode of having been unreason' (p. 90 below).

Perhaps the key to Foucault's commentary lies in the way it illuminates a self-conscious figure of madness, albeit fictional, which embodies both unreason and reason. After Foucault, the reader of *Rameau's Nephew* has to adjust to a new articulation of sanity and insanity, or of reason and madness: it is here, in Diderot's piece, that reason talks and communicates with its other, instead of being irrevocably estranged from a madness that is destined, during the nineteenth century, to become mental illness - that is, a meaningless delirium which can be relieved only by drugs, rather than by being communicated.

On Madness in *Rameau's Nephew**

> I supplied them with a complete madhouse.
>
> (*Rameau's Nephew*)

'One afternoon there I was, doing much looking, seldom speaking, and listening as little as I could, when I was accosted by one of the oddest characters in this land of ours where God has not allowed any lack of them. He was a mixture of highness and lowness, good sense and unreason.'[1]

When doubt confronted its major threats, Descartes realised that he could not be mad. Although he was to acknowledge for a long time to come that all the powers of unreason kept vigil around his thought, as a philosopher, resolutely undertaking to doubt, he could not be 'one of these insane ones'. Rameau's nephew, though, well knows – and this is the most abiding of his fleeting certainties – that he is mad. '(Before beginning he fetches a deep sigh, and puts both hands to his forehead. Then he recovers an appearance calm and says:) You know of course that I am an ignoramus, a fool, a lunatic, rude, lazy.'[2]

This consciousness of being mad is still quite fragile. It is not a self-enclosed, secret and sovereign consciousness communicating with the profound powers of unreason; Rameau's Nephew's is a servile consciousness, open to the winds and transparent to the gaze of others. He is mad because he is told as much and treated as such: 'people wanted me to be ridiculous, and I have made myself that way.'[3] Unreason in him is all surface, nothing more than opinion, subjected to what is least free and denounced by what is most precarious in reason. Unreason is entirely at the level of the futile madness of men. It is nothing else, perhaps, than this mirage.

What, then, is the significance of this unreasonable existence Rameau's Nephew gives rise to in a way which is still a secret for his contemporaries, but is decisive for our retrospective gaze?

It is an existence which goes way back in time, reuniting some very ancient figures – among others, a profile of buffoonery recalling the Middle Ages – but also announcing the most modern forms of unreason: those contemporary with Nerval, Nietzsche and Antonin Artaud. To interrogate Rameau's Nephew in the paradox of his clairvoyant and unassuming existence in the eighteenth century is to back away slightly from the evolutionary chronicle; but it is at the same time to allow oneself to notice, in their general form, the grand structures of unreason – those which lie in Western culture at a level a little below historical time. And perhaps *Rameau's Nephew* will hastily teach us, by way of images jostled by these contradictions, what was most essential in the upheavals which renewed the experience of unreason in the classical age. It is necessary to interrogate it as a foreshortened paradigm of history. And since, during the illumination of an instant, it describes a great broken line which runs from the Ship of Fools to Nietzsche's last words and perhaps to Artaud's vociferations, we shall try to find out what this character is hiding, how reason, madness and unreason confront each other in Diderot's text, and what new relations are established between them. The history I am going to write in this last part is lodged inside the space opened by the word of the Nephew; but it will obviously be far from covering it in its entirety. As the last person in whom madness and unreason are united, Rameau's Nephew is the one in whom the moment of their separation is also foreshadowed. In the final section of *Histoire de la folie* I attempt to retrace the movement of this separation in its first anthropological phenomena. But it is only in the last texts of Nietzsche or Artaud that it will take on, for Western culture, its philosophical and tragic significance.

*

Thus, the character of the madman makes its reappearance in Rameau's Nephew. It is a reappearance in the form of buffoonery. Like the buffoon of the Middle Ages, the Nephew lives within forms of reason – a little on the margin, no doubt, since he is *not* like others, but nevertheless integrated, since he is there like a thing at the disposition of reasonable people, a piece of property that is shown, transmitted and possessed like an object. But immediately he himself denounces the equivocal nature of this possession. For if he is, for reason, an appropriated object, it is because reason needs him as its object. This is a need which touches the very content and meaning of reason's existence: without madmen, reason would be deprived of its reality; it would be a monotonous void, boredom itself, a sensory desert making present to itself its own contradiction: 'Now that they no longer have me, what can they do? They become bored like dogs.'[4] But a reason that is itself only the possession of madness can no longer define itself through an immediate identity with self; and so it alienates itself in this belonging: 'A really sensible person would not have a jester [*un fou*]. So anyone who has a jester is not sensible, and if he is not sensible he must be a jester and perhaps, if he is a king, his jester's jester [*le fou de son fou*].'[5] Unreason becomes the reason of reason – even to the extent that reason recognises itself only in the mode of having been unreason.

That which was only buffoonery in the *derisory* character of the importunate host reveals, in the final account, an imminent *power of derision*. The adventure of Rameau's Nephew recounts the necessary instability and ironic reversal of every form of judgement which denounces unreason as being exterior and inessential to it. Unreason goes back little by little towards that which condemns it, imposing on it a kind of retrospective servitude; for a wisdom which believes in instituting with madness a pure relation of judgement and definition – 'this is a *madman*' – has immediately posited a relation of possession and obscure belonging: 'this is *my* madman', to the extent that I have sufficient reason for recognising his madness, and that this recognition is a mark, a sign, like the emblem of my reason. Reason cannot draw up a report on madness without compromising itself in the act of doing so. Unreason is not *outside* of reason, but precisely *within* it, invested, possessed by it and made a thing; unreason is, for reason, what is most interior, and also most transparent, most on display. Whereas wisdom and truth are always indefinitely separated from reason, madness is only ever what reason can possess of itself. 'For long ages there was an official King's Jester [*le fou du roi*], but at no time has there been an official King's Wise Man.'[6]

Now, the triumph of madness again announces itself in a double return: reflux of unreason towards reason where the latter's certitude is assured only in the possession of madness; return towards an experience where both are indefinitely implied: 'it would mean being mad by another trick of madness not to be mad ...'. And yet this implication is of a style different to the one which menaced Western reason at the end of the Middle Ages and during the Renaissance. It no longer designates obscure and inaccessible regions which were transcribed for the imaginary in the fantastic mixture of worlds at some final point in time; it reveals the irreparable fragility of relations of belonging, reason's immediate fall brought about by having it there where it searches for its being: *reason alienates itself in the very movement whereby it takes possession of unreason.*

In these few pages by Diderot, the relations of reason and unreason assume an entirely new face. The destiny of madness in the modern world is strangely prefigured there, and is already almost engaged with. From there, this improbable trajectory goes broadly in a straight line up to Antonin Artaud.

*

At first glance, one would like to situate Rameau's Nephew within the ancient lineage of madmen and jesters, and restore to him all the powers of irony which have been attributed to them. In the revelation of truth, does he not play the role, for so long unique to him in the theatre, of casual agent, a role which classicism has completely forgotten? Does it not often happen that truth shines forth in the wake of his impertinence? These mad people:

> break the tedious uniformity that our social conventions and set politenesses have brought about. If one of them appears in a company of people he is the speck of yeast that leavens the whole and restores to each of us a portion of his natural individuality. He stirs people up and gives them a shaking, makes them take sides, brings out the truth, shows who is really good and unmasks the villains.[7]

But if madness thus has the task of having truth wend its way throughout the world, this is no longer because its blindness communicates with the essential through strange forms of knowledge, but through blindness, and this alone; its power comes only from error: 'If we say something good it is just by accident, like lunatics or visionaries.'[8] This means, no doubt, that chance is the only necessary link between truth and error, the only path to a paradoxical certainty; and to this extent, madness, that exaltation of chance – a chance neither wished for nor sought, but given up to itself – appears as the truth of truth, just as it is revealed error. For revealed error, borne along in full light of day, is both that being that it is, and that non-being which makes it become error. And it is here that madness takes on a new meaning for the modern world.

On the one hand, unreason is what is most immediately close and deeply embedded in a living being: all of wisdom, of truth, of reason that it can sacrifice or abolish renders pure and insistent the being that it reveals. For this being, every retardation, every withdrawal, even every mediation, is unbearable: 'I would rather exist, even as an impudent argufier, than not exist at all.'[9]

Rameau's Nephew is hungry, and says so. Whatever voraciousness or shamelessness there is in the Nephew, however much cynicism might arise in him, it is not a hypocrisy which decides to give up its secrets, for his secret is precisely to be unable to be a hypocrite; Rameau's Nephew is not the other side of Tartuffe; he shows only this immediate pressure to be in

unreason and the impossibility of mediation.[10] But at the same time, unreason is given over to the non-being of illusion, and exhausts itself in the
night. If, in terms of significance, unreason boils down to what is most immediate in being, it equally mimes what is most distant, most fragile and the
least consistent in appearance. It is at one and the same time the urgency
of being and the pantomime of non-being, the immediate necessity, and the
mirror's infinite reflection. 'The worst thing is the subservient posture in
which you are kept by need. The necessitous man doesn't walk like anybody else, he jumps, crawls, twists himself up, creeps along. He spends his
life taking up positions and carrying them out.'[11] With the rigour of need
and the silliness of the useless, unreason is, in a single movement, this self-
contained egoism and this fascination for what is most exterior in the
inessential. Rameau's Nephew is this simultaneity itself, this extravagance
pushed, in a systematic will to delirium, to the point of its being done quite
consciously, and as a total experience of the world: 'Good heavens, what
you call a beggars' pantomime is what makes the whole world go round.'[12]
To be this noise oneself, this music, this spectacle, this comedy, to concre-
tise oneself as a thing and as an illusory thing, thus to be not only a thing,
but a void and a nothingness, to be the absolute void of this absolute plenitude through which one is fascinated by the outside; to be, finally, the vertigo of this void and this being in their voluble circle and, at one and the
same time, the being of an enslaved consciousness to the point of annihilation and the supreme glorification of a sovereign consciousness – such, no
doubt, is the meaning Rameau's Nephew proffers in the middle of the eighteenth century, well before the total spread of the word of Descartes: a les-
son far more anti-Cartesian than all of Locke, all of Voltaire or all of Hume.

Rameau's Nephew, in his human reality, in this frail life which escapes
anonymity only by way of a name which is not even his – shadow of a
shadow – is, beyond and within all truth, a delirium, realised as existence,
of the being and the non-being of the real. When, on the other hand, we
reflect that Descartes's project was to support doubt provisionally until the
truth appeared in the reality of the clear idea, we see indeed that the non-
Cartesianism of modern thought, in terms of what is decisive, does not start
with a discussion of innate ideas, or with the incrimination of the ontological argument, but indeed with this text, *Rameau's Nephew*, with this existence that it designates in a reversal which could not be understood in
Hölderlin's and Hegel's era. What is put in question there is indeed what is
again at issue in *The Paradox of the Comedian*; but this is also another aspect
of it: it is not just a question of what part of reality should be elevated to
the non-being of comedy by a cold heart and a lucid intelligence, but also
of what part of the non-being of existence can be realised in the shallow
plenitude of appearance – and this through the medium of a delirium that
reaches the most extreme point of consciousness. It is no longer necessary,
after Descartes, to encounter courageously all the uncertainties of delirium,
of dream, of illusions; it is no longer necessary once to surmount the perils
of unreason; it is even from the heart of unreason that we can ponder the
nature of reason; and the possibility is again opened up of recapturing the
essence of the world in the whirling of a delirium which totalises the being
and non-being of the real in an illusion equivalent to the truth.

*

At the heart of madness, delirium takes on a new meaning. Until then, it was defined entirely in the space of error as: illusion, false belief, an opinion poorly based but obstinately held. It enveloped all that thought could produce when it was no longer placed in the domain of truth. Now delirium is the place of a perpetual and instantaneous confrontation between: need and fascination, the solitude of being and the sparkle of appearance, immediate plenitude and the non-being of illusion. Nothing is untied from its old links with dream; but the face of their resemblance has changed; delirium is no longer the demonstration of what is most subjective in the dream; it is no longer the slide towards what Heraclitus had already called ἴδιος ξδσμος. If it is still allied with dream, this is via everything in it related to the play of luminous appearance and silent reality, to the insistence of needs and the constraint of fascinations, to everything related to dialogue without a language of day and light. Dream and delirium no longer communicate in the night of blindness, but in this clarity where the most immediate in being confronts what is indefinitely reflected in the mirages of appearance. Delirium and dream englobe and demonstrate this tragic element in the uninterrupted rhetoric of their irony.

As a tragic confrontation, announcing Freud and Nietzsche, of need and illusion in a dreamlike mode, Rameau's Nephew's delirium is at the same time an ironical repetition of the world – its destructive rebuilding in the theatre of illusion:

> shouting, singing, throwing himself about like a mad thing: a one-man show featuring dancers, male and female, singers of both sexes, a whole orchestra, a complete opera-house, dividing himself into twenty different stage parts, tearing up and down, stopping, like one possessed, with flashing eyes and foaming mouth.... He wept, laughed, sighed, his gaze was tender, soft or furious: a woman swooning with grief, a poor wretch abandoned in the depth of despair, a temple rising into view, birds falling silent at eventide ... night with its shadows, darkness and silence.[13]

Unreason is encountered not in some furtive, otherworldly presence, but in this world, in the emerging transcendence of every expressive act, from the source of language to this equally initial and terminal moment where man becomes external to himself, accommodating in his intoxication the innermost part of the world. Unreason no longer wears the strange faces through which it was recognised in the Middle Ages, but now bears the imperceptible mask of the familiar and the identical. Unreason is both the world itself and the same world, separated from itself only by the thin surface of pantomime; its powers are no longer based in disorientation; giving rise to what is radically other is no longer specific to it, for now it has the world whirl round in the circle of the same.

But in this vertigo, where the truth of the world is maintained only inside an absolute void, man, at the moment when he passes from interior dreams to forms of exchange, also meets the ironical perversion of his own truth. Unreason then represents another malign genie – no longer the one who would exile man from the truth of the world, but one who simultaneously mystifies and demystifies, who enchants, to the point of extreme disenchantment, this truth about himself that man has entrusted to his hands, his face, his word; this is a malign genie who no longer works when man wants to accede to the truth, but when he wants to restore to the world a truth which is properly his own, and, thrown into the intoxication of the senses where he becomes lost, he remains, finally, 'motionless, dazed, astonished.'[14] The possibility of the malign genie is no longer lodged in *perception*, but in *expression*. There indeed is the height of irony: man is given over to the unreason of immediacy and the senses – is alienated in them – by this mediation that he is himself.

Rameau's Nephew's laughter foreshadows in advance and lessens the whole nineteenth-century anthropological movement; in all of post-Hegelian thought, man will go from certitude to truth via the work of mind and reason; but for a long time already, Diderot had made it understood that man is incessantly sent back from reason to the non-true truth of immediacy, and this by a mediation without work, a mediation always-already carried out in the depths of time. This mediation without patience – simultaneously extreme distance and absolute promiscuity, entirely negative, because it has only subversive force, and entirely positive, because it is fascinated by what it suppresses – is the delirium of unreason - the enigmatic figure in which we recognise madness. In its effort, through expression, to restore the sensory intoxication of the world and the urgent game of need and of appearance, delirium remains ironically alone: the suffering of hunger remains an immense pain.

*

Half remaining in the shadows, this experience of unreason has, from Rameau's Nephew to Raymond Roussel and Antonin Artaud, silently maintained itself. Were it a question of demonstrating its continuity, it would be necessary to free it from the pathological notions with which it has been covered up. The return to immediacy in the last of Hölderlin's poems, the sacralisation of perception in Nerval, can offer only a distorted and superficial meaning if we try to understand them in terms of a positivist view of madness. It is necessary to ask about their true meaning at the moment of unreason in which they are situated. For it is from the very centre itself of this experience of unreason – which is their concrete condition of possibility – that we can understand the two movements of poetic conversion and psychological evolution: they are not bound one to another by a relation of cause and effect; they do not develop by complementarity or the reverse. They both rest on the same foundation – that of a submerged unreason, the experience of which, as Rameau's Nephew has already shown, includes the intoxication of perception, fascination in immediacy, and the painful irony which announces delirium's solitude. This concerns not the nature of madness but the essence of unreason. If this essence has passed unnoticed, it is not only because it is hidden but because it becomes caught up in everything that enables it to see the light of day. For – and this is perhaps one of the fundamental traits of our culture – it is not possible to continue in a decisive and indefinitely resolute manner within the distance of unreason. This distance must be forgotten and abolished, just as soon as it is measured in the vertigo of perception and the isolation of madness. For their part, Van Gogh and Nietzsche have testified to it: fascinated by the delirium of the real, by sparkling appearances, by time abolished and entirely regained through the justice of enlightenment, gripped by immutable solidity of the most frail appearance, they were, for this very reason, rigorously excluded and left isolated inside an inexorable pain, which represented madness, not only for others, but for themselves in their truth, one again become immediate certainty. The moment of *Ja-sagen* at the irruption of the perceptible is also a withdrawal into the shadow of madness.

But for us, these two moments are distinct and distant like poetry and silence, day and night, the fulfilment of language in its actualisation and its loss in the infinity of delirium. Again, for us, the confrontation with unreason in its formidable unity has become impossible. The nineteenth century, in its spirit of seriousness, found it necessary to cut up this indivisible domain that would point to the irony of *Rameau's Nephew*; then it marked out, between formerly inseparable entities, the abstract frontier of the pathological. In the middle of the eighteenth century this unity, in a flash, had been brightly illuminated; but it took more than half a century for someone to dare again to fix it in his sights: in the wake of Hölderlin, Nerval, Nietzsche, Van Gogh, Raymond Roussel, Artaud ventured there, to the point of tragedy - that is, to the point of the alienation of this experience of unreason in the renunciation of madness. And each of these lives, each of these words which make up these lives, repeats, in the insistence of time, the same question, which no doubt concerns the essence of the modern world itself: Why is it not possible to sustain oneself in the difference of unreason? Why is it always necessary for the latter to become separated from itself, fascinated in the delirium of feeling, taking refuge in madness? How is it that it was able to be deprived of language? What is this power which petrifies those who come face to face with it, and condemns to *madness* all those who have tried the text of *Unreason*?

Translated by John Lechte

Notes

* Translator's title.
1. Denis Diderot, *Le Neveu de Rameau*, in *Œuvres*, Paris: Gallimard, 'Bibliothèque de la Pléiade', 1951, p. 396.
2. Denis Diderot, *Rameau's Nephew*, trans. Leonard Tancock, Harmondsworth: Penguin Classics series, 1966, p. 45. Translation modified.
3. ibid., p. 83.
4. ibid., p. 47.
5. ibid. p. 83.
6. ibid.
7. ibid., p. 35.
8. ibid., p. 40.
9. ibid., p. 43.
10. The significance of Rameau's Nephew is seen precisely in the pressure to be this absence of mediation. The same movement of thought is found in Sade; beneath an

apparent proximity, this is the reverse of a philosophy of 'significance' (mediation towards truth and reason) that is regularly encountered in the eighteenth century.

11. *Rameau's Nephew*, trans. Tancock, p. 120.
12. ibid., p. 122.
13. ibid., pp. 103–4.
14. ibid., p. 104.

5

Michel Foucault, 'Madness, Absence of an Œuvre', in *Histoire de la folie à l'âge classique, suivi de 'Mon corps, ce papier, ce feu' et 'La folie, l'absence d'œuvre'.*

Paris: Gallimard, 'Bibliothèque des histoires', 1972, pp. 575–82.

Editor's Introduction

The central thesis of this hitherto neglected 'Appendix' to the 1972 edition of Foucault's famous history of madness is that the truth of madness lies in the way that it has, in the nineteenth and twentieth centuries, become medicalised. It has become mental illness. But, Foucault speculates, those madmen who have until recently been forced to the margins of European history and culture may one day come to be seen as integral to its cultural identity. What was thought to be irrevocably other, in effect, may well enter the order of the Same. Although the aim of medicalisation is to eliminate madness, Foucault suggests that in mental illness, where madness is in fact hiding, the truth of contemporary experience may yet be revealed.

An important aspect of Foucault's study concerns both the notion of madness as forbidden and censored speech, and Freud's insights as to its significance. What Freud discovered, Foucault avers, is that language always refers back to itself; it is a 'white region of auto-implication', where madness and literature are intertwined. Literature and madness are linked because, since Mallarmé, the uniqueness of writing has become inseparable from the almost incommunicable singularity constitutive of individuality. Literature in the twentieth century has, in effect, become fundamentally poetic, but as poetry, literature does not speak to anyone; it is not a vehicle of communication; it does not, therefore, constitute a community. It simply exists in its 'sovereign silence', and as such cannot be heard as a coherent voice. It is the absence of a coherent *œuvre*, or work. How this silence can be known, perceived, or written about in its sovereignty is precisely the challenge Foucault takes up with his archaeological method.

Madness, Absence of an *Œuvre*

Perhaps one day we will indeed no longer know what madness was. Its figure will be closed in upon itself, no longer allowing us to decipher the traces that it will have left. Will these traces themselves be anything other, for an ignorant gaze, than simple black marks? At the very most they will be part of configurations which we would now be incapable of delineating, but which will be, in the future, the indispensable grids through which we render readable ourselves and our culture. Artaud will belong to the basis of our language, and not to its rupture; neuroses, to forms constitutive of (and not deviating from) our society. All that we experience today in the mode of a limit or strangeness, or as unbearable, will have been reunited with the serenity of the positive. And what for us currently designates this Exterior indeed risks, one day, designating us – us.

Only the enigma of this Exteriority will remain. What then, someone will wonder, was this strange delimitation working at the heart of the Middle Ages up to the twentieth century and perhaps beyond? Why did Western culture push to its margins that in which it could just as well have recognised itself – in fact did recognise itself in an oblique fashion? Why has it clearly proposed since the nineteenth century – but also since the Classical Age – that madness was the naked truth of man, yet placed it in a neutral and pale space where it was apparently cancelled out? Why take down Nerval's and Artaud's words, why recognise oneself in their works but not in the men themselves?

This is how the vibrant image of reason on fire will fade. The very familiar game of reflecting ourselves at the other extremity of ourselves in madness and of setting ourselves to listen to voices which, having come from afar, tell us from close up that we are this game, with its rules, its tactics, its inventions, its ruses, its tolerated illegalities, will for ever be no more than a complex ritual, the significations of which will have been reduced to ashes. It would be something like the great ceremonies of exchange and rivalry in archaic societies, or like the ambiguous attention that Greek reason paid to its oracles. Or, since the fourteenth century of Christianity, like the twin institutions of the practices and trials of sorcery. In the hands of historical cultures, there will remain only the codified measures of internment, medical techniques and, on the other hand, the sudden, irruptive inclusion in our language of the words of the excluded.

What will be the technical base for this mutation? The possibility for medicine to master mental illness like any other organic ailment? The precise pharmacological control of all psychical symptoms? Or a definition of behavioural deviations rigorous enough for society to prepare the appropriate mode of neutralisation for each one? Or again, will there be other modifications, none of which, perhaps, will really rid us of mental illness, but which will each signify the effacement of the face of madness from our culture?

I know that in proposing this last hypothesis I am contesting what is ordinarily accepted: that medical progress could indeed lead to the disappearance of mental illness, like leprosy and tuberculosis; although one thing will remain, which is man's relation to his fantasies, to his impossible, to his pain without the body, to his night-time carcass; and that once the pathological is put out of play, the sombre belonging of man to madness will be an ageless memory of an evil effaced in its form of an illness, but persisting as a misfortune. The truth is that this idea supposes as unalterable what, no doubt, is the most precarious part of all, much more precarious than the constancies of the pathological: the relation of a culture to precisely what it excludes and, more precisely, the relation of our culture to this truth about itself, distant and near, which it discovers and recovers in madness.

That which is not going to wait to die, that which is already dying in us (and whose death precisely bears our present language) is *homo dialecticus* – the being of departure, of return and of time, the animal who forfeits its truth and finds it again illuminated, the stranger to oneself who becomes familiar. This man was the sovereign subject and the serf object in all discourses for a long time held about man, and especially about alienated man. And, fortunately, he died under the weight of their chatter.

Does not this mean that we will no longer know how man was able to put this figure of himself into the background, or how he was able to have what was bonded to him, and to which he was bonded, pass to the other side of the limit? No thought will any longer be able to think this movement where even until very recently Western man found his freedom. It is the relationship to madness (not a specific knowledge of mental illness or a specific attitude towards human madness) which will for ever be lost. All that will be known is that we others, Westerners of five centuries' standing, were a people on the surface of the globe who, among other fundamental traits, had this strangest trait of all: we maintained with mental illness a profound and moving relationship, one perhaps difficult to formulate for ourselves, but impenetrable to anyone else, in which we experienced the most profound of our dangers and perhaps the closest of our truths. It will be said not that we were at a *distance* from madness, but that we were *in the distance* of madness. Thus the Greeks were not isolated from hubris (ὕβρισ) because they condemned it; they were, rather, in the space (*l'éloignement*) of this excess, at the heart of the remote region where they conserved it.

To a future generation will fall the task of thinking this enigma (a little as we do, since today we are trying to grasp how Athens was able to be enamoured of, and lost its fondness for, Alcibiades' folly): how were men able to search for their truth, their essential speech and their signs, in the risk which made them tremble, and in relation to which they could not stop themselves averting their eyes as soon as they caught a glimpse of it? And this will seem much stranger to them than asking for the truth of man in death; for it says what everything will be. Madness, on the other hand, is a rare danger, a chance which counts for little compared to the obsessive fear to which it gives birth and the questions addressed to it. How, in a single culture, can such an unlikely eventuality possess such power of revelatory dread?

To answer this question, those who will be looking over their shoulder at us will doubtless not have much at their disposal. Just a few charred signs: the same fear, endlessly recapitulated over the centuries, of seeing madness rise up and submerge the world; the rituals including and excluding the insane; the attentive listening, since the nineteenth century, so as to surprise in madness something that could indicate the truth of man; the same impatience with which the words of madness are rejected and welcomed, the hesitation in recognising their inanity or their decisiveness.

For the rest, we have: this single movement by which we come to meet the madness we are moving away from, this appalling recognition, this will to fix the limit and immediately compensate for it with the fabric of a unitary meaning – all this will be reduced to silence, just as today the Greek trilogy of μανία, ὕβρισ, ἀλογία is mute for us, or as the posture of the 'mania, hubris, alogia' shamanistic deviation in a given primitive society is mute.

We are at this point, at this refolding of time, where a certain technical control of illness conceals more than it reveals of the movement which shuts the experience of madness in on itself. But it is exactly this fold which allows us to open out what for centuries remained implied: mental illness and madness – two different configurations which were joined and merged together from the seventeenth century onwards, and are now becoming separated before our eyes, or rather, in our language.

To say that madness is disappearing today means undoing what was implied both in psychiatric knowledge and in a reflection of an anthropological kind. But this is not to say, for all that, that what disappeared was the general form of transgression whose visible face, for centuries, was madness. Nor is it to say that this transgression was not in train at the very moment when we wonder what madness is in the process of giving rise to a new experience.

There is not a single culture in the world where everything is permitted. And we have known for a long time that man did not begin with freedom but with the limit and the impassable line. We know the systems which forbidden acts obey; we have been able to distinguish for each culture the regime of prohibitions on incest. But we still have much to learn about the organisation of the interdictions of language. The two systems of restriction are not superimposed on one another, as if one were only the verbal version of the other: what must not appear at the level of speech is not in any necessary way what is proscribed at the level of the gesture. The Zuni, who forbade it, tell of the incest of brother and sister; the Greeks tell the legend of Oedipus. Conversely, the French penal code of 1808 abolished the old laws against sodomy, but the language of the nineteenth century was much more intolerant of homosexuality (at least in its masculine form) than were previous epochs. And it is probable that psychological concepts like compensation and symbolic expressions cannot by any means account for such a phenomenon.

One day the domain of language interdictions should be studied in its autonomy. No doubt it is still too early to know exactly how to carry out an analysis. Would it be by using the currently acknowledged divisions in language? Here, to begin with, we would recognise, at the limit of the interdiction and the impossible, the laws concerning the linguistic code (what are called, so clearly, *grammatical errors*); then inside the code and among existing words, or expressions, we would recognise those one is forbidden to use (the whole religious, sexual, and magic series of *blasphemous words*); then the statements authorised by the code, allowed in the act of speaking, but whose signification is intolerable for the culture in question at a given moment: here the detour of metaphor is no longer possible, for it is meaning itself which is the object of *censorship*. Finally, there also exists a fourth form of excluded language: it consists in submitting a speech, apparently conforming to the recognised code, to another code whose key is given in the speech itself, so that the latter is internally split: it says what it says, but it adds a mute surplus which silently states what it says and gives the code according to which it says it. Here it is a question not of an encoded language, but of a structurally esoteric language. That is to say, it does not communicate a forbidden signification while hiding it; it is located from the beginning in an essential recess of speech. This is a recess which hollows it out from the inside, perhaps to infinity. Little does it matter then what is said in such a language or what significations it delivers up. It is this obscure and central liberation of speech at the heart of itself, its uncontrollable flight towards an always un-illuminated source, that no culture can accept immediately. Such a speech is transgressive – not in its meaning, nor in its verbal matter, but in its *play*.

It is quite probable that every culture, whatever it may be, knows, practises and tolerates (to a certain extent), but equally represses and excludes these four forms of forbidden speech.

In Western history, the experience of madness has moved along this continuum. In truth, it has long occupied an indistinct region, difficult for us to clarify, between the interdiction of action and that of language: hence the exemplary importance of the *furor–inanitas* couple which practically organised, at the levels of gesture and speech, the world of madness until the end of the Renaissance. The era of Confinement (the general hospitals, Charenton, Saint-Lazare, organised in the seventeenth century) marks a migration of madness towards the regions of the insane: madness hardy keeps more than a moral relationship with forbidden acts (it remains essentially attached to sexual taboos), but it is included in the universe of linguistic interdictions; classical confinement incorporates, with madness, the libertine use of thought and speech, obstinate impiety or heterodoxy, blasphemy, sorcery, alchemy – in short, all that characterises the forbidden *spoken* world of unreason. Madness is an excluded language – one which, against the code of language, pronounces words without signification (the 'insane', the 'imbeciles' and the 'demented'), or utters words regarded as sacred (the 'violent' and the 'furious'), or again where someone produces forbidden significations (the 'libertines', the 'pigheaded'). Pinel's reform is much more the visible culmination of this repression of madness as forbidden speech than it is a modification of it.

The latter really took place only with Freud, when the experience of madness shifted towards the last form of the interdiction of language that we were speaking about earlier. Then it ceased to to be a language error, a proffered blasphemy, or an intolerable signification (and in this sense psychoanalysis is indeed, as Freud himself defined it, the great lifting of interdictions); it appeared as a speech closed in upon itself, saying something else beneath what it says and at the same time being the only possible code: an esoteric language, if you like, since it keeps its language (*langue*) inside a speech (*parole*)) which finally says nothing other than this implication.

It is therefore necessary to take Freud's *œuvre* for what it is; it does not reveal that madness is caught in a network of significations common to everyday language, thereby authorising us to speak of it in the everyday platitude of the vocabulary of psychology. It brings European experience of madness forward in order to situate it in the perilous, always transgressive region (therefore still forbidden, but in a particular mode) which is that of languages implying themselves – that is to say, stating (*énonçant*) in their statement the language (*langue*) in which they are stating it. Freud did not discover the lost identity of a meaning; he outlined the irruptive figure of a signifier which is *absolutely not* like others. That should have sufficed to protect his *œuvre* from all the psychologising interpretations with which our half-century has covered it, in the (derisory) name of the 'human sciences' and their asexual unity.

And by this very fact, madness appeared not as the ruse of a hidden signification, but as a prodigious *reserve* of meaning. Even so, it is necessary properly to understand this word 'reserve': much more than a provision, it is a question of a figure which retains and suspends meaning, organising a void where only a still incomplete possibility is proposed, so that some specific meaning comes to lodge itself there, then another, or still a third, and so on perhaps to infinity. Madness opens up a lacunary reserve which outlines and makes visible this hollow where language (*langue*) and speech (*parole*) imply each other, are formed, the one on the basis of the other, and where they say nothing other than their still mute relationship. Since Freud, Western madness has become a non-language because it has become a double language (a language (*langue*) which exists only in this speech (*parole*), a speech which speaks only its language) – that is to say, a womb of language which, in the strictest sense, says nothing. Here is the fold of the spoken which is an absence of a work (*absence d'œuvre*).

One day it will be necessary to do Freud justice for not forcing to *speak* a madness which for centuries was precisely a language (*langage*) (an excluded language, an inane chatter, an ordinary speech indefinitely outside the reflective silence of reason); on the contrary, he exhausted the Logos of unreason; he dried it up; he referred words back to their source – back to this white region of auto-implication where nothing is said.

What is now happening is, for us, still in an uncertain light. Nevertheless, we can see a strange movement taking shape in our language. Literature (and this no doubt since Mallarmé) is, little by little, in the process of becoming in its turn a language in which speech states, at the same time as that which it speaks and in the same movement, the language (*langue*) which makes it decipherable as speech. Before Mallarmé, to write meant to establish the written word (*parole*) inside a given language (*langue*), so that the work (*œuvre*) of language (*langage*) was of the same nature as every other language: except for the (indeed majestic) signs of Rhetoric, the Subject of Images. At the end of the nineteenth century (at the time when psychoanalysis was discovered, or close to it), literature had become a speech which inscribed within itself its own principle of decipherment; or, in any case, it supposed, beneath each of its sentences, under each of its words, the power to modify, with all sovereignty, the values and significations of the language [*langue*] to which, despite everything (and in fact), it belonged. It suspended the reign of language (*langue*) in the actual gesture of writing.

Hence the necessity for secondary languages (what are, in sum, called criticism): they no longer function now as exterior additions to literature (judgements, mediations, relays that one thought useful to establish between a work, referred back to the psychological enigma of its creation, and the consuming act of reading); henceforth they make up, at the heart of literature, part of the void that it institutes in its own language; they are the necessary but necessarily unfinished movement by which speech (*parole*) is brought back to language (*langue*), and language (*langue*) is established in speech.

Hence, too, this strange proximity between madness and literature, to which one must not attribute the meaning of a psychological parent finally revealed. Discovered as a language keeping silent while being superimposed on itself, madness neither shows nor recounts the birth of an *œuvre* (or of anything which, with genius or luck, could have become an *œuvre*); it outlines the empty form from whence this *œuvre* comes – that is to say, the place from which it does not cease to be absent, where one will never find it because it was never there. There in this faint region, under this essential hiding-place, the twin incompatibility of the work and madness reveals itself; this is the blind spot of the possibility of each, and of their mutual exclusion.

But since Raymond Roussel, since Artaud, this is also the place from which language grows nearer to literature. But it does not approach it in the way of something which it would have the task of stating (*énoncer*). It is time to notice that the language of literature is not defined by what it says, nor by the structures which allow it to signify, but that it has a being, and it is around this being that it must be interrogated. What is this being at the moment? Something, no doubt, which has to do with auto-implication, with the double and the void buried within it. In this sense, the being of literature, as it has emerged since Mallarmé and comes to our own day, is taking over the region where, since Freud, the experience of madness has formed.

In the eyes of who knows what future culture – and maybe it is already near – it will be we who brought closest together these two sentences never really uttered, and as contradictory and impossible as the famous 'I lie', which both refer to the same empty self-referent: 'I write' and 'I am delirious'. We will thus figure beside a thousand other cultures which have connected 'I am mad' with 'I am an animal', or 'I am God', or 'I am a sign' or, again, with 'I am a truth', as was the case for the whole of the nineteenth century up until Freud. And if this culture has a taste for history, it will in fact remember that Nietzsche, becoming mad, had proclaimed (this was in 1887) that he was the truth (why I am so wise, why I know so much, why I write such good books, why I am a destiny). And less than fifty years later, Roussel – the day before his suicide, in *How I Wrote Certain of My Books* – wrote the twin story of his madness and the devices he used to write. And people will, without any doubt, be astonished that we were able to recognise such a strange parentage between what was for a long time dreaded as a cry, and what for a long time was expected as a song.

But maybe this mutation will precisely not seem to merit any astonishment. It is we today who are astonished to see two languages communicating (that of madness and that of literature) whose incompatibility has been built by our history. Since the seventeenth century, madness and mental illness have occupied the same space in the field of excluded languages (in general, that of the insane). In entering another domain of excluded language (the one defined, sacralised, dreaded, vertically drawn up above itself, linked to itself in a useless and transgressive Fold we call literature), madness undoes its relationship – old or recent, according to the continuum one chooses – with mental illness.

The latter – and there is no doubt about it – will enter a continually better-controlled technical space. In hospitals, pharmacology has already transformed wards of agitated patients into warm aquariums. But below these transformations, and for reasons which appear strange in terms of them (at least to our present gaze), a *dénouement* is now emerging: madness and mental illness are dismantling their membership of the same anthropological unity. This unity is itself disappearing, along with man, its temporary postulate. Madness, the lyrical halo of mental illness, continues to pass away. And far from the pathological, in the region of language, there where it withdraws still without saying anything, an experience is in the process of being born where our thought is at stake; its imminence, already visible but empty, absolutely cannot yet be named.

Translated by John Lechte

6

Julia Kristeva 'Nom de mort ou de vie' ('Name of Death or of Life'), in Jacques Sédat, ed., *Retour à Lacan?*

Paris: Fayard, 1981, pp. 163–82.

Editor's Introduction

Although Julia Kristeva's text pivots around 'borderline' experience, which forms the main trajectory of the chapter, it also addresses the question of the nature of psychoanalysis as a therapy. In this regard, Kristeva asks what the analyst can offer to the analysand who suffers, without analysis becoming a process of normalisation. The answer, in part, is that the analyst can propose theoretical fictions which 'expand the limits of the signifiable'; these serve to express the inexpressible, just as great writing does.

'Borderline' experience, Kristeva's analysis suggests, is one where the capacity to be both actor (we are involved in life) and impresario (we are also detached spectators, or observers of life) becomes immensely troubling. Borderline experience often oscillates between the positions of actor and spectator (impresario), the barrier between the two positions being

unstable and fluid. How the psychoanalyst can deal with borderline situations – and what psychoanalysis is in the light of borderline experience –
is precisely at issue. Somehow, the analyst must walk a tightrope in an
attempt to find the right amount of detachment and involvement with a borderline patient's plight. No doubt this is to admit that – to a certain extent,
at least – the analyst mimes the very borderline condition he or she is trying to alleviate.

The pretext for Kristeva's discussion of the borderline state is Lacan's
question: What is a metalanguage? – Lacan being the one who says that
'there is no metalanguage'. Against Lacan, Kristeva argues for 'metalanguage', and she goes on to show that metalanguage (equivalent to the
position of impresario) is the source of meaning and identity. The absence
or failure of metalanguage can result in psychosis.

On the other hand, it is equally illusory to assume (as does a certain
Positivist tendency) that there is only metalanguage – or only an objectifying discourse. Were this the case, some of the greatest experiments in
modern poetry and language (see the work of Mallarmé) would not have
been realised.

All through the piece Kristeva refers back to the division, or split, constituting the subject. This split repeats the poetry–metalanguage, actor–
impresario opposition already mentioned. Ego psychology, for its part,
tends not to recognise this split. Rather, it sees the ego as an undivided
unity which is only ever at risk in a contingent sense, never in any structural sense. A proper name, which might seem to be the proof of identity
– because it refers inexorably to *one* individual, person, or subject – in fact
has no real signified; or rather, says Kristeva, it opens the way to a 'cascade' of signifieds, to heterogeneity and otherness. We should not conclude from this that the proper name, and the accompanying unity which
keeps heterogeneity in check, is unimportant. Neither should we ignore
the importance and necessity of meaningful dialogue – also based on the
proper name. The point is to tread a path which glorifies neither a rigid
unity nor the impossible fluidity of a borderline experience. Writing, we can
ssume, brings to the fore the very tenuousness of borderline subjectivity. For writing is simultaneously a gesture which objectifies and the act of
an actor.

Hamlet, for Kristeva, opens the way to an investigation and a clarifica-
tion of the borderline state in literature. By comparison with Freud's theory of neurosis (see Freud, 'Psychopathic Characters on the Stage', in
Section Three of this volume), Hamlet's 'To be or not to be' is the rever-
beration of one about to fall out of the symbolic and become – perhaps –
psychotic, and linguistically incoherent. Here, by implication, *Hamlet* brings
the question of the mother to the fore in relation to the symbolic order, as
much as the question of the father. Or rather, with Hamlet it is the oscillation between father and son ('Am I father or son? – or both?') which is
so riveting.

Dostoevsky, too, occupies the position of the successful borderline, particularly in a work like *The Devils.* For his is a polyphonic text constituted
through a plurality of positions (this is Dostoevsky as impresario), and also
through the writer being involved with each of his characters (this is

Dostoevsky as actor). Or – as Kristeva would have it – like Shakespeare, Dostoevsky is both father (impresario) and son (actor) of his own creations.

Kristeva's lasting question becomes: is not the writer's position just enunciated also the position of any analyst worthy of the name? This position is one where the treatment - based on aesthetic appreciation and theological sensitivity (faith) – can bring about a transformation in the patient, one which means that the analyst may also be transformed.

Name of Death or of Life*

To speak (about) psychoanalysis is beyond words.

Not only because one ends up finding solace in a supposedly analytic community, thus calling the public to the bedside of a narcissism no longer able to be private. Not only because one would hope that *they* will end up understanding – as if a head-on *resistance* could thus be overcome other than by a masochistic and/or sacralising Assumption. Not only because we presuppose, for modest Freudian discoveries, the power of a *Weltanschauung* likely to pick holes in knowledge, and in university knowledge in particular – in this case, in relation to language. Not only because it is necessary, or because it is good to 'pretend', to 'hope', to 'presuppose' when we speak, but ... I should now forget about all of this.

Psychoanalytic speech is no doubt guilt-ridden – and therefore jubilatory – and Lacan brought to the fore, for those who remain impervious to the revelations of contemporary art, precisely this sublime and derisory discontent, thus signalling that it is the profound logic of this 'theatre of cruelty', of this histrionic drama, which modulates human speech.

The above summarises my position as presented to an audience of American academics gathered together to discuss the concept of language in today's sciences (human and inhuman). That the American university (not psychoanalysis, except at its margins) lends an interested ear to these deliberations is a poor reason for taking the risk in speaking about it. A more profound justification is provided for me by the noticeable wave of psychoanalytic discourse in diverse domains of modern culture, and by the effect it can produce – as treatment or theory – on individuals, rare as they are, who allow themselves to be penetrated by it. Different effects occur because this is not a homogeneous discourse, and the differences, far from simply originating in a formalist or doctrinal quarrel, reveal ethical options that can be interrogated. Such would be the reason – since one is necessary – I give to readers for returning to this lecture given in New York.

To begin with, the following may be understood as a response to the question addressed to me by Jacques Lacan at his seminar, after the publication of one of my books: 'But what is a metalanguage?' Metalanguage and the division in the subject, such as I understand them today – or, if one prefers, *metalanguage* and *psychosis* – is where I now propose briefly to venture. I begin with three associations, for these seem to me to clarify the very particular status of the subject of metalanguage, if not the risks on which it rests.

Hamlet

The first association is the conclusion drawn by the father of semantics, Michel Bréal, who attached his name to it in his first *Essai de sémantique* (1897),[1] and who writes:

> If it is true, as has sometimes been claimed, that language is a play where words appear as actors and where grammatical organisation reproduces movement, it is necessary to correct this comparison on one special point: the impresario frequently intervenes in the action in order to mix with it his reflections and personal feelings – not like Hamlet, who, although interrupting his actors, remains foreign to the drama, but as we do ourselves in a dream when we are simultaneously an interested spectator and the author of events. This intervention is what I propose to call the subjective side of language. (p. 254)

The speaking subject obtains, by this reasoning, to a particular destiny: he is not the *author* (it is through social necessity, chance or a divinity that philosophical speculations on language attribute, as we know, a causal or authorial character to language), he is *actor* and *impresario*: he acts and observes himself acting, he delegates to a system but also intervenes in it. Essentially split (*dédoublé*) ('the splitting of the human personality', writes Bréal, p. 262), he reminds us of Hamlet. Having launched this comparison with the Shakespearian character, Bréal immediately withdraws from it; for at the moment when he directs his actors, the Danish Prince is not yet mad; a distance remains between him, the characters and the ghost: he is 'foreign to the drama'. But it is with private madness, protected by sleep – in dream, therefore – that the first semanticist compares our condition in language: possessed by the system of language (*langue*), we nevertheless take charge of it as a discourse on which we leave our personal mark as authors.... Naturally it is a modest and tenacious impresario – the linguist – who speaks *about* language, and thus raises the split in the subject in language (*langage*) yet another notch, since he presents the essential truths of the drama to others. It is the linguist-impresario, then, who is the first to discover the speaking subject's *Spaltung*. Question: would the subject of metalanguage be closer than others not only to the haunting obsession ('to be or not to be') epitomised by Hamlet, but also to the division in the ego which is, as we know, the basis of psychosis? Rather than answering this question, let us simply recall, in the light of the juxtapositions between the linguist and Hamlet suggested by Bréal, that this division (in Hamlet as in the linguist) is based on the murder of a father and on a failed attempt at revenge. Hamlet seems to say: 'I am the one who understands what there is to understand (language, the play): now, what there is to understand is that the father is dead; but it was not I who killed him, and I will prove it to you by killing the wrong person (Polonius rather than Claudius); it is simply that from misunderstanding to misunderstanding, from slip of the tongue to slip of the tongue, the void carries away all the protagonists. The father is dead; I have not killed him; I will not avenge him, or rather, I will avenge him only in dying; I will be reunited with the father; I am the dead father.'

Father or son, meaning or non-meaning, to be or not to be? Just when I prove the meaning – as, simultaneously, actor, author, stage director – *I* completely disappear(s). I – subject of the meaning, of the Whole meaning – am (is) the mad – or dead – subject.

The metalinguistic approach implicitly rivals the meaning of the theological possession of Meaning; we are haunted by the father, by one without transcendence. Now, this mastery seems destined to have three outcomes: that of not raising the question of subjectivity in language; that of reducing subjectivity to a phenomenology of univocal consciousness – its ultimate horizon being the Husserlian transcendental ego; or that of drawing all the consequences of the 'split' – which could drive metalinguistic discourse, on the edge of psychosis, towards what relieves it: fiction....

Ghosts and Poetry

The second association is provided for me by Ferdinand de Saussure. He seems to be wondering about how to separate 'linguistic reality' from what he *knows* about it, since he is inside it. Far from suggesting some sort of agnosticism, or rehabilitating the old adage that 'language lies', Saussure raises a new epistemological question when, at the heart of the very possibility of a science of language, he places the *inside/outside* problematic, which, in other respects, is the key question preoccupying today's analyst faced with psychotic discourse. 'For there are also ghosts created by linguists.'[2] Or again:

> Writing this piece is for me an unimaginable torture, one entirely disproportionate to the importance of the effort put in. When it is a question of linguistics, this situation is intensified for me by the fact that every clear theory, to the extent that it is clear, cannot be expressed linguistically; for in fact I propose that no term whatever in this science has ever been based on a clear idea. Also, between the beginning and the end of a sentence one is tempted to redo it five or six times.[3]

The difficulty Saussure speaks of can be attributed to the instability of early linguistics; but maybe this is characteristic of every linguistic formulation since, in the light of the split topos of the subject, as suggested above, every 'unity' designated by theory is already not only ambivalent, but presupposes readings which would constitute an 'ensemble of articulations'.[4]

Finally, the third association: at an international conference in Warsaw, the great French linguist Emile Benveniste, whose name should be mentioned here, told me, between giving two distinguished university lectures: 'In the last century there have in the end been only two French linguists: Mallarmé and Artaud.' It is a question, as you know, of two poets whose subjective dramas embrace phobia in one case and schizophrenia in the other.

I now conclude these associations inspired for me by metalanguage. I hope that the evocation of psychosis in relation to metalanguage has sown a more than Cartesian – let us say Freudian – doubt in your minds as far as the solidity of knowledge is concerned. And to the extent that doubt pricks the pride of research, I will now touch on the more technical aspects of 'subjectivity in language' - namely: what is language for the psychoanalyst? What modification of the object, 'language', is the psychoanalyst led to make in the light of psychotic discourse?

The Division in the Subject

For the analyst, language (*langage*) (I will deliberately keep the imprecise breadth this term has in French[5]) is simply a place, the subject's only place: a system of signs, quite singular at each occurrence, which integrates all psychic experiences (perceptions, affects, fantasies, intellections, etc.), and because of this it announces itself with the singularity of an idiolect. If one is at a wall – and I shall return later to this 'wall' in one patient's dream – it has meaning only in relation to both of its two sides – this side and the other side of where it stands. Language (*langage*), for the analyst, is the only *vehicle of the transference*: a means of revealing and concealing the truth and the lie. Even if it does not say everything, it wants to say and mean everything; but it cannot. The analyst therefore hears an always incomplete 'totality', because this totality is addressed to an other. Analytic listening thus begins from the presupposition of the locally decidable incompleteness of language in the undecidable process of the transference.

It was when he was faced with unconscious defences (for example, unconscious guilt) that Freud abandoned his first argument about the unconscious in order to propose a second in terms of the striking immersion of the ego in the id and the division of the ego, leaving to one side the idea of an energetic, biological, and fundamentally drive-based unconscious. Through listening to psychoses, Lacan went much further and, at the risk of closing the opening towards the unknown and the heterogeneous in the drive sense of these terms – an opening present in Freud – he proposed, with equal ease, both his scandalous formulation 'The unconscious is structured like a language' and his triad of 'real–symbolic–imaginary'. The question we will ask here is: faced with the division in the ego and psychosis, what is it that prompts us to modify our understanding of the psyche and, more particularly, of language?

Words–Things

I shall begin, for my commentary on the first of the above propositions, with Hanna Segal's work and, in particular, her article 'Notes on Symbol Formation'.[6] Having discussed Jones's position (see Ernest Jones, *The Theory of Symbolism*, 1916) according to which only what is symbolised is repressed – symbols appearing, according to him, when the affect invested in the idea symbolised is not manifested – Segal refutes this conception. According to her, symbol formation is specific to the ego, which seeks to elaborate anxieties born out of its relation with an object. In the phase Melanie Kleine called 'projective identification', the first projections and identifications (with another subject or with objects) constitute the point of departure of the process of symbol formation. However, these first 'symbols' are experienced by the ego not as symbols or as substitutes, but as symbolic *equations*. In this way, then, the phase of projective identification extends its logic to the point of constituting the first symbolic tools, the 'symbolic equations', which endure as the concrete thought of schizophrenics. And it is only the so-called depressive position, occurring previously, which establishes the feeling that the object (the mother) is total, as much as the differentiation between the ego and the object. Guilt, anguish, mourning and the effort to re-create the object characterise this ambivalent phase where introjection takes precedence over projection – a fact which leads to a certain level of drive inhibition. Symbols, then, really do become inhibitions: far from being the equivalent of the object, they differentiate themselves from it and are henceforth able to assure their role of restoring and re-creating the object; they become the means of sublimation. The symbol henceforth will serve not to deny the loss of the object, but to overcome loss: such would be the basis of verbal thought.

I use Hanna Segal's position – which I assume to be known to an Anglo-American public - in order to lead my reflection elsewhere.

First of all, nothing in the so-called projective identification phase, to the extent that we accept its existence, allows one to speak of an 'ego' and of an 'object'. On the contrary, their non-differentiation seems, at the dawning of the speaking being, to characterise the fusional dyad that the subject forms with its generatrice. But it is in lacking any reference to a Third Party – to the paternal function – that this primitive communication of needs and frustrations structures itself. Such communication is constituted by aggressivity and mimeticism in the isolated space articulated by *unstable* dichotomies, which do not stop moving and condensing. The adult speaking subject knows only how to fantasise this modality as a conflictual identification with the mother: as an *abjection* – an ab-ject: an impossible object that is not yet an object – as well as something foul, unclean, and as a ravaging intrusion into a territory that has not yet become one's own (*propre*[7]). As far as language (*langage*) is concerned, we see it being reduced (during the fusional dyad, and in those states which recall this) to its construction as a signifier, deprived of a signified and gaining the immediate value of an intervention, a need, an act, or magic. An evocation of this modality of language (*langage*) which, in other respects, psychotics show to us, is found in Plato's 'chora' (see *Timaeus*): it is a maternal receptacle prior to the Name of the Father. Even the name of a syllable is unsuitable for it. . . . Let us then rectify Segal's position: it is not to an object but to an ab-ject[8] that – not an ego, but a not-yet-ego refers by way of the semiotic code made of pure signifiers, condensing the affect equivalent to a way towards the act (*passage à l'acte*). When such a use of the ab-ject and of the language (*langage*) corresponding to it is found in an adult, it is not regression which is at issue, but a *restructuration* specific to the triadic relation which props up the place of the subject as much as the symbolic function. What is this structuration? We will find it by touching upon other aspects of the division.

Problematic Repression

The analyst is struck by another feature of psychotic discourse, one also present in the discourse recently arrived on that couch that we call 'borderline'. As if repression were problematic (Fairburn, Kernberg), these patients very easily evoke the sexually traumatic causes of their malaise, but also painlessly reverse the obvious contents of the discourse they have just proffered, in order to unveil the hidden 'unconscious'. From unveiling to unveiling, from reversal to reversal, from memory to memory, from a denuding of the body to a radiography of the part bared – where is the unconscious? Listening to them, one has the impression that the repressed (or what one calls the repressed in a neurotic) can arrive at *meaning*, but not at *signification*. For what the subject says is not under control: the subject speaks, but in fragments, without coherence; he does not know what he says. Less than *repression* it is, rather, a question of *misrecognition*; rather than an *unconscious*, it is an *unawareness (insu)* which speaks. Through a discourse without a subject.

The first conclusion one is tempted to draw in listening to such speech is that it is, as a result of the division, cut off from affect. But we quickly notice that in the transference it is, for the most part, logical after all, with links and connections which initially give rise to *signification*, and also to affect, thus suppressing psychic and somatic pain. For signification exists when discourse, far from exhausting itself in referring to some object without a desire for anybody, on the contrary, moves away from the hallucination inevitably accompanying such a reference to the void, and finds something to be transferred to the same boat as the Third Party. Clearly, the analyst simultaneously occupies, in this accession of signification, the maternal and paternal place – the place of desire and death.

It is as if, in the borderline's treatment, one saw, on the divided and painful body – because bereft of signification – a wall of repression (phallic symbol if ever there was one) establish itself as the condition of language's position. I think of the patient who, after long months of complaints about 'emptiness', a 'false self', 'foreignness' and diverse pains, came to me with a dream: 'He arrived by bicycle at a town divided in two by a wall. To the right, the wall allowed a glimpse of a sunny garden where a beautiful and welcoming brunette lived. Yet the danger of crossing this wall, guarded by a powerful gendarmerie, made him look to the left, but if all the bridges facilitating a return to the place of pain were not cut, hostile watchmen were there who petrified the self and froze the patient in anguish in this divided space.' Only in the light of this dream, however, can the patient proffer words of love for the maternal place and embark on a long journey in search of an evanescent father – a journey where nothing is acquired, but one which contains all the relapses and regressions well known to borderline treatments.

Nevertheless, this wall of repression never remains solid for the borderline person, whatever the constructive role (at least initially) of the transference. I would rather compare it with a *fold*, in the sense used in René Thom's catastrophe theory, where each element of the fold belongs to at least two surfaces and two structures which are, for example, like two sides of a folded sheet of paper. To be the inhabitant of this frontier, the 'borderline' person has a latently aesthetic discourse. It is impossible not to see the mastery of connotations (in Hjelmslev's sense) in this folded subjectivity; the borderline possesses the virtualities of the actor, and is a manipulator of seeming, a seducer who uses masks which remain more or less foreign to him; he also tends to be a commentator, a theoretician, a commander of signs, a philosopher, and the metaphysician of his time.

I will take two linguistic elements of borderline discourse in order to illustrate how this *fold* language is constructed, and from where we could have
direct access to it.

The Signifier of the Proper Name

Access could, first of all, come from the *signifier*, privileged place of a meaning which has slipped past the full force of signification, becoming with the
borderline the place where the split is spoken with the greatest condensation. This is even more the case when the signifier at issue is a *proper name*
– which, as we know, does not signify (it denotes, but, according to John
Stuart Mill, does not connote) – or when it is equivalent to a demonstrative
like *this* (Russell). Hence the analytic session involving a long dissertation
on an image of Christ bearing a little girl, which brings to light the division
(*dédoublement*) in both the female analyst (bearer and child) and the
(female) patient, each playing in turn both roles of the pair. Other divisions
found in the clinical picture of the patient could also be read in this splitting in two, namely: subject or object, man or woman, breast (*sein* (*saint*))
or penis – even reading this, as André Green has suggested, as: neither subject nor object, neither man nor woman, neither breast nor penis.... Being
tied to the analyst's own name (the (krist)), this condensed hallucination
stemming from division led, at the end of the session, to what for some
would be a regression, but what I would call an emergence of signification,
even at the same level as an – until then – isolated signifier which, for this
patient, sounded like a void evoking the threat of the idiocy she dreaded.
Here is the emergence of signification: 'I was adopted by some people, the
Juliens....' Apparently, what is at stake is an invention, a deception, a desire
to be adopted by the analyst, to be reborn through her (for the name of the
patient's adoptive family is entirely different...). 'Hold on, I don't know
why I said that,' she says, as if it had just dawned on her. 'I hadn't thought
that it could have anything to do with you...'.

We thus hear what plays the role of 'holding' [English in the text] (in
Winnicott's sense), and even what overturns (Hanna Segal's) 'symbolic
equivalences' where signs would refer to objects; the unifying role of the
transfer emerges and, in particular, the Proper Name, the ultimate mark of
an identity – the mark of One which is not a pure signifier, or is so only
apparently. For if it is true that the Proper Name has no signified, its signifier is far from being self-sustaining; on the contrary, it opens up a cascade
of signifieds in which experiences, as much ideological (in the case cited: a
'resurrection' is inaugurated in the patient through the adoptive family;
there is an expectation that the analyst will indeed finally bring about the
hoped-for renaissance; religious education is an issue, etc.) as physical (the
Calvary, the Passion of the Christly body, but also the bad 'holding' by the
unstable mother evoking psychosomatic pains in the patient) or phantasmic
(is the mother a man?), etc. But the signifier of the Proper Name acts like
the figure, 1, which allows the subject to represent – not this time as symbolic equivalences, but as signs (signifier/signified) – all heteroclite (perceptive, coenesthetic, phantasmic, ideological, etc.) experiences unable until

then to find a signification, having remained 'unnameable' within language. Borderline discourse will, however, always keep its status as a scar between unnameable *meaning* on the one hand, and the empty *signifier* on the other. This is a scar which constitutes the category of the Proper Name and which these patients, inhabitants of frontiers, are affected by in all other categories and articulations of discourse.

Alternative Negativism

The second trait of borderline discourse on which I will focus is its notice-able negativism, which is in fact a tendency to oscillate between antonyms: 'It is perhaps All but it is also Nothing', or: 'It is neither All nor Nothing'; 'She is the one who makes me live, but in fact she devitalises me', etc. It is impossible to say here that one of these antonyms (or a disavowed antonym) represents 'unconscious' thoughts or desires. The subject is literally locked between the two poles of this dyad, for what is barred from symbolisation is on neither one side nor the other of the opposition, but is outside it. Within it or beyond it? The point within is necessarily an affect which is not yet a sign, and is invisible and unrepresented. 'You were in front – no, you were behind; in fact you were neither in front nor behind; but how is that possible? It reminds me of the concave mirror at a Luna Park I used to visit as a child', one male patient says. As in the famous mirror scene in the Marx Brothers' film *Duck Soup*, what is going to let him escape from this mimetic oscillation where he is stuck – being simultaneously the same and other because he is on neither side of the mirror – is the appearance of a Third Party. The analyst as a Third Party, or the Object of the analyst's desire as a Third Party threatening the narcissistic dyad without which the borderline would get all caught up – this is what, by appearing in the transference, brings down the masks of false selves where this patient has become alien-ated, and gives rise to sadness, disarray, tears: a feeling of abjection of self and of others which, if it does not lead to mysticism, is a way of signifying the division of the subject (neither subject nor object but ab-ject). The pos-sibility of speaking creatively – not by repeating more or less intelligent stereotypes, but by dressing up in words the subject's own experience (the specific place where the subject is located – can be produced only after this crisis.

The strange advent of the Third Party who releases the patient from his imprisonment in a tourniquet of anonymity obviously has a name (proper or common). It is the *vocal* signifier of this name which detaches itself from the pair of antonyms, and in the end finds the signified of affect that I would not say is repressed, but *unknown*. 'I am not a solitary [*solitaire*] person, no, I am perhaps a person in solidarity [*solidaire*] with my own self, or rather, neither the one nor the other. . . .' Then comes the patient's evolution of a royal sta-tus, impressing the child, in the full sunlight, dazzling in the school yard where he roams about, deprived of a father. . . . Embarrassment and shame arise before the patient says that his father was – neither a person of solidarity (*solidaire*) nor solitary (*solitaire*), but permanently 'drunk'. And after this confession he can rework the long trajectory of a rejected, even foreclosed, love – one whose restoration will lead to the torments and delights of a notice-able homosexuality through a clearly anal resurrection of the father.

What I would like to indicate in passing is that to form an amorous iden-tification with a Third Party, which is for the boy an amorous identification with the same sex, is to attach oneself to the *voice*. I make this point in order to emphasise that access to the split (the drive or affect) cannot be made by way of the visible, the representable or the signified, but through what is buried there, like the ghost of Hamlet's father, which persists only as a voice in the vocal signifier....

We can go still further and argue that if primary identification with the maternal object seeks out the image and the look, as Oedipus saw only after putting out his eyes, it is, on the contrary, through vocal, intonational or phonematic articulations that language and the Third, paternal Party are simultaneously constituted. This implies that the human speaker, whether knowing it or not – that is to say, in playing his or her own Hamlet, as actor or as linguist – will have disputes with the Father – that is to say, with another man in relation to whom it will or will not be a question of conceding author-ity (hence the homosexual tenor of every institution, colloquium or group desirous of accomplishing or simply clarifying the social and/or symbolic contract). Whereas a woman – when she does not become unequivocally mad like Ophelia but, in place of Hamlet, tries to act out the play, all the time searching for signification – will never forget that the Voice of the Father and, at a pinch, language itself, is only a shadow. With her gaze fixed on the body – of her mother, and thus on her own – she searches for mean-ing, but always a bit sceptically – obligated as she is by an imaginary debt to believe in non-verbal forms. As linguist or metalinguist, always a bit scep-tical, her obvious rationalism is supported by an implicit belief in the unnameable, which can be the source of religion as much as of analysis. In the light of this implication of the subject in language, what can analytic lis-tening do?

The Ways Open to Analytic Listening

The most imaginative response – the least reductive and the most generous in its direct humanism – comes from Winnicott. Having heard this hetero-geneity of borderline discourse that I have just briefly outlined, he consid-ers treatment as, in sum, an imaginary identification with the analyst, allowing the patient to play with the analyst, but also to play *tout court*. Better than the normative tendencies of ego psychology, Winnicott's way aims, in substance, to liberate the artistic capacities of patients, which means that if they do not come to refer to a reality in univocal signs (which bear witness to castration and the paternal function) at least they domesticate this space of play – a split space, a fold or a catastrophe – in a language which is simultaneously meaningful and a pure signifier, with a more or less decidable signification. This comprehensive and warm minimalism which seduces – for it represents an introduction to perversion in Anglo-Saxon Protestantism – is part of a medical attitude: it allows for a more or less gratifying socialisation. It does not lead to the truth.

This truth is what Jacques Lacan pursues in his teaching when he indicates that the end of the treatment is the subject's experience of unbeing (*désêtre*): the subject is nothing other than its language reduced to the capacity to develop a style (that is to say, a knot between real/symbolic/imaginary). It has no other existence likely to procure narcissistic gratification: neither through the hysterical fantasy of an unnameable body-part, nor through the oral–anal manipulation of subjects, objects or material signifiers – which, in the last instance, only leave the patient dependent on the mother.

The fascinating rigorism of Lacanian theory reminds me of Dostoevsky's *Devils*, and more particularly – by way of all these characters who are *possessed* only because they have lost any reference to absolute and divine Truth – it reminds me, as a footnote, that the Russian writer borrowed a famous passage from St Luke: Christ chased the devils from the possessed. The possessed person of the Gospels very much recalls our borderline cases: he speaks disjointedly, is unaware of contraries (he lives in tombs), hesitates regarding inside and outside, his and the other's, the forbidden and the permitted (therefore, he does not wear clothes), and so on. Christ frees him by asking him: 'What is your name?' The unfortunate man then admits that his 'name is Legion', meaning: 'My name is what is opposed to the Name' (in its unifying function, in what one could call its *erotic consistency*). Let us recall in passing that for Freud erotic means 'unifying', in opposition to the dissolution brought by Thanatos. In this sense, Christ would be an 'erotic' hero. The possessed person thus admits to the disarray in which he finds himself, and it is only then that he becomes capable of opting, one supposes, for unity. His demons then leave his body and go into the pigs, and catharsis is produced.

The recognition of the signifier, One, unifying and condensing all the heterogeneity of bodily experiences – experiences which would, without it, remain a demoniacal pigsty – a recognition *of the place of language*, in sum, is what separates the social exercise of discourse from psychosis. Lacanian exigency is not foreign to the word of the Gospel, and this is perhaps why, at bottom, it provokes so much resistance ('religious' and anti-religious).

However, we should not forget that, in the story from St Luke, it is the possessed person who first of all addresses Christ by asking him what he wants – which signifies that it is he, the possessed one, who already wants something from the healer, and thus that he is on the way to believing in an imposing person. The question which we ask is, therefore: can we suppose a similar power for the analytic function so that the transference turns into an act of faith? And assuming that such a phenomenon were to be possible today, would it always be a question of an analysis or, far from that, of a heretical capitalisation, by which I mean being deprived: deprived of transcendence, of divine revelation, and therefore of something perverse?

Dostoevsky's response to the possessed person is not exactly that of St Luke. Ideologue of his time, it is nevertheless through his aesthetic performance, through the polyphony of his text, that Dostoevsky is opposed to Stavrogin or Verhovensky, who have banished from their discourse and from their lives the possibility of truth (truth as an exact denotation of a reference, as well as truth as the presupposed rigour of discourse itself). In a way, Dostoevsky is not content to name, or to have an identifying name spoken

– as does Christ in the Gospel of St Luke. Nor does he do *less* than his demoniacal characters bereft of true words, and lost in semblances and masks, battling for a power without any place. He does more and better than they do: he verbalises from the same place as them, but, *in addition*, he views them from a distance and puts them on stage; he is himself Father and his own Son. One could say this of every writer, but Dostoevsky's novels, because of their polyphony (analysed by Bakhtin) without a centre of ideological values or enunciation, constitute one of the most striking examples of this writing function – which is to bring about a resurrection of the subject, that is, the subject's accession to the place of the Father through the intermediary of language.

Joyce in *Ulysses*, besides reflecting on Hamlet, notes that Shakespeare's dead son was called ... Hamlet, and that it was, moreover, the death of the dramatist's father – John Shakespeare – which seems to haunt Elsinore castle in the play *Hamlet*. And Joyce further insinuates, as every writer does implicitly, that it is the author's place – the author being the father of his imaginary formations - which simultaneously allows: the healing of Hamlet's wound (Hamlet: the one who speaks and hears himself speak to madness), the competition with the paternal authority which is only a 'legal fiction', and the equalling of the sacred mystery of religion: its overturning. For the meaning of the sacred, like all meaning - since it relates back to the Third Party, to the Father – is only constructed over a void.... The only vehicle for Hamlet's madness will thus be ... the dramatist, Shakespeare, who does not, like Hamlet, have to die in order to grasp the meaning (of the Father), but who is father-*and*-son: a resurrection accomplished in signs.

Between the aesthetic and the theological solution (whether transcendent or privatised) of the division in the subject in language, it is difficult for the analyst to search for a third way. Seeing the limits and advantages of both solutions (aesthetic and theological), it perhaps remains for him to use them selectively and unpredictably, arrogating to himself the right to the unusual in the search for what can only be the undecidable truth of the subject's place in language. There is meaning, but it is polyvalent (fictional) and heterogeneous (it insists within and beyond the signification of speech). Such would be the postulate of an interpretative attitude that allows us to avoid blocking the outcome of the treatment through (creative) perversion, or through allegiance to a master of language (who stands out behind the theory of the 'unbeing' (*désêtre*) – thus, without denying either of them – and to arrange for the possibility of a resurrection in signs for those whose suffering is to be strangers to language.

This encounter of psychoanalysis with aesthetics on the one hand, and with religion on the other, does not win it many friends in the field of classical humanism – quite the contrary. Being dependent on a reduction of the symbolic field to Cartesian, Kantian, or phenomenological consciousness, classical humanism retains from *signifiance*[9] only that which can be systematised as an effect of signification. Nevertheless, the vast field of symptoms, of the pain of a murder passing through the unsaid, leads us to our condition of being divided in and by language. I have tried to give a reading of this division which is neither that of an unnameable unconscious nor that of an always-already-structured signifier. For I am persuaded that faced with

the fundamental choice 'to be or not be', the exact statement of my position would be this: to propose or not to propose theoretical fictions in order
to expand the limits of the signifiable and push back the frontiers of ghosts,
visions, experiences of possession.... An endless enterprise, in fact, which
could be characterised as follows: language is what makes me be more and
more by way of non-being. The more I happen not to be, the more I reach
being. I am never *more* than the place where I was not, but there it was
already speaking, 'before me'. *Wo Es war soll Ich werden.* There, where it
was speaking me without my being there, I must come to speak as if I were
not.

Translated by John Lechte

Notes

* This is a variation of a lecture given in English at Columbia University in 1979.
1. Michel Bréal, *Essai de sémantique*, Paris: Hachette, 1897. In English as
Semantics: Studies in the Science of Meaning, trans. Mrs Henry Cust, New York:
Dover, 1964.
2. R. Gödel, *Les Sources manuscrites du cours de linguistique générale de Ferdinand
de Saussure*, Geneva: Droz, 1957, p. 68.
3. J. Starobinski, 'Le Texte dans le texte', *Tel Quel*, 37, Spring 1969, p. 3.
4. See *Langages* (Paris), no. 24, 'Epistémologies et linguistique'.
5. The French word *langage* can mean both language in general, and a particular
(non-natural) language – as in the language of philosophy, or the language of flow-
ers. (Translator's Note (TN))
6. Hanna Segal, 'Notes on Symbol Formation', *International Journal of Psycho-
Analysis*, vol. XXXVII, no. 38 (1957), pp. 391–7.
7. *Propre* connotes 'clean' as well as 'own'. Kristeva is trying to make the link
between what is clean, or pure (the realm of the object, and thus of the
subject–object relation) and the formation of identity. (TN)
8. A discussion of the notion of *abject*, in relation to the *subject* and to the *object*,
is proposed in my book *Powers of Horror: An Essay on Abjection*, trans. Leon S.
Roudiez, New York: Columbia University Press, 1983.
9. For Kristeva, *la signifiance* is more than the symbolic (meaning) aspect of language and includes its material, or semiotic, dimension. In a sense, *la signifiance* is
the (heterogeneous) process of the semiotic. More precisely: 'What we call *signifiance* ... is precisely this unlimited and unbounded generating process, this unceas-
ing operation of the drives toward, in, and through language; toward, in, and through
the exchange system and its protagonists – the subject and its institutions.' (Julia
Kristeva, *Revolution in Poetic Language*, trans. Margaret Waller, New York:
Columbia University Press, 1984, p. 17.) (TN)

SECTION THREE

Freud on Literature – A Selection

7

Sigmund Freud 'Psychopathic Characters on the Stage' (1942) [1905–6], *S.E.*, 7.

Trans. James Strachey, London: Hogarth Press and Institute of Psycho-Analysis, 1961, pp. 303–10.

Editor's Introduction

Freud moves, in a series of reflections in this piece, from an explanation of drama *per se* as a 'rebellion against the gods', through the various kinds of struggle embodied in drama, to that kind of drama which is founded on the conflict between 'a conscious impulse and a repressed one'. This is drama which can be enjoyed by neurotics; it is, Freud says, 'psychopathological drama' – exemplified, for instance, by *Hamlet*.

The key to *Hamlet*, says Freud, is that the hero is struggling against an unconscious impulse which emerges only as the play progresses. The difficulty for any playwright in putting a psychopathic character on stage is that the unconscious impulse largely constitutive of the character cannot have a name. This situation tends to deprive the 'normal' spectator (i.e. the one who is not neurotic) of a certain pleasure; for he or she is unable to identify with the neurosis of the character.

Freud thus lays weight, in speaking about the structure of drama, on the spectator's pleasure, derived through identification – even if this be an identification with the suffering of the hero. What the spectator cannot identify with – although it can be experienced – is the unnamed, unconscious impulse, an impulse that Freud effectively conflates with the death of art. Neurosis, we recall Freud saying, is a 'failed work of art'.

This piece may profitably be compared to Kristeva's 'Name of Death or of Life'.

Psychopathic Characters on the Stage

If, as has been assumed since the time of Aristotle, the purpose of drama is to arouse 'terror and pity'[1] and so 'to purge the emotions', we can describe that purpose in rather more detail by saying that it is a question of opening up sources of pleasure or enjoyment in our emotional life, just as, in the case of intellectual activity, joking or fun open up similar sources, many of which that activity had made inaccessible. In this connection the prime factor is unquestionably the process of getting rid of one's own emotions by 'blowing off steam'; and the consequent enjoyment corresponds on the one hand to the relief produced by a thorough discharge and on the other hand, no doubt, to an accompanying sexual excitation; for the latter, as we may suppose, appears as a by-product whenever an affect is aroused, and gives people the sense, which they so much desire, of a raising of the potential of their psychical state. Being present as an interested spectator at a spectacle or play[2] does for adults what play does for children, whose hesitant hopes of being able to do what grown-up people do are in that way gratified. The spectator is a person who experiences too little, who feels that he is a 'poor wretch to whom nothing of importance can happen', who has long been obliged to damp down, or rather displace, his ambition to stand in his own person at the hub of world affairs; he longs to feel and to act and to arrange things according to his desires – in short, to be a hero. And the playwright and actor enable him to do this by allowing him *to identify himself* with a hero. They spare him something, too. For the spectator knows quite well that actual heroic conduct such as this would be impossible for him without pains and sufferings and acute fears, which would almost cancel out the enjoyment. He knows, moreover, that he has only *one* life and that he might perhaps perish even in a *single* such struggle against adversity. Accordingly, his enjoyment is based on an illusion; that is to say, his suffering is mitigated by the certainty that, firstly, it is someone other than himself who is acting and suffering on the stage, and, secondly, that after all it is only a game, which can threaten no damage to his personal security. In these circumstances he can allow himself to enoy being a 'great man', to give way without a qualm to such suppressed impulses as a craving for freedom in religious, political, social and sexual matters, and to 'blow off steam' in every direction in the various grand scenes that form part of the life represented on the stage.

Several other forms of creative writing, however, are equally subject to these same preconditions for enjoyment. Lyric poetry serves the purpose, more than anything, of giving vent to intense feelings of many sorts – just as was at one time the case with dancing. Epic poetry aims chiefly at making it possible, to feel the enjoyment of a great heroic character in his hour of triumph. But drama seeks to explore emotional possibilities more deeply and to give an enjoyable shape even to forebodings of misfortune; for this reason it depicts the hero in his struggles, or rather (with masochistic satisfaction) in defeat. This relation to suffering and misfortune might be taken as characteristic of drama, whether, as happens in serious plays, it is only *concern* that is aroused, and afterwards allayed, or whether, as happens in tragedies, the suffering is actually realized. The fact that drama originated out of sacrificial rites (cf. the goat and the scapegoat) in the cult of the gods cannot be unrelated to this meaning of drama.[3] It appeases, as it were, a rising rebellion against the divine regulation of the universe, which is responsible for the existence of suffering. Heroes are first and foremost rebels against God or against something divine; and pleasure is derived, as it seems, from the affliction of a weaker being in the face of divine might – a pleasure due to masochistic satisfaction as well as to direct enjoyment of a character whose greatness is insisted upon in spite of everything. Here we have a mood like that of Prometheus, but alloyed with a paltry readiness to let oneself be soothed for the moment by a temporary satisfaction.

Suffering of every kind is thus the subject-matter of drama, and from this suffering it promises to give the audience pleasure. Thus we arrive at a first precondition of this form of art: that it should not cause suffering to the audience, that it should know how to compensate, by means of the possible satisfactions involved, for the sympathetic suffering which is aroused. (Modern writers have particularly often failed to obey this rule.) But the suffering represented is soon restricted to *mental* suffering; for no one wants *physical* suffering who knows how quickly all mental enjoyment is brought to an end by the changes in somatic feeling that physical suffering brings about. If we are sick we have one wish only: to be well again and to be quit of our present state. We call for the doctor and medicine, and for the removal of the inhibition on the play of phantasy which has pampered us into deriving enjoyment even from our own sufferings. If a spectator puts himself in the place of someone who is physically ill he finds himself without any capacity for enjoyment or psychical activity. Consequently a person who physically ill can only figure on the stage as a piece of stage property and not as a hero, unless, indeed, some peculiar physical aspects of his illness make psychical activity possible – such, for instance, as the sick man's forlorn state in the *Philoctetes* or the hopelessness of the sufferers in the class of plays that centre round consumptives.

People are acquainted with mental suffering principally in connection with the circumstances in which it is acquired; accordingly, dramas dealing with it require some event out of which the illness shall arise and they open with an exposition of this event. It is only an apparent exception that some plays, such as the *Ajax* and the *Philoctetes*, introduce the mental illness as already fully established; for in Greek tragedies, owing to the familiarity of the material, the curtain rises, as one might say, in the middle of the play. It is easy to give an exhaustive account of the preconditions governing an event of the kind that is here in question. It must be an event involving conflict and it must include an effort of will together with resistance. This precondition found its first and grandest fulfilment in a struggle against divinity. I have already said that a tragedy of this kind is one of rebellion, in which the dramatist and the audience take the side of the rebel. The less belief there comes to be in divinity, the more important becomes the *human* regulation of affairs; and it is this which, with increasing insight, comes to be held responsible for suffering. Thus the hero's next struggle is against human society, and here we have the class of *social* tragedies. Yet another fulfilment of the necessary precondition is to be found in a struggle between individual men. Such are tragedies of *character*, which exhibit all the excitement of an 'agon' (ἀγών, conflict), and which are best played out between outstanding characters who have freed themselves from the bond of human institutions – which, in fact, must have *two* heroes. Fusions between these two last classes, with a hero struggling against institutions embodied in powerful characters, are of course admissible without question. Pure tragedies of character lack the rebellious source of enjoyment, but this emerges once again no less forcibly in social dramas (in Ibsen for instance) than it did in the historical plays of the Greek classical tragedians.

Thus *religious* drama, *social* drama and drama of *character* differ essentially in the terrain on which the action that leads to the suffering is fought out. And we can now follow the course of drama on to yet another terrain, where it becomes *psychological* drama. Here the struggle that causes the suffering is fought out in the hero's mind itself – a struggle between different impulses, and one which must have its end in the extinction, not of the hero, but of one of his impulses; it must end, that is to say, in a renunciation. Combinations of any kind between this precondition and the earlier types are, of course, possible; thus institutions, for instance, can themselves be the cause of internal conflicts. And this is where we have tragedies of love; for the suppression of love by social culture, by human conventions, or the struggle between 'love and duty', which is so familiar to us in opera, are the starting-point of almost endless varieties of situations of conflict: just as endless, in fact, as the erotic day-dreams of men.

But the series of possibilities grows wider; and psychological drama turns into psychopathological drama when the source of the suffering in which we take part and from which we are meant to derive pleasure is no longer a conflict between two almost equally conscious impulses but between a conscious impulse and a repressed one. Here the precondition of enjoyment is that the spectator should himself be a neurotic, for it is only such people who can derive pleasure instead of simple aversion from the revelation and the more or less conscious recognition of a repressed impulse. In anyone who is *not* neurotic this recognition will meet only with aversion and will call up a readiness to repeat the act of repression which has earlier been successfully brought to bear on the impulse: for in such people a single expenditure of repression has been enough to hold the repressed impulse completely in check. But in neurotics the repression is on the brink of failing; it is unstable and needs a constant renewal of expenditure, and this expenditure is spared if recognition of the impulse is brought about. Thus it is only in neurotics that a struggle can occur of a kind which can be made the subject of a drama; but even in them the dramatist will provoke not merely an *enjoyment* of the liberation but a *resistance* to it as well.

The first of these modern dramas is *Hamlet*.[4] It has as its subject the way in which a man who has so far been normal becomes neurotic owing to the peculiar nature of the task by which he is faced, a man, that is, in whom an impulse that has hitherto been successfully suppressed endeavours to make its way into action. *Hamlet* is distinguished by three characteristics which seem important in connection with our present discussion. (1) The hero is not psychopathic, but only *becomes* psychopathic in the course of the action of the play. (2) The repressed impulse is one of those which are similarly repressed in all of us, and the repression of which is part and parcel of the foundations of our personal evolution. It is this repression which is shaken up by the situation in the play. As a result of these two characteristics it is easy for us to recognize ourselves in the hero: we are susceptible to the same conflict as he is, since 'a person who does not lose his reason under certain conditions can have no reason to lose'.[5] (3) It appears as a necessary precondition of this form of art that the impulse that is struggling into consciousness, however clearly it is recognizable, is never given a definite name; so that in the spectator too the process is carried through with his attention averted, and he is in the grip of his emotions instead of taking stock of what is happening. A certain amount of resistance is no doubt saved in this way, just as, in an analytic treatment, we find derivatives of the repressed material reaching consciousness, owing to a lower resistance, while the repressed material itself is unable to do so. After all, the conflict in *Hamlet* is so effectively concealed that it was left to me to unearth it.

It may be in consequence of disregarding these three preconditions that so many other psychopathic characters are as unserviceable on the stage as they are in real life. For the victim of a neurosis is someone into whose conflict we can gain no insight if we first meet it in a fully established state. But, *per contra*, if we recognize the conflict, we forget that he is a sick man, just as, if he himself recognizes it, he ceases to be ill. It would seem to be the dramatist's business to induce the same illness in *us*; and this can best be achieved if we are made to follow the development of the illness along with the sufferer. This will be especially necessary where the repression does not already exist in us but has first to be set up; and this represents a step further than *Hamlet* in the use of neurosis on the stage. If we are faced by an unfamiliar and fully established neurosis, we shall be inclined to send for the doctor (just as we do in real life) and pronounce the character inadmissible to the stage.

This last mistake seems to occur in Bahr's *Die Andere*,[6] apart from a second one which is implicit in the problem presented in the play – namely, that it is impossible for us to put ourselves with conviction into the position of believing that one particular person has a prescriptive right to give the girl complete satisfaction. So that her case cannot become ours. Moreover, there remains a third mistake: namely that there is nothing left for us to discover and that our entire resistance is mobilized against this predetermined condition of love which is so unacceptable to us. Of the three formal preconditions that I have been discussing, the most important seems to be that of the diversion of attention.

In general, it may perhaps be said that the neurotic instability of the public and the dramatist's skill in avoiding resistances and offering forepleasures can alone determine the limits set upon the employment of abnormal characters on the stage.

Notes

1. [The German '*Mitleid*' has the meaning of 'sympathetic suffering'.]
2. ['*Schauspiel*' is the ordinary German word for a dramatic performance. Freud writes it here with a hyphen '*Schau-spiel*' to bring out the word's two components: '*Schau*', 'spectacle', and '*Spiel*', 'play' or 'game'. Freud returned to this topic in his subsequent paper on creative art and phantasy 'Creative Writers and Day-Dreaming', *S.E.*, 9) and again, many years later, at the end of Chapter II of *Beyond the Pleasure Principle* (*S.E.*, 18).]
3. [The subject of the Hero in Greek tragedy was discussed by Freud in his *Totem and Taboo* (1912–13), in Section 7 of the fourth essay.]
4. [Freud's first published discussion of *Hamlet* was in *The Interpretation of Dreams*

(Chapter V, Section D (β); *S.E.* 4, 264 ff.).]
  5. [Lessing, *Emilia Galotti*, Act IV, Scene 7.]
  6. [This play by Hermann Bahr, the Austrian novelist and playwright (1863–1934), was first produced at the end of 1905. Its plot turns upon the dual personality of its heroine, who is unable, in spite of every effort, to escape from an attachment (based on her physical feelings) to a man who has her in his power. – This paragraph was omitted from the 1942 translation.]

8

Sigmund Freud, 'Dostoevsky and Parricide', *S.E.*, 21.

Trans. James Strachey, London: Hogarth Press and Institute of Psycho-Analysis, 1961, pp. 173–94.

Editor's Introduction

In this chapter, which does not present any major theoretical difficulties, the reader will note how Freud seems to be uncomfortable with Dostoevsky's writing as writing. Should we be surprised at this when, early on in the essay, Freud refers to Dostoevsky's 'unanalysable artistic gift'? The answer is partly 'yes', because Freud goes to such lengths to explain the themes of Dostoevsky's novels – especially *The Brothers Karamazov* – in terms of the writer's personality – read: his neurosis – characterised by an exaggerated fear of death. While, therefore, it may at first glance seem that Freud has given up on explaining Dostoevsky's artistic side (maybe because, as Freud claimed, the poet always preceded him, thus leaving him little to say), he says that three of the greatest works of literature of all time – *Oedipus Rex, Hamlet* and *The Brothers Karamazov* – deal with parricide. Great literature and psychoanalysis appear to be made for each other: psychoanalysis's central concern – Oedipus, core of the symbolic order, according to Lacan – is similarly the central concern of literature. Of course, in Dostoevsky's case, Freud is mostly talking about a real father, not a symbolic father.

  Even if Freud's hypothesis (that *The Brothers Karamazov* is the result of Dostoevsky's desire for his own father's death) could be understood literally, we should note that Dostoevsky's father is actually absent when he is writing. The desire for the father's death leading Dostoevsky, as Freud notes, to identify with Dimitri, the criminal, in the novel in question, can thus only be the result of a memory of a traumatic event. Memory would be a distancing from the traumatic event of the son's encounter with the father – in short, a means of displacement. In this sense, memory and writing are inseparable, and the father progressively becomes symbolic.

  The question that Freud's piece on Dostoevsky and parricide raises is whether, in order to write successfully about parricide, one has to be a parricide oneself. One could, indeed, pretend not to be a parricide, but do so by pushing one's wager to the limit by pretending to be one? Whatever the position taken on this, it is surely language – always saying something other than what it says (Lacan) – which enables the user to hide in it. Language – writing – throws down the gauntlet to the interpreter and dares its recipient to make a final claim about it. What better way for the true parricide to hide, then, than to write about parricide? Would a true parricide draw attention to himself in such a way? Then again, is not this just what Dostoevsky anticipates – that the astute reader will assume that the writer is no fool, and that he is playing around with the theme of parricide so as to throw us off the track? After all, 'in reality', Dostoevsky, as Sollers reminds us, was himself a father.[1] Or maybe pretence had not crossed Dostoevsky's mind, leaving the reader of his novels to deal precisely with a writing effect.

Notes

1. Philippe Sollers, 'Dostoïevski, Freud, la roulette', in *Théories des exceptions*, Paris: Seuil, 1986, p. 71.

Dostoevsky and Parricide

Four facets may be distinguished in the rich personality of Dostoevsky: the creative artist, the neurotic, the moralist and the sinner. How is one to find one's way in this bewildering complexity?

The creative artist is the least doubtful: Dostoevsky's place is not far behind Shakespeare. *The Brothers Karamazov* is the most magnificent novel ever written; the episode of the Grand Inquisitor, one of the peaks in the literature of the world, can hardly be valued too highly. Before the problem of the creative artist analysis must, alas, lay down its arms.

The moralist in Dostoevsky is the most readily assailable. If we seek to rank him high as a moralist on the plea that only a man who has gone through the depths of sin can reach the highest summit of morality, we are neglecting a doubt that arises. A moral man is one who reacts to temptation as soon as he feels it in his heart, without yielding to it. A man who alternately sins and then in his remorse erects high moral standards lays himself open to the reproach that he has made things too easy for himself. He has not achieved the essence of morality, renunciation, for the moral conduct of life is a practical human interest. He reminds one of the barbarians of the great migrations, who murdered and did penance for it, till penance became an actual technique for enabling murder to be done. Ivan the Terrible behaved in exactly this way; indeed this compromise with morality is a characteristic Russian trait. Nor was the final outcome of Dostoevsky's moral strivings anything very glorious. After the most violent struggles to reconcile the instinctual demands of the individual with the claims of the community, he landed in the retrograde position of submission both to temporal and spiritual authority, of veneration both for the Tsar and for the God of the Christians, and of a narrow Russian nationalism – a position which lesser minds have reached with smaller effort. This is the weak point in that great personality. Dostoevsky threw away the chance of becoming a teacher and liberator of humanity and made himself one with their gaolers. The future of human civilization will have little to thank him for. It seems probable that he was condemned to this failure by his neurosis. The greatness of his intelligence and the strength of his love for humanity might have opened to him another, an apostolic, way of life.

To consider Dostoevsky as a sinner or a criminal rouses violent opposition, which need not be based upon a philistine assessment of criminals. The real motive for this opposition soon becomes apparent. Two traits are essential in a criminal: boundless egoism and a strong destructive urge. Common to both of these, and a necessary condition for their expression, is absence of love, lack of an emotional appreciation of (human) objects. One at once recalls the contrast to this presented by Dostoevsky – his great need of love and his enormous capacity for love, which is to be seen in manifestations of exaggerated kindness and caused him to love and to help where he had a right to hate and to be revengeful, as, for example, in his relations with his first wife and her lover. That being so, it must be asked why there is any temptation to reckon Dostoevsky among the criminals. The answer is that it comes from his choice of material, which singles out from all others violent, murderous and egoistic characters, thus pointing to the existence of similar tendencies within himself, and also from certain facts in his life, like his passion for gambling and his possible confession to a sexual assault upon a young girl.[1] The contradiction is resolved by the realization that Dostoevsky's very strong destructive instinct, which might easily have made him a criminal, was in his actual life directed mainly against his own person (inward instead of outward) and thus found expression as masochism and a sense of guilt. Nevertheless, his personality retained sadistic traits in plenty, which show themselves in his irritability, his love of tormenting and his intolerance even towards people he loved, and which appear also in the way in which, as an author, he treats his readers. Thus in little things he was a sadist towards others, and in bigger things a sadist towards himself, in fact a masochist – that is to say the mildest, kindliest, most helpful person possible.

We have selected three factors from Dostoevsky's complex personality, one quantitative and two qualitative: the extraordinary intensity of his emotional life, his perverse innate instinctual disposition, which inevitably marked him out to be a sado-masochist or a criminal, and his unanalysable artistic gift. This combination might very well exist without neurosis; there are people who are complete masochists without being neurotic. Nevertheless, the balance of forces between his instinctual demands and the inhibitions opposing them (plus the available methods of sublimation) would even so make it necessary to classify Dostoevsky as what is known as an 'instinctual character'. But the position is obscured by the simultaneous presence of neurosis, which, as we have said, was not in the circumstances inevitable, but which comes into being the more readily, the richer the complication which has to be mastered by the ego. For neurosis is after all only a sign that the ego has not succeeded in making a synthesis, that in attempting to do so it has forfeited its unity.

How then, strictly speaking, does his neurosis show itself? Dostoevsky called himself an epileptic, and was regarded as such by other people, on account of his severe attacks, which were accompanied by loss of consciousness, muscular convulsions and subsequent depression. Now it is highly probable that this so-called epilepsy was only a symptom of his neurosis and must accordingly be classified as hystero-epilepsy – that is, as severe hysteria. We cannot be completely certain on this point for two reasons – firstly, because the anamnestic data on Dostoevsky's alleged epilepsy are defective and untrustworthy, and secondly, because our understanding of pathological states combined with epileptiform attacks is imperfect.

To take the second point first. It is unnecessary here to reproduce the whole pathology of epilepsy, for it would throw no decisive light on the problem. But this may be said. The old *morbus sacer* is still in evidence as an ostensible clinical entity, the uncanny disease with its incalculable, apparently unprovoked convulsive attacks, its changing of the character into irritability and aggressiveness, and its progressive lowering of all the mental faculties. But the outlines of this picture are quite lacking in precision. The attacks, so savage in their onset, accompanied by biting of the tongue and incontinence of urine and working up to the dangerous *status epilepticus* with its risk of severe self-injuries, may, nevertheless, be reduced to brief periods of *absence*, or rapidly passing fits of vertigo, or may be replaced by short spaces of time during which the patient does something out of character, as though he were under the control of his unconscious. These attacks, though as a rule determined, in a way we do not understand, by purely physical causes, may nevertheless owe their first appearance to some purely mental cause (a fright, for instance) or may react in other respects to mental excitations. However characteristic intellectual impairment may be in the overwhelming majority of cases, at least *one* case is known to us (that of Helmholtz) in which the affliction did not interfere with the highest intellectual achievement. (Other cases of which the same assertion has been made are either disputable or open to the same doubts as the case of Dostoevsky himself.) People who are victims of epilepsy may give an impression of dullness and arrested development just as the disease often accompanies the most palpable idiocy and the grossest cerebral defects, even though not as a necessary component of the clinical picture. But these attacks, with all their variations, also occur in other people who display complete mental development and, if anything, an excessive and as a rule insufficiently controlled emotional life. It is no wonder in these circumstances that it has been found impossible to maintain that 'epilepsy' is a single clinical entity. The similarity that we find in the manifest symptoms seems to call for a functional view of them. It is as though a mechanism for abnormal instinctual discharge had been laid down organically, which could be made use of in quite different circumstances – both in the case of disturbances of cerebral activity due to severe histolytic or toxic affections, and also in the case of inadequate control over the mental economy and at times when the activity of the energy operating in the mind reaches crisis-pitch. Behind this dichotomy we have a glimpse of the identity of the underlying mechanism of instinctual discharge. Nor can that mechanism stand remote from the sexual processes, which are fundamentally of toxic origin: the earliest physicians described coition as a minor epilepsy, and thus recognized in the sexual act a mitigation and adaptation of the epileptic method of discharging stimuli.[2]

The 'epileptic reaction', as this common element may be called, is also undoubtedly at the disposal of the neurosis whose essence it is to get rid by somatic means of amounts of excitation which it cannot deal with psychically. Thus the epileptic attack becomes a symptom of hysteria and is adapted and modified by it just as it is by the normal sexual process of discharge. It is therefore quite right to distinguish between an organic and an 'affective' epilepsy. The practical significance of this is that a person who suffers from the first kind has a disease of the brain, while a person who suffers from the second kind is a neurotic. In the first case his mental life is subjected to an alien disturbance from without, in the second case the disturbance is an expression of his mental life itself.

It is extremely probable that Dostoevsky's epilepsy was of the second kind. This cannot, strictly speaking, be proved. To do so we should have to be in a position to insert the first appearance of the attacks and their subsequent fluctuations into the thread of his mental life; and for that we know too little. The descriptions of the attacks themselves teach us nothing and our information about the relations between them and Dostoevsky's experiences is defective and often contradictory. The most probable assumption is that the attacks went back far into his childhood, that their place was taken to begin with by milder symptoms and that they did not assume an epileptic form until after the shattering experience of his eighteenth year – the murder of his father.[3] It would be very much to the point if it could be established that they ceased completely during his exile in Siberia, but other accounts contradict this.[4]

The unmistakable connection between the murder of the father in *The Brothers Karamazov* and the fate of Dostoevsky's own father has struck more than one of his biographers, and has led them to refer to 'a certain modern school of psychology'. From the standpoint of psychoanalysis (for that is what is meant), we are tempted to see in that event the severest trauma and to regard Dostoevsky's reaction to it as the turning-point of his neurosis. But if I undertake to substantiate this view psychoanalytically, I shall have to risk the danger of being unintelligible to all those readers who are unfamiliar with the language and theories of psychoanalysis.

We have one certain starting-point. We know the meaning of the first attacks from which Dostoevsky suffered in his early years, long before the incidence of the 'epilepsy'. These attacks had the significance of death: they were heralded by a fear of death and consisted of lethargic, somnolent states. The illness first came over him while he was still a boy, in the form of a sudden, groundless melancholy, a feeling, as he later told his friend Soloviev, as though he were going to die on the spot. And there in fact followed a state exactly similar to real death. His brother Andrey tells us that even when he was quite young Fyodor used to leave little notes about before he went to sleep, saying that he was afraid he might fall into this death-like sleep during the night and therefore begged that his burial should be postponed for five days. (Fülöp-Miller and Eckstein, 1925, p. lx.)

We know the meaning and intention of such death-like attacks.[5] They signify an identification with a dead person, either with someone who is really dead or with someone who is still alive and whom the subject wishes dead. The latter case is the more significant. The attack then has the value of a punishment. One has wished another person dead, and now one *is* this other person and is dead oneself. At this point psychoanalytical theory brings in the assertion that for a boy this other person is usually his father and that the attack (which is termed hysterical) is thus a self-punishment for a death-wish against a hated father.

Parricide, according to a well-known view, is the principal and primal crime of humanity as well as of the individual. (See my *Totem and Taboo*, 1912–13.) It is in any case the main source of the sense of guilt, though we do not know if it is the only one: researches have not yet been able to establish with certainty the mental origin of guilt and the need for expiation. But it is not necessary for it to be the only one. The psychological situation is complicated and requires elucidation. The relation of a boy to his father is, as we say, an 'ambivalent' one. In addition to the hate which seeks to get rid of the father as a rival, a measure of tenderness for him is also habitually present. The two attitudes of mind combine to produce identification with the father; the boy wants to be in his father's place because he admires him and wants to be like him, and also because he wants to put him out of the way. This whole development now comes up against a powerful obstacle. At a certain moment the child comes to understand that an attempt to remove his father as a rival would be punished by him with castration. So from fear of castration – that is, in the interests of preserving his masculinity – he gives up his wish to possess his mother and get rid of his father. In so far as this wish remains in the unconscious it forms the basis of the sense of guilt. We believe that what we have here been describing are normal processes, the normal fate of the so-called 'Oedipus complex'; nevertheless it requires an important amplification.

A further complication arises when the constitutional factor we call bisexuality is comparatively strongly developed in a child. For then, under the threat to the boy's masculinity by castration, his inclination becomes strengthened to diverge in the direction of femininity, to put himself instead in his mother's place and take over her role as object of his father's love. But the fear of castration makes *this* solution impossible as well. The boy understands that he must also submit to castration if he wants to be loved by his father as a woman. Thus both impulses, hatred of the father and being in love with the father, undergo repression. There is a certain psychological distinction in the fact that the hatred of the father is given up on account of fear of an *external* danger (castration), while the being in love with the father is treated as an *internal* instinctual danger, though fundamentally it goes back to the same external danger.

What makes hatred of the father unacceptable is *fear* of the father; castration is terrible, whether as a punishment or as the price of love. Of the two factors which repress hatred of the father, the first, the direct fear of punishment and castration, may be called the normal one; its pathogenic intensification seems to come only with the addition of the second factor, the fear of the feminine attitude. Thus a strong innate bisexual disposition becomes one of the preconditions or reinforcements of neurosis. Such a disposition must certainly be assumed in Dostoevsky, and it shows itself in a viable form (as latent homosexuality) in the important part played by male friendships in his life, in his strangely tender attitude towards rivals in love and in his remarkable understanding of situations which are explicable only by repressed homosexuality, as many examples from his novels show.

I am sorry, though I cannot alter the facts, if this exposition of the attitudes of hatred and love towards the father and their transformations under the influence of the threat of castration seems to readers unfamiliar with psychoanalysis unsavoury and incredible. I should myself expect that it is precisely the castration complex that would be bound to arouse the most general repudiation. But I can only insist that psychoanalytic experience has put these matters in particular beyond the reach of doubt and has taught us to recognize in them the key to every neurosis. This key, then, we must apply to our author's so-called epilepsy. So alien to our consciousness are the things by which our unconscious mental life is governed!

But what has been said so far does not exhaust the consequences of the repression of the hatred of the father in the Oedipus complex. There is something fresh to be added: namely that in spite of everything the identification with the father finally makes a permanent place for itself in the ego. It is received into the ego, but establishes itself there as a separate agency in contrast to the rest of the content of the ego. We then give it the name of super-ego and ascribe to it, the inheritor of the parental influence, the most important functions. If the father was hard, violent and cruel, the super-ego takes over those attributes from him and, in the relations between the ego and it, the passivity which was supposed to have been repressed is re-established. The super-ego has become sadistic, and the ego becomes masochistic – that is to say, at bottom passive in a feminine way. A great need for punishment develops in the ego, which in part offers itself as a victim to Fate, and in part finds satisfaction in ill-treatment by the super-ego (that is, in the sense of guilt). For every punishment is ultimately castration and, as such, a fulfilment of the old passive attitude towards the father. Even Fate is, in the last resort, only a later projection of the father.

The normal processes in the formation of conscience must be similar to the abnormal ones described here. We have not yet succeeded in fixing the boundary line between them. It will be observed that here the largest share in the outcome is ascribed to the passive component of repressed femininity. In addition, it must be of importance as an accidental factor whether the father, who is feared in any case, is also especially violent in reality. This was true in Dostoevsky's case, and we can trace back the fact of his extraordinary sense of guilt and of his masochistic conduct of life to a specially strong feminine component. Thus the formula for Dostoevsky is as follows: a person with a specially strong innate bisexual disposition, who can defend himself with special intensity against dependence on a specially severe father. This characteristic of bisexuality comes as an addition to the components of his nature that we have already recognized. His early symptoms of death-like attacks can thus be understood as a father-identification on the part of his ego, which is permitted by his super-ego as a punishment. 'You wanted to kill your father in order to be your father yourself. Now you *are* your father, but a dead father' – the regular mechanism of hysterical symptoms. And further: 'Now your father is killing *you*.' For the ego the death symptom is a satisfaction in phantasy of the masculine wish and at the same time a masochistic satisfaction; for the super-ego it is a punitive satisfaction – that is, a sadistic satisfaction. Both of them, the ego and the super-ego, carry on the role of father.

To sum up, the relation between the subject and his father-object, while retaining its content, has been transformed into a relation between the ego and the super-ego – a new setting on a fresh stage. Infantile reactions from the Oedipus complex such as these may disappear if reality gives them no further nourishment. But the father's character remained the same, or rather, it deteriorated with the years, and thus Dostoevsky's hatred for his father and his death-wish against that wicked father were maintained. Now it is a dangerous thing if reality fulfils such repressed wishes. The phantasy has become reality and all defensive measures are thereupon reinforced. Dostoevsky's attacks now assumed an epileptic character; they still undoubtedly signified an identification with his father as a punishment, but they had become terrible, like his father's frightful death itself. What further content they had absorbed, particularly what sexual content, escapes conjecture.

One thing is remarkable: in the aura of the epileptic attack, one moment of supreme bliss is experienced. This may very well be a record of the triumph and sense of liberation felt on hearing the news of the death, to be followed immediately by an all the more cruel punishment. We have divined just such a sequence of triumph and mourning, of festive joy and mourning, in the brothers of the primal horde who murdered their father, and we find it repeated in the ceremony of the totem meal.[6] If it proved to be the case that Dostoevsky was free from his attacks in Siberia, that would merely substantiate the view that they were his punishment. He did not need them any longer when he was being punished in another way. But that cannot be proved. Rather does this necessity for punishment on the part of Dostoevsky's mental economy explain the fact that he passed unbroken through these years of misery and humiliation. Dostoevsky's condemnation as a political prisoner was unjust and he must have known it, but he accepted the undeserved punishment at the hands of the Little Father, the Tsar, as a substitute for the punishment he deserved for his sin against his real father. Instead of punishing himself, he got himself punished by his father's deputy. Here we have a glimpse of the psychological justification of the punishments inflicted by society. It is a fact that large groups of criminals want to be punished. Their super-ego demands it and so saves itself the necessity for inflicting the punishment itself.[7]

Everyone who is familiar with the complicated transformation of meaning undergone by hysterical symptoms will understand that no attempt can be made here to follow out the meaning of Dostoevsky's attacks beyond this beginning.[8] It is enough that we may assume that their original meaning remained unchanged behind all later accretions. We can safely say that Dostoevsky never got free from the feelings of guilt arising from his intention of murdering his father. They also determined his attitude in the two other spheres in which the father-relation is the decisive factor, his attitude towards the authority of the State and towards belief in God. In the first of these he ended up with complete submission to his Little Father, the Tsar, who had once performed with him in *reality* the comedy of killing which his attacks had so often represented in *play*. Here penitence gained the upper hand. In the religious sphere he retained more freedom: according to apparently trustworthy reports he wavered, up to the last moment of his life, between faith and atheism. His great intellect made it impossible for him to overlook any of the intellectual difficulties to which faith leads. By an individual recapitulation of a development in world-history he hoped to find a way out and a liberation from guilt in the Christ ideal, and even to make use of his sufferings as a claim to be playing a Christ-like role. If on the whole he did not achieve freedom and became a reactionary, that was because the filial guilt, which is present in human beings generally and on which religious feeling is built, had in him attained a super-individual intensity and remained insurmountable even to his great intelligence. In writing this we are laying ourselves open to the charge of having abandoned the impartiality of analysis and of subjecting Dostoevsky to judgements that can only be justified from the partisan standpoint of a particular *Weltanschauung*. A conservative would take the side of the Grand Inquisitor and would judge Dostoevsky differently. The objection is just; and one can only say in extenuation that Dostoevsky's decision has every appearance of having been determined by an intellectual inhibition due to his neurosis.

It can scarcely be owing to chance that three of the masterpieces of the literature of all time – the *Oedipus Rex* of Sophocles, Shakespeare's *Hamlet* and Dostoevsky's *The Brothers Karamazov* – should all deal with the same subject, parricide. In all three, moreover, the motive for the deed, sexual rivalry for a woman, is laid bare.

The most straightforward is certainly the representation in the drama derived from the Greek legend. In this it is still the hero himself who commits the crime. But poetic treatment is impossible without softening and disguise. The naked admission of an intention to commit parricide, as we arrive at it in analysis, seems intolerable without analytic preparation. The Greek drama, while retaining the crime, introduces the indispensable toning-down in a masterly fashion by projecting the hero's unconscious motive into reality in the form of a compulsion by a destiny which is alien to him. The hero commits the deed unintentionally and apparently uninfluenced by the woman; this latter element is, however, taken into account in the circumstance that the hero can only obtain possession of the queen mother after he has repeated his deed upon the monster who symbolizes the father. After his guilt has been revealed and made conscious, the hero makes no attempt to exculpate himself by appealing to the artificial expedient of the compulsion of destiny. His crime is acknowledged and punished as though it were a full and conscious one – which is bound to appear unjust to our reason, but which psychologically is perfectly correct.

In the English play the presentation is more indirect; the hero does not commit the crime himself; it is carried out by someone else, for whom it is not parricide. The forbidden motive of sexual rivalry for the woman does not need, therefore, to be disguised. Moreover, we see the hero's Oedipus complex, as it were, in a reflected light, by learning the effect upon him of the other's crime. He ought to avenge the crime, but finds himself, strangely enough, incapable of doing so. We know that it is his sense of guilt that is paralysing him; but, in a manner entirely in keeping with neurotic processes, the sense of guilt is displaced on to the perception of his inadequacy for fulfilling his task. There are signs that the hero feels this guilt as a super-individual one. He despises others no less than himself: 'Use every man after his desert, and who should 'scape whipping?'

The Russian novel goes a step further in the same direction. There also the murder is committed by someone else. This other person, however, stands to the murdered man in the same filial relation as the hero, Dmitri; in this other person's case the motive of sexual rivalry is openly admitted; he is a brother of the hero's, and it is a remarkable fact that Dostoevsky has attributed to him his own illness, the alleged epilepsy, as though he were seeking to confess that the epileptic, the neurotic, in himself was a parricide. Then, again, in the speech for the defence at the trial, there is the famous mockery of psychology – it is a 'knife that cuts both ways':[9] a splendid piece of disguise, for we have only to reverse it in order to discover the deepest meaning of Dostoevsky's view of things. It is not psychology that deserves the mockery, but the procedure of judicial enquiry. It is a matter of indifference who actually committed the crime; psychology is only concerned to know who desired it emotionally and who welcomed it when it was done.[10] And for that reason all of the brothers, except the contrasted figure of Alyosha, are equally guilty – the impulsive sensualist, the sceptical cynic and the epileptic criminal. In *The Brothers Karamazov* there is one particularly revealing scene. In the course of his talk with Dmitri, Father Zossima recognizes that Dmitri is prepared to commit parricide, and he bows down at his feet. It is impossible that this can be meant as an expression of admiration; it must mean that the holy man is rejecting the temptation to despise or detest the murderer and for that reason humbles himself before him. Dostoevsky's sympathy for the criminal is, in fact, boundless; it goes far beyond the pity which the unhappy wretch has a right to, and reminds us of the 'holy awe' with which epileptics and lunatics were regarded in the past. A criminal is to him almost a Redeemer who has taken on himself the guilt which must else have been borne by others. There is no longer any need for one to murder, since *he* has already murdered; and one must be grateful to him, for, except for him, one would have been obliged oneself to murder. That is not kindly pity alone, it is identification on the basis of similar murderous impulses – in fact, a slightly displaced narcissism. (In saying this, we are not disputing the ethical value of this kindliness.) This may perhaps be quite generally the mechanism of kindly sympathy with other people, a mechanism which one can discern with especial ease in this extreme case of a guilt-ridden novelist. There is no doubt that this sympathy by identification was a decisive factor in determining Dostoevsky's choice of material. He dealt first with the common criminal (whose motives are egotistical) and the political and religious criminal; and not until the end of his life did he come back to the primal criminal, the parricide, and use him, in a work of art, for making his confession.

The publication of Dostoevsky's posthumous papers and of his wife's diaries has thrown a glaring light on one episode in his life, namely the period in Germany when he was obsessed with a mania for gambling (cf. Fülöp-Miller and Eckstein, 1925), which no one could regard as anything but an unmistakable fit of pathological passion. There was no lack of rationalizations for this remarkable and unworthy behaviour. As often happens with neurotics, Dostoevsky's sense of guilt had taken a tangible shape as a burden of debt, and he was able to take refuge behind the pretext that he was trying by his winnings at the tables to make it possible for him to return to Russia without being arrested by his creditors. But this was no more than a pretext and Dostoevsky was acute enough to recognize the fact and honest enough to admit it. He knew that the chief thing was gambling for its own sake – *le jeu pour le jeu*.[11] All the details of his impulsively irrational conduct show this and something more besides. He never rested until he had lost everything. For him gambling was a method of self-punishment as well. Time after time he gave his young wife his promise or his word of honour not to play any more or not to play any more on that particular day; and, as she says, he almost always broke it. When his losses had reduced himself and her to the direst need, he derived a second pathological satisfaction from that. He could then scold and humiliate himself before her, invite her to despise him and to feel sorry that she had married such an old sinner; and when he had thus unburdened his conscience, the whole business would begin again next day. His young wife accustomed herself to this cycle, for she had noticed that the one thing which offered any real hope of salvation – his literary production – never went better than when they had lost everything and pawned their last possessions. Naturally she did not understand the connection. When his sense of guilt was satisfied by the punishments he had inflicted on himself, the inhibition upon his work became less severe and he allowed himself to take a few steps along the road to success.[12]

What part of a gambler's long-buried childhood is it that forces its way to repetition in his obsession for play? The answer may be divined without difficulty from a story by one of our younger writers. Stefan Zweig, who has incidentally devoted a study to Dostoevsky himself (1920), has included in his collection of three stories *Die Verwirrung der Gefühle* [*Confusion of Feelings*] (1927) one which he calls 'Vierundzwanzig Stunden aus dem Leben einer Frau' ['Four-and-Twenty Hours in a Woman's Life']. This little masterpiece ostensibly sets out only to show what an irresponsible creature woman is, and to what excesses, surprising even to herself, an unexpected experience may drive her. But the story tells far more than this. If it is subjected to an analytical interpretation, it will be found to represent (without any apologetic intent) something quite different, something universally human, or rather something masculine. And such an interpretation is so extremely obvious that it cannot be resisted. It is characteristic of the nature of artistic creation that the author, who is a personal friend of mine, was able to assure me, when I asked him, that the interpretation which I put to him had been completely strange to his knowledge and intention, although some of the details woven into the narrative seemed expressly designed to give a clue to the hidden secret.

In this story, an elderly lady of distinction tells the author about an experience she has had more than twenty years earlier. She has been left a widow when still young and is the mother of two sons who no longer need her. In her forty-second year, expecting nothing further of life, she happens, on one of her aimless journeyings, to visit the Rooms at Monte Carlo. There, among all the remarkable impressions which the place produces, she is soon fascinated by the sight of a pair of hands which seem to betray all the feelings of the unlucky gambler with terrifying sincerity and intensity. These hands belong to a handsome young man – the author, as though unintentionally, makes him of the same age as the narrator's elder son – who, after losing everything, leaves the Rooms in the depth of despair, with the evident intention of ending his hopeless life in the Casino gardens. An inexplicable feeling of sympathy compels her to follow him and make every effort to save him. He takes her for one of the importunate women so common there and tries to shake her off; but she stays with him and finds herself obliged, in the most natural way possible, to join him in his apartment at the hotel, and finally to share his bed. After this improvised night of love, she exacts a most solemn vow from the young man, who has now apparently calmed down, that he will never play again, provides him with money for his journey home and promises to meet him at the station before the departure of his train. Now, however, she begins to feel a great tenderness for him, is ready to sacrifice all she has in order to keep him and makes up her mind to go with him instead of saying goodbye. Various mischances delay her, so that she misses the train. In her longing for the lost one she returns once more to the Rooms and there, to her horror, sees once more the hands which had first excited her sympathy: the faithless youth had gone back to his play. She reminds him of his promise, but, obsessed by his passion, he calls her a spoilsport, tells her to go, and flings back the money with which she has tried to rescue him. She hurries away in deep mortification and learns later that she has not succeeded in saving him from suicide.

The brilliantly told, faultlessly motivated story is of course complete in itself and is certain to make a deep effect upon the reader. But analysis shows us that its invention is based fundamentally upon a wishful phantasy belonging to the period of puberty, which a number of people actually remember consciously. The phantasy embodies a boy's wish that his mother should herself initiate him into sexual life in order to save him from the dreaded injuries caused by masturbation. (The numerous creative works that deal with the theme of redemption have the same origin.) The 'vice' of masturbation is replaced by the addiction to gambling;[13] and the emphasis laid upon the passionate activity of the hands betrays this derivation. Indeed, the passion for play is an equivalent of the old compulsion to masturbate; 'playing' is the actual word used in the nursery to describe the activity of the hands upon the genitals. The irresistible nature of the temptation, the solemn resolutions, which are nevertheless invariably broken, never to do it again, the stupefying pleasure and the bad conscience which tells the subject that he is ruining himself (committing suicide) – all these elements remain unaltered in the process of substitution. It is true that Zweig's story is told by the mother, not by the son. It must flatter the son to think: 'if my mother only knew what dangers masturbation involves me in, she would certainly save me from them by allowing me to lavish all my tenderness on her own body'. The equation of the mother with a prostitute, which is made by the young man in the story, is linked up with the same phantasy. It brings the unattainable woman within easy reach. The bad conscience which accompanies the phantasy brings about the unhappy ending of the story. It is also interesting to notice how the *façade* given to the story by its author seeks to disguise its analytic meaning. For it is extremely questionable whether the erotic life of women is dominated by sudden and mysterious impulses. On the contrary, analysis reveals an adequate motivation for the surprising behaviour of this woman who had hitherto turned away from love. Faithful to the memory of her dead husband, she had armed herself against all similar attractions; but – and here the son's phantasy is right – she did not, as a mother, escape her quite unconscious transference of love on to her son, and Fate was able to catch her at this undefended spot.

If the addiction to gambling, with the unsuccessful struggles to break the habit and the opportunities it affords for self-punishment, is a repetition of the compulsion to masturbate, we shall not be surprised to find that it occupied such a large space in Dostoevsky's life. After all, we find no cases of severe neurosis in which the auto-erotic satisfaction of early childhood and of puberty has not played a part; and the relation between efforts to suppress it and fear of the father are too well known to need more than a mention.[14]

Notes

1. See the discussion of this in Fülöp-Miller and Eckstein (1926). Stefan Zweig (1920) writes: 'He was not halted by the barriers of bourgeois morality; and no one can say exactly how far he transgressed the bounds of law in his own life or how much of the criminal instincts of his heroes was realized in himself.' For the intimate connection between Dostoevsky's characters and his own experiences, see René Fülöp-Miller's remarks in the introductory section of Fülöp-Miller and Eckstein (1925), which are based upon N. Strakhov (1921).–[The topic of a sexual assault on an immature girl appears several times in Dostoevsky's writings – especially in the posthumous *Stavrogin's Confession* and *The Life of a Great Sinner*.]

2. [Cf. Freud's earlier paper on hysterical attacks (1909, 234).]

3. See René Fülöp-Miller (1924). [Cf. also the account given by Aimée Dostoevsky (1921) in her life of her father.] Of especial interest is the information that in the novelist's childhood 'something terrible, unforgettable and agonizing' happened, to which the first signs of his illness were to be traced (from an article by Suvorin in the newspaper *Novoe Vremya*, 1881, quoted in the introduction to Fülöp-Miller and Eckstein, 1925, p. xlv). See also Orest Miller (1921, 140): 'There is, however, another special piece of evidence about Fyodor Mikhailovich's illness, which relates to his earliest youth and brings the illness into connection with a tragic event in the family life of his parents. But, although this piece of evidence was given to me orally by one who was a close friend of Fyodor Mikhailovich, I cannot bring myself to reproduce it fully and precisely since I have had no confirmation of this rumour from any other quarter.' Biographers and scientific research workers cannot feel grateful for this discretion.

4. Most of the accounts, including Dostoevsky's own, assert on the contrary that the illness only assumed its final, epileptic character during the Siberian exile. Unfortunately there is reason to distrust the auto-biographical statements of neurotics. Experience shows that their memories introduce falsifications which are designed to interrupt disagreeable causal connections. Nevertheless, it appears

certain that Dostoevsky's detention in the Siberian prison markedly altered his pathological condition. Cf. Fülöp-Miller (1924, 1186).

5. [The explanation had already been given by Freud in a letter to Fliess of 8 February, 1897 (Freud, 1950, Letter 58).]

6. See *Totem and Taboo* [(1912-13), Section 5 of Essay IV, 140].

7. [Cf. 'Criminals from a Sense of Guilt', the third essay in Freud's 'Some Character-Types Met with in Psycho-Analytic Work' (1916, 332).]

8. The best account of the meaning and content of his attacks was given by Dostoevsky himself, when he told his friend Strakhov that his irritability and depression after an epileptic attack were due to the fact that he seemed to himself a criminal and could not get rid of the feeling that he had a burden of unknown guilt upon him, that he had committed some great misdeed, which oppressed him. (Fülöp-Miller, 1924, 1188.) In self-accusations like these psychoanalysis sees signs of a recognition of 'psychical reality', and it endeavours to make the unknown guilt known to consciousness.

9. [In the German (and in the original Russian) the simile is 'a stick with two ends'. The 'knife that cuts both ways' is derived from Constance Garnett's English translation. The phrase occurs in Book XII, Chapter X, of the novel.]

10. [A practical application of this to an actual criminal case is to be found in Freud's comments on the Halsmann Case (1931), where *The Brothers Karamazov* is again discussed.]

11. 'The main thing is the play itself,' he writes in one of his letters. 'I swear that greed for money has nothing to do with it, although Heaven knows I am sorely in need of money.'

12. 'He always remained at the gaming tables till he had lost everything and was totally ruined. It was only when the damage was quite complete that the demon at last retired from his soul and made way for the creative genius.' (Fülöp-Miller and Eckstein, 1925, p. lxxxvi.)

13. [In a letter to Fliess of 22 December 1897, Freud suggested that masturbation is the 'primal addiction', for which all later addictions are substitutes (Freud, 1950, Letter 79).]

14. Most of the views which are here expressed are also contained in an excellent book by Jolan Neufeld (1923).

References

Dostoevsky, A. (1921). *Fyodor Dostoyevsky*, London.

Freud, S. (1909). 'Some General Remarks on Hysterical Attacks', *S.E.*, 9.

—— (1950). *The Origins of Psycho-Analysis*, New York, 1954. (Partly including 'A Project for a Scientific Psychology', *S.E.*, 1.)

—— (1912–13). *Totem and Taboo*, *S.E.*, 13.

—— (1916). 'Some Character-Types Met with in Pyscho-Analytic Work', *S.E.*, 14.

—— (1931). 'The Expert Opinion in the Halsmann Case', S.E, 21.

Fülöp-Miller, R. (1924). 'Dostojewskis heilige Kranheit', *Wissen und Leben*, 19–20, Zurich.

—— and Eckstein, F. (1925) (eds). *Dostojewski am Roulette*, Munich.

—— (1926) (eds). *Der unbekannte Dostojewski*, Munich.

—— (1928) (eds). *Die Urgestalt der Brüder Karamasoff*, Munich.

Miller, O. (1921). 'Zur Lebensgeschichte Dostojewskis', in F.M. Dostojewski, *Autobiographische Schriften*, Munich. (Russian original, 1983.)

Neufeld, J. (1923). *Dostojewski: Skizze zu seiner Psychoanalyse*, Vienna.

Strakhov, N. (1921). 'Über Dostojewskis Leben und literarische Tätigkeit', in F.M. Dostojewski, *Literarische Schriften*, Munich. (Russian original, 1983.)

Zweig, S. (1920). *Drei Meister* (vol. I of *Die Baumeister der Welt*), Leipsig.

SECTION FOUR

Writing with Psychoanalysis

9

Jacques Lacan, 'Homage to Marguerite Duras, on *Le Ravissement de Lol V. Stein*', in *Duras on Duras*.

San Francisco: City Lights Books, 1987, pp. 122–9.

Editor's Introduction

To appreciate Lacan's remarks, it is obviously helpful for the reader to know Duras's story – now available in English – *The Ravishing of Lol V. Stein*. And, especially in this case, there is no substitute for reading the primary text; its narrative structure and the diegesis embedded in it open up the possibility of a range of interpretative stances. However, the reader will be greatly helped by Leslie Hill's reading of Duras, both here and elsewhere,[1] and he or she may also like to consult the entry on Duras in my *Fifty Key Contemporary Thinkers*.[2] Lacan's own reconstruction of the novel is also extremely significant, and calls for interpretation in its own right.

To appreciate Leslie Hill's reading of 'Lacan with Duras' (a play on Lacan's 'Kant avec Sade'), it is essential to read Lacan. Reproduced here, then, is the English translation of Lacan's short article, which was first published in French in 1965.

The issue at stake is this: does Lacan, as Hill suggests, use Duras's story as a ready-made illustration of certain psychoanalytic principles of a Lacanian sort? Does he try to frame the text? A response to these questions – as well as including a reading of *The Ravishing of Lol V. Stein* – will have to include Lacan's own claim that, as with Freud, the writer precedes him, and his own commentary is superfluous. Could we go so far as to say that it might be possible to understand Lacanian psychoanalysis better than it understands itself by reading Duras? One of the aims of the present collection is to show that there is no easy or straightforward answer to such a question. There can only be the working towards a possible answer – a 'working through', as it were, where certain obstacles are overcome, but absolute certainty is impossible.

If, as Lacan claims, he can add nothing to what Duras has written, what is the point of his piece? Might not the disclaimer be another way for the author of a 'return to Freud' to secure the prestige of his own interpretation? After all, many readers with certain intellectual pretensions are often in search of the challenge that the defiles of intersubjectivity throw up: he has revealed himself – but no! He has revealed himself only in order to hide himself all the more surely. When we thus query Lacan's true motives, he becomes (in Lacanian terms) a signifier – just as certain aspects of Duras's story become a signifier: the ball at the beginning, for instance, is just such a signifier. Did it ever really take place? And if it did, what really happened there?

Some readers (and I am one) will feel that if the point of Duras's story were only, or mainly, to evoke issues surrounding the desire for know-ledge of an event – or a non-event – if, indeed, it is the ambiguity surrounding the ball and the triangular positioning of the protagonists which is at stake, the story is much diminished in terms of its uniqueness. If, in contrast, the ball, and, more importantly, Lol V. Stein's loss of her fiancé, did take place – if we say the trauma is real – a very different complexion comes over the work. For as the trauma is unknowable, we move into the realm of experience where knowledge (of origins) is foreclosed. An almost hyper-geometrical and rationalistic organisation of space gives way to the impossibility of escaping from a given emotional state – that state which is Lol V. Stein's.

These, then, are some of the issues opened up by Lacan's text.

Notes

1. See Leslie Hill, *Marguerite Duras: Apocalyptic Desires*, London: Routledge, 1993.
2. John Lechte, *Fifty Key Contemporary Thinkers: From Structuralism to Postmodernity*, London: Routledge, 1994, pp. 240–1.

Homage to Marguerite Duras, on *Le Ravissement de Lol V. Stein**

Le ravissement – this word is enigmatic. Does it have an objective or a subjective dimension – is it a ravishing or a being ravished – as determined by Lol V. Stein?

Ravished. We think of the soul, and of the effect wrought by beauty. But we shall free ourselves, as best we can, from this readily available meaning, by means of a symbol.

A woman who ravishes is also the image imposed on us by this wounded figure, exiled from things, whom you dare not touch, but who makes you her prey.

The two movements, however, are knotted together in a cipher that is revealed in a name skilfully crafted in the contour of writing: Lol V. Stein.

Lol V. Stein: paper wings, V, scissors, Stein, stone, in love's guessing game you lose yourself.

One replies: O, open mouth, why do I take three leaps on the water, out of the game of love, where do I plunge?

Such artistry suggests that the ravisher is Marguerite Duras, and we are the ravished. But if, to quicken our steps behind Lol's steps, which resonate through the novel, we were to hear them behind us without having run into anyone, is it then that her creature moves within a space which is doubled; or is it rather that one of us has passed through the other, and which of us, in that case, has let himself be traversed?

Or do we now realize that the cipher is to be calculated in some other way: for to figure it out, one must count *oneself* three.

But let us read.

The scene of which the entire novel is but a recollection describes the enrapturing of two in a dance that fuses them together before the entire ball and under the eyes of Lol, the third, who endures the abduction of her fiancé by a woman who had only suddenly to appear.

And to get at what Lol is seeking from this moment on, must we not have her say, '*Je me deux*,' to conjugate, with Apollinaire, '*douloir?*'[1]

But, precisely, she cannot say that she suffers.

Thinking along the lines of some cliché, we might say she is repeating the event. But we should look more closely than this.

This is roughly what we discern in this scene, to which Lol will return many times, where she watches a pair of lovers in whom she has found, as if by chance, a friend who was close to her before the drama, and who helped her even as it unfolded: Tatiana.

This is not the event, but a knot retying itself there. And it is what this knot ties up that actually ravishes – but then again, whom?

The least we can say is that at this point the story puts one character in balance, and not only because Marguerite Duras has invested this character with the narrative voice: the other partner of the couple. His name, Jacques Hold.

Nor is he what he appears to be when I say: the narrative voice. He is, rather, its anguish. Once again the ambiguity returns: is it his anguish, or that of the narrative? He does not, in any case, simply display the machinery, but is in fact one of its mainsprings, and he does not know just how taken up in it he is.

This allows me to introduce Marguerite Duras here, having moreover her consent to do so, as the third ternary, of which one of the terms remains the ravishment of Lol V. Stein caught as an object in her own knot, and in which I myself am the third to propose a ravishment, in my case, a decidedly subjective one.

What I have just described is not a madrigal, but a limit of method, one whose positive and negative value I hope to affirm here. A subject is a scientific *term*, something perfectly calculable, and this reminder of its status should terminate what can only be called by its name, boorishness: let us say the pedantry of a certain kind of psychoanalysis. This frivolous aspect of psychoanalysis, to remain sensitive, one hopes, to those who immerse themselves in it, ought to indicate to them that they are sliding towards stupidity; for example, by attributing an author's avowed technique to some neurosis: boorishness. Or again, by showing it to be an explicit adoption of certain mechanisms which would thereby make an unconscious edifice of it: stupidity.

I think that even if I were to hear it from Marguerite Duras herself that, in her entire *œuvre*, she doesn't know where Lol has come from, and even if I could glean this from the next sentence she says to me, the only advantage that the psychoanalyst has the right to draw from his position, were this then to be recognized as such, is to recall with Freud that in his work the artist always precedes him, and that he does not have to play the psychologist where the artist paves the way for him.

This is precisely what I acknowledge to be the case in the ravishing of Lol V. Stein, where it turns out that Marguerite Duras knows, without me, what I teach.

In this respect, I do not wrong her genius in bringing my critique to bear on the virtue of her talents.

In paying homage to her, all that I shall show is that the practice of the letter converges with the workings of the unconscious.

Let me assure whoever might read these lines by the dimming or rising footlights – indeed, from those future shores where Jean-Louis Barrault, through his *Cahiers*,[2] would harbor the unique conjunction of the theatrical act – that the thread I will be unraveling takes its bearings at every moment, and to the letter, from the ravishing of Lol V. Stein; and furthermore, that work going on today at my school certainly crosses paths with it. Moreover, I do not so much address myself to this reader as I draw upon his inmost being in order to practise the knot I unravel.

This thread is to be picked up in the first scene, where Lol is robbed of her lover; that is to say, it is to be traced in the motif of the dress which sustains the phantasm (to which Lol is soon to become fixed) of a beyond that she cannot find the word for, this word which, as it closes the doors on the three of them, might have espoused her at the moment her lover was to raise up the woman's black dress to unveil her nakedness. Will this go further? Yes, to this unspeakable nakedness that insinuates itself into the place of her own body. There everything stops.

Is this not enough to reveal to us what has happened to Lol, and what it says about love; that is, about this image, an image of the self in which the other dresses you and in which you are dressed, and which, when you are robbed of it, lets you be just what underneath? What is left to be said about that evening, Lol, in all your passion of nineteen years, so taken with your dress which wore your nakedness, giving it its brilliance?

What you are left with, then, is what they said about you when you were a child, that you were never all there.

But what exactly is this vacuity? It begins to take on a meaning: you were, yes, for one night until dawn, when something in that place gave way, the center of attention.

What lies concealed in this locution? A centre is not the same on all surfaces. Singular on a flat surface, everywhere on a sphere, on a more complex surface it can produce an odd knot. This last knot is ours.

Because you sense that all this has to do with an envelope having neither an inside nor an outside, and in the seam of its centre every gaze turns back into your own, that these gazes are your own, which your own saturates and which, Lol, you will forever crave from every passerby. Let us follow Lol as she passes from one to the other, seizing from them this talisman which everyone is so eager to cast off: the gaze.

Every gaze will be yours, Lol, as the fascinated Jacques Hold will say to himself, for himself, ready to love 'all of Lol.'

There is in fact a grammar of the subject which has taken note of this stroke of genius. It will return under the pen which pointed it out to me.

You can verify it, this gaze is everywhere in the novel. And the woman of the event is easy to recognize, since Marguerite Duras has depicted her as non-gaze.

I teach that vision splits itself between the image and the gaze, that the first model for the gaze is the stain,[3] from which is derived the radar that the splitting of the eye offers up to the scopic field.

The gaze spreads itself as a stroke on the canvas, making you lower your own gaze before the work of the painter.

Of that which requires your attention one says, '*ça vous regarde:*' this looks at you.

But rather, it is the attention of that which is regarding you that has to be obtained. For you do not know the anguish of what gazes at you without, however, regarding you.

It is this anguish that takes hold of Jacques Hold when, from the window of the cheap hotel where he awaits Tatiana, he discovers, stretched out at the edge of the rye field before him, Lol.

Do you read on a comic level his panicky agitation, be it violent or only dreamed, before, significantly, he gets a grip on himself, before he tells himself that Lol can probably see him. Just a little more calm, and then the next phase, when she knows that he can see her.

Still, he must show her Tatiana, propitiatory at the window, no longer moved by the fact that Tatiana hasn't noticed anything, cynical at having already sacrificed her to the law of Lol, since it is in the certainty of obeying Lol's desire that he will go through the motions with his lover, upsetting her with those words of love whose floodgates, he knows, can only be opened by the other, but these same cowardly words tell him that this is not what he wants, not for her.

Above all, do not be deceived about the locus of the gaze here. It is not Lol who looks, if only because she sees nothing. She is not the voyeur. She is realized only in what happens.

Only when Lol, with the appropriate words, elevates the gaze to the status of a pure object for the still innocent Jacques Hold is its place revealed.

'Naked, naked under her black hair,' these words from the lips of Lol mark the passage of Tatiana's beauty into a function of the intolerable stain which pertains to this object.

This function is no longer compatible with the narcissistic image in which the lovers try to contain their love, and Jacques Hold immediately feels the effects of this.

From that moment on, in their dedication to realizing Lol's phantasm, they will be less and less themselves.

What is manifest in Jacques Hold, his division of the subject, will no longer concern us here. We are interested rather in how he fits into this threefold being, in which Lol is suspended, laying over his emptiness the 'I think' of a bad dream which makes up the content of the book. But in so doing, he contents himself with giving her a consciousness of being that is sustained outside of herself, in Tatiana.

It is Lol, however, who puts together this threefold being. And it is because the 'thought' of Jacques Hold comes to haunt Lol too insistently at the end of the novel, when he accompanies her on a pilgrimage to the scene of the event, that Lol goes mad.

The episode in fact contains signs of this, but I would point out that I heard this from Marguerite Duras.

The last sentence of the novel, which brings Lol back to the rye field, seems to me to bring about a much less decisive end than my remark would suggest. One suspects from it a caution against the pathos of understanding. Lol is not to be understood, she is not to be saved from ravishment.

Even more superfluous is my own commentary on what Marguerite Duras has done in giving a discursive existence to her creature.

For the very thought by means of which I would restore to her a knowledge which was always hers could never encumber her with the consciousness of being an object, since she has already recuperated this object through her art.

This is the meaning of sublimation, something that still confounds psychoanalysts because, in handing down the term to them, Freud's mouth remained sewn shut.

His only warning was that the satisfaction it brings should not be considered illusory.

But clearly he didn't speak out loudly enough since, thanks to them, the public remains persuaded to the contrary. And the public will remain so if the psychoanalysts don't come around to acknowledging that sublimation is to be measured by the number of copies sold for the author.

This leads us to the ethics of psychoanalysis, a topic which, in my seminar, produced a schism within the unsteady ranks of the audience.

In front of everyone, however, I confessed one day that throughout the entire year my hand had been held in some invisible place by another Marguerite, Marguerite of the *Heptameron*.[4] It is not without consequence that I find here this coincidence of names.

It seems quite natural to me to find in Marguerite Duras that severe and militant charity that animates the stories of Marguerite d'Angoulême, when they can be read free from those prejudices which are intended solely to screen us off from their locus of truth.

This is the idea of the 'gallant' story. In a masterful work, Lucien Febvre has tried to expose the trap it sets.

I would draw attention to the fact that Marguerite Duras has received from her readers a striking and unanimous affirmation of this strange way of loving: of that particular way of loving which the character – whom I placed in the role not of narrator but of subject – brings as an offering to Lol, the third person indeed, but far from being the excluded third.

I am delighted to see this proof that the serious still have some rights after four centuries in which the novel feigned sentimentality, firstly to pervert the techniques of the convention of courtly love into a mere fictional account, and then to cover up the losses incurred – losses parried by the convention of courtly love – as it developed into the novel of marital promiscuity.

And the style which you adopt, Marguerite Duras, throughout your Heptameron, might well have paved the way for the great historian I mentioned earlier to attempt to understand some of these stories for what they really are: true stories.

But sociological reflections on the many changing moods of life's pain are but little when compared to the relationship that the structure of desire, which is always of the Other, has with the object that causes it.

Take the exemplary tale in Book X of Amador, who is not a choir boy. Devoted even unto death to a love which, for all its impossibility, is in no way Platonic, he sees his own enigma all the more clearly by not viewing it in terms of the ideal of the Victorian happy ending.

For the point at which the gaze turns back into beauty, as I have described it, is the threshold between-two-deaths, a place I have defined, and which is not merely what those who are far removed from it might think: it is the place of misery.

It seems to me, Marguerite Duras, from what I know of your work, that your characters are to be found gravitating around this place, and you have situated them in a world familiar to us in order to show that the noble women and gentlemen of ancient pageantry are everywhere, and they are just as valiant in their quests; and should they be caught in the thorns of an uncontrollable love, towards that stain, celestial nocturne, of a being offered up to the mercy of all ..., at half past ten on a summer's evening.

You probably could not come to the aid of your creations, new Marguerite, bearing a myth of the personal soul. But does not the rather hopeless charity with which you animate them proceed from the faith which you have in such abundance, as you celebrate the taciturn wedding of an empty life with an indescribable object.

Translated by Peter Connor

Notes

Le Ravissement de Lol V. Stein was published in America under the title *The Ravishing of Lol Stein*, New York: Grove Press, 1966.

1. *Je me deux* is the first person reflexive form of the now archaic French infinitive, meaning to feel sorrow. It means, therefore, 'I feel sorrow,' but also, read in another way, it can mean literally, 'I two myself.' No English verb captures the ambiguity of the French; the closest approximation might be, 'I am rent,' which suggests the splitting of the subject of which Lacan will be speaking. (TN)

2. This article first appeared in the *Cahiers Renault-Barrault*, December 1965. (TN)

3. For an understanding of the function of the stain in Lacan's theory of the gaze, see his 'The Split between the Eye and the Gaze', in *The Four Fundamental Concepts of Psychoanalysis*, trans. Alan Sheridan, New York: Norton, 1977, pp. 67–78. (TN)

4. 'Marguerite d'Angoulême (1492–1549), author of the *Heptameron*, published posthumously in 1558–9. The seventy-two tales of the *Heptameron*, told by a group of travellers delayed by a flood on their return from a Pyrenean spa, illustrate the triumph of virtue and honor. (TN)

10

Leslie Hill, 'Lacan with Duras'.

Journal of the Institute of Romance Studies, 1 (1992), pp. 405–24.

Editor's Introduction

Hill introduces his own essay very well, and gives detailed background information for most of the key ideas and issues he discusses. We need, as a result, to focus on only one or two points in the hope of further sharpening the reader's appreciation of the discussion.

According to Hill, a key element in our appreciation of Lacan's reading of Duras has to do with the way in which Lacan's attempt to frame Duras's novel *The Ravishing of Lol V. Stein* ends up by framing him. This is what Hill calls covert transference: in trying to frame Duras's story, Lacan is forced to repeat the act of story-telling, rather than tell the truth of story-telling – particularly the truth of the telling of *The Ravishing of Lol V. Stein*. It is not for want of trying, however, that the analyst fails to get to the truth. For Lacan, according to Hill, makes the partial narrator, Jacques Hold – and not Lol – the true subject of the story. The narrating position – easily gendered masculine because of its claim to detachment (the third person) – thus becomes the de-centred centre of Duras's novel.

Hill also argues that Lacan uses *The Ravishing of Lol V. Stein* and the tenth story from the sixteenth-century collection entitled *L'Heptaméron* (*The Heptameron*) as 'allegorical models of sublimation', rather than as enactments of sublimation accessible only through analysis. In effect, Hill discovers an 'applied' element in Lacan's approach to writing. One effect of this 'allegorising', which valorises Jacques Hold, is to underplay the importance of Lol herself in Duras's novel – Lol, the character whose name appears in the title, and who is fundamentally implicated in the opening scene of the ball, becomes insignificant. Indeed, Hill claims that Lacan's gesture is little short of subjecting Lol to 'an act of erasure'.

Finally, Hill argues that the so-called triangular scene at the ball where Lol's fiancé, Michael Richardson, goes off with Anne-Marie Stretter is not in fact triangular – not, at least, from the point of view of separation. For Lacan omits to consider the dawn – the dawn being a sign of the separation of day and night, but itself neither day nor night. Hill goes on to say that 'the distinction between fusion and separation is hopelessly blurred'.

Whether the reader agrees with Hill or not is less important than the fact that, through this piece, we are led to the intimate link between writing, fusion and separation. Lol seems to be in the third position in the triangle – which might entail her being the story's narrator. However, as others have suggested, Duras is able to link writing not simply to the symbolisation of loss, but also to an experience of loss. Where, therefore, does psychoanalysis stand with regard to the link between writing and experience? This is the discussion's most insistent question.

Lacan with Duras

> Elle m'aime, un peau, beaucoup, passionnément, à la folie, pas du tout...
>
> [She loves me, a little, a lot, passionately, madly, not at all...]
>
> (French rhyme to be recited while plucking daisies)

The history of relations between psychoanalysis and literature is long and complex. But it is a story that depends for much of its plot and several of its peripateia on a small number of privileged examples: witness, for instance, the part played in the work of subsequent commentators by, say, Freud's 1907 account of Jensen's *Gradiva*, the subject of one of the earliest accounts of fantasy and dream by psychoanalysis in a literary text, or the even more frequently cited discussion of Hoffmann's story 'The Sandman' in Freud's celebrated paper on 'The Uncanny' (1919), or, more recently, the role of Lacan's much-glossed seminar of 1955 on 'The Purloined Letter' by Edgar Allan Poe, itself a return to a text already brought within the realm of analytic inquiry by Marie Bonaparte in 1933.[1] This repeated recourse to the same canonic cases is itself no doubt symptomatic, like much else affecting the transmission of psychoanalytic theory. Regarding the relations between analysis and literature, the result is not unlike the circular unfolding of a familial melodrama, in which scenes from the past constantly return to haunt the present; and it is perhaps no surprise therefore that, as though to re-enact the drama of origins yet again, the analytic tradition, in its dealings with the literary, has tended to privilege a certain type of text or genre, notably that of the Gothic tale or Romantic *conte* with its familiar repertoire of sexual enigma, violence, and obsession.

The reasons for this preference stem no doubt in part from the literary tastes and enthusiasms of the pioneers of psychoanalytic criticism; but they also reflect, as Freud quickly realised, the explicit parallel often made in the Gothic tale itself (particularly in the case of Hoffmann) between narrative and fantasy, story-telling and day-dreaming (*Phantasieren*).[2] But this privileging of the nineteenth-century short story by Freud and his immediate followers has also meant that readers wishing to apply analytic methods to more recent – modernist or postmodernist – fiction have often had to look elsewhere in analytic theory, to Freudian dream interpretation, for instance, or to some of Freud's later case studies, in order to develop a method of reading better equipped to deal with the structural indeterminacies characteristic of modern writing. The case is particularly acute with Lacan. The linguistic self-consciousness that Lacan's own work displays, with regard to its own theoretical agenda as well as its manner of presentation, has usually been taken as proof for the claim that Lacanian theory has a particularly rich contribution to make to the psychoanalytic understanding of modern texts. But, notwithstanding these expectations, there is in fact little that is explicit in Lacan's work that might sustain this enterprise, save a number of repeated, but none the less brief and programmatic remarks on Joyce.[3]

In this chapter I want to turn my attention to a short text by Lacan which, though no more than seven pages long, constitutes a rare exception to this rule: his review of the novel *Le Ravissement de Lol V. Stein* by Marguerite Duras. He was initially shown the novel, it seems, by Michèle Montrelay, who went on, in June 1965, to give a presentation of the book to Lacan's seminar. Lacan's own essay, published in December that year, under the rather grandiloquent title of 'Hommage fait à Marguerite Duras, du ravissement de Lol V. Stein', deserves attention as a particularly seductive piece of writing, one which deals with a story of seduction, but also, by way of the homage it pays to the novel's author, enacts – or acts out – its own desire to seduce.[4] In its turn, it is clear that the essay has seduced many of its own readers, many of them women, to the extent that for some of them, even including Lacan himself, Duras becomes, by the end of the essay, a Lacanian writer. What I want to trace in this paper are some of the key moments in this scenario of seduction and identification.

Let me first begin with two vignettes, two glimpses of Jacques Lacan at work. Both are memories or associations, supplied by Duras herself, the first in an interview from 1969, the second five years later. This is the first:

> Il m'a donné rendez-vous un jour, à minuit, dans un bar, Lacan. Il m'a fait peur. Dans un sous-sol. Pour parler de *Lol V. Stein*. Il m'a dit que c'était un délire *cliniquement* parfait. Il a commencé à me questionner. Pendant deux heures. Je suis sortie de là un peu chancelante.[5]

> [Lacan arranged for us to meet one day, at midnight, in a bar. I was terrified. It was in a basement. He wanted to talk about *Lol V. Stein*. He told me it was a *clinically* perfect case of delusion. He started questioning me. It went on for two hours. I was rather shaken when I finally emerged.]

Duras's second recollection comes from a conversation with Xavière Gauthier, the context of which is the claim, developed at the time by Hélène Cixous and others, that writing by 'women', or *écriture féminine*, as it is now generally known, is subject to a different, more multiplicitous, subversive economy than texts authored by 'men' (and in a celebrated footnote to 'Le Rire de la Méduse' Cixous named Colette, Genet, and Duras as the only three such 'women' in modern French literature). Here, at any rate, is Duras in 1974:

> La plus belle chose qu'on m'ait dite, à propos de *Lol V. Stein* c'est un critique, c'est ceci: '*Lol V. Stein*, c'est moi qui l'ait [*sic*] écrit.' Mais le pire article que j'ai eu sur ce livre, c'est quand même Jacqueline Piatier qui l'a écrit dans *Le Monde*, c'est-à-dire une femme. Et qui a sorti Lol V. Stein de son cercueil? C'est quand même un homme, c'est Lacan.[6]

> [The most wonderful thing anybody said to me about *Lol V. Stein* was from a critic who said that *he* was the one who wrote it. But the most awful review I got for the book was written by a woman, by Jacqueline Piatier in *Le Monde*. And who was the one who did the most to raise Lol V. Stein from her coffin? It was of course a man, it was Lacan.]

In these memories there are the traces of a complex intersubjective scene, a scene that might be called a scene of interpretation, involving an author, an analyst, another woman, a coffin, a death and a resurrection, madness, desire, fear, indeed, all the elements of another fantasy scenario. It is not clear, of course, how much of what Duras tells her interviewers is true. In itself this is probably not important. For what Duras's words imply is the more crucial realisation that the story of the relations between authors and analysts, or between literature and interpretation, is no less eventful or full of ambivalence than any of the things that get said or narrated within literary texts themselves or, for that matter, analytic sessions. Any reading will bear the marks of transferential overdetermination, and all the scene between Duras and Lacan might be suggesting, therefore, is that interpretation cannot remain untouched by the fantasy investments that characterise all products of the unconscious, whether these are literary texts, transferential narratives, dreams or parapraxes in general.

So much seems clear from the way Duras charges her memories of Lacan with a mixture of hostility and approval. But Lacan's own position is not immune from such transferential passion or drama. For as Lacan pays homage to Duras, he is arguably also paying his dues to another lady writer, a failed novelist with an obsession with the Prince of Wales, whom Lacan also once raised from her coffin so she could take on the role of something resembling his own psychiatric muse. I am referring here to another, earlier Marguerite who figures importantly in Lacan's career, and to whom his future work as an analyst was indebted. The name of this early would-be novelist was Marguerite Anzieu. But she is better known under the clinical pseudonym of 'Aimée', the 'loved one', given to her by Lacan in his doctoral dissertation of 1932, *De la psychose paranoïaque dans ses rapports avec la personnalité*, which is largely based on a consideration of her single case.[7] 'Aimée', for Lacan's thesis, is an exemplary figure, and constitutes a paradigm of what he theorises at the time as paranoid psychosis; but her figure continued to dominate, albeit silently, much of the rest of Lacan's analytic career in his ambition to theorise – to some extent in tandem – two important but neglected areas of the Freudian legacy, the questions of psychosis and of female desire. It was these two issues together that the story of 'Aimée' embodied so eloquently for Lacan.

So, at the outset of Lacan's career, almost in anticipation of the story of Lol V. Stein, there is another clinically perfect case, in which a would-be novelist, already subject to delusions of persecution and other psychotic disturbances, falls victim to a sudden shift of energy and resorts to an act of erotically charged violence by attacking, with a knife, a famous actress as she leaves the theatre one evening. Shortly after, as she feels the force of the law deployed against her, it seems her delusions begin to subside. And in that place of authority, there appears a young psychiatrist called Jacques, Jacques Lacan, as it happens, who goes on to write the story of 'Aimée', and thereby gain a much noticed doctorate. (As I hope to show, some of the terms of this opening scene seem possessed of a curiously infectious energy; and they return with a disturbing insistence.)

Lacan's review of Duras's novel is arguably a minor, occasional piece, but, while in its author's view – unlike other review articles – it did not merit inclusion in the *Écrits* published the following year, it occupies a more central role than it might appear, judging from its relative neglect by Lacanian literary theorists. It draws, for instance, quite extensively on material first presented in Lacan's seminar of 1959–60 on 'L'Éthique de la psychanalyse' (not published till 1986). It is also closely linked to Lacan's account of

Hamlet in the 1958–9 seminar on 'Le Désir et son interprétation', and rehearses arguments from the 1964 series on 'Les Quatre Concepts fondamentaux de la psychanalyse'. It also in other ways looks forward to the seminar of 1972–3 on female sexuality, 'Encore'.[8]

In the context of Duras's work, on the other hand, *Le Ravissement de Lol V. Stein* marks something of a turning point. It inaugurates a series of texts and films dealing not only with the figure of Lol (who recurs, in changed guise, in 1971 and 1973 in Duras's *L'Amour* and *La Femme du Gange*) but also with the enigmatic, languishing figure of Anne-Marie Stretter, who returns in the novel *Le Vice-consul* ten years later, in works like *India Song* and *Son nom de Venise dans Calcutta désert*. To this day, *Le Ravissement de Lol V. Stein* is the text of Duras's which has given rise to the greatest amount of critical commentary. Much of this, largely in the wake of Lacan, has been framed by issues derived either from psychoanalytic theory or from feminism, if not from both, and questions of desire, sexual difference, and gender identity loom large in discussions of the novel.[9] To what extent, critics have asked, is female desire in general commanded by the logic of exclusion, speechlessness, and repetition that seems to motivate the behaviour and desires of Duras's heroine? Does the novel offer a true account of the radical nature of female desire or does it provide merely an alienated and distorted version of that desire? Is it the case that the novel's male narrator simply usurps for himself the story of Lol V. Stein, even to the point of seemingly stealing her gaze and substituting his point of view for her own? But does Lol, who virtually never speaks in the text, nevertheless manage to steal the novel back from the ostensible narrator and somehow voice in the text her own specific desires and gender identity?

The debate about these issues is far from closed, and there is much disagreement about Lacan's particular reading of the novel. For some readers it evidently offers an accurate account of the truth of female desire and the character of Lol V. Stein as a female subject; for others Lacan's intervention is more like a phallocentric appropriation of the novel that entirely misses the subversive potential of Duras's writing. But over and beyond the detail of Lacan's reading, it is in the way this controversy has developed that Lacan's influence may be detected. Time and again, the questions raised by the discontinuities and fictional ambiguities of Duras's novel are abandoned in favour of an argument about truth. Critics of the novel, it seems, whether sympathetic or hostile to Lacan (or Duras), seem to endorse this supposed equivalence between desire and truth. Debate about Duras's writing, then, has often been about the paradigmatic or exemplary character of that writing and the extent to which readers, particularly women readers, should – or should not – subscribe to what, for many readings of the novel, is claimed to be a fundamental – or perversely essentialised – truth about female desire.

It is clear that the main destination of Lacan's reading of Duras's novel (as it is of his account of 'The Purloined Letter') is the claim that the text, this text, is an exemplary manifestation of truth. Provided we can tell it, as well as tell what it is (and Lacan himself tells us in *Télévision* that we can't – tell it all, that is[10]), what this truth tells us is something to do with the essential structure of female desire. (And we must remember here that for

Lacan women and truth, at least for man – men –, are synonymous: 'J'ai dit', he says in 1973, 'que l'une et l'autre, au moins pour l'homme, c'était la même chose' ['I have said that the one and the other, at least as far as man is concerned, are the very selfsame thing', *S*, XX, 108].) Admittedly, in Lacan, truth is an elusive entity, irreducible to plain words or even to words at all. But literary texts, for Lacan, are nevertheless always paradigmatic; like Hamlet, they are always typical to the precise extent that they are atypical.[11] They always serve to make manifest essential structural verities. These truths fall beyond the scope of any psychobiographical approach to literature, and it is this that, in Lacan's view, disqualifies the thematic approach, particularly of the sort practised on Poe, for instance, by the much-reviled Princess Marie Bonaparte. *Le Ravissement de Lol V. Stein*, as analysed by Lacan, speaks to us then not of an individual case, with all the messy accidents and contingencies of desire and individual history which this would entail, but of the transcendental truth that makes that case possible. But, Lacan claims, if we realise this, we must also realise, if we read Lacan properly, that it is only in Lacanian theory that truth finds its proper and properly coherent articulation.

In *Le Ravissement de Lol V. Stein*, then, writes Jacques, in a phrase that has been diversely interpreted as representing either the height of arrogance or the depths of humility, 'Marguerite Duras s'avère savoir sans moi ce que j'enseigne' ['Marguerite Duras turns out already to know without me that which I teach', *MD*, 133]. The gesture is one of rhetorical appropriation, but it is also a necessarily transferential one, with Duras's text – and in a more covert way the author herself, twice brought into Lacan's text as a source of extratextual knowledge – playing the part of the subject supposed to know, the 'sujet supposé savoir'. And at the same time, of course, Lacan himself receives the text of his transference as a message reverting to him like a fragment drawn from his own theoretical elaborations.

But before I go any further, let me recall the main events of Duras's novel. It is the story of a doctor, by the name of Jacques Hold, who at the age of thirty-six comes to work in the town of S. Tahla. (Throughout the whole of the scene of interpretation and seduction that I am reconstructing here, names are like strangely talkative symptoms; they fall subject to odd laws of repetition and division, and Lacan's readers need to be alert to the slippages of names that take place in this encounter with Duras.) Jacques has an affair with a woman called Tatiana Karl; he learns that Tatiana has a former schoolfriend called Lola Valérie Stein. Ten years earlier, it seems, Lol, accompanied by Tatiana, had gone one evening to the ball in the nearby town of T. Beach with her fiancé, Michael Richardson. (In almost all Duras's texts or films there is a dance scene, and what it invariably describes is a scene of desire deferred and thus intensified.) Enter the mysterious figure of Anne-Marie Stretter, in a low-cut black dress. Lol's fiancé dances with this newcomer, and she and he depart together at dawn, leaving Lol in the state of *ravissement* to which the title refers: ecstatic, but also ravished, doubled up and beside herself with an intensity that is neither pain nor pleasure, loss nor excess, but somehow their common origin. Jacques finally meets Lol, who has not ceased to fascinate him, and his feelings for her become more and more intense, while Lol, for her part, embarks on a massive reprise of her own past. Her desire, she says, had always been *to see* Michael Richardson undressing Anne-Marie Stretter after the ball ('Les voir', she explains (*R*, 103)); and she goes about realising this desire, belatedly, by revisiting, together with Jacques, the scene of her abandonment by Michael Richardson, all the while re-enacting that scene from the past by getting Jacques to stand in for Michael Richardson, while Tatiana takes on the role of Anne-Marie Stretter, in what seems to be a kind of diabolically voyeuristic triangular game.

Such, one might say, reduced to its essentials, is the *fabula* of Duras's novel. But the way Duras narrates this story introduces into the narrative a number of unsettling inconsistencies that considerably trouble its coherence. The first seven sections of the book (out of a total of eighteen) are in the form of an avowedly hazardous reconstruction – by an as yet unnamed narrator – of the initial ballroom scene and the events that followed it. The reader is told that the narrative is based mainly on second-hand information gleaned from a variety of unreliable sources (ranging from Tatiana Karl to Lol's husband and her mother), but it also depends on a high degree of empathic identification between the narrator and his central character. However, the narrative voice in the text oscillates uncertainly between two heterogeneous and incompatible positions. At first, despite assurances to the contrary, the narrator seems to occupy a privileged place outside of the fictional world that he is reconstructing. This is what enables him, for instance, to stage much of the opening description of the ballroom scene from the point of view of Lol herself. But, at the same time, the text continually stresses how much the process of reconstruction is speculative and to what extent the narrator is impeded by all the restrictions implicit in being an intradiegetic, second-hand observer.

About two-fifths of the way through the book (*R*, 75), the first-person narrator is named as Jacques Hold. It is then with some surprise that the reader realises, for instance, that the man seen earlier emerging from the cinema in S. Tahla by Lol herself (*R*, 52–7), and identified by her in the text as Tatiana Karl's current lover, is none other than the actual narrator. Earlier, however, the text had withheld the narrator's identity and the scene outside the cinema was told from the point of view of Lol herself. Speaking and seeing, voice and vision, are split apart, and the position of focalising subject is no longer attributed to the first-person intradiegetic narrator. The result is mimetic incoherence, and the figure of the narrator no longer controls the narrative that nevertheless appears under his name.

Once identified, Jacques recounts the rest of the story in an equally disconcerting double manner. At crucial moments he loses his status as first-person narrator and slides into the third person. This often happens under the contagious effect of Lol's gaze, as for example when Jacques goes to his regular assignation at the Hôtel des Bois with Tatiana and realises, in the half-light of dusk, that Lol is waiting for them to appear in the window. Here the narrative, as though to echo Jacques's loss of control over events, which are coming to be dictated increasingly by the 'despotic' Lol (*R*, 112), suddenly and without warning switches from the first person to the third (*R*, 123). And some pages later, a similar dissociation occurs, also under the influence of Lol's gaze, with Jacques being referred to in the third person while a first-person voice, that of the book's narrator – but somehow not the Jacques of before – carries on the task of narrating the text (*R*, 134).

In instances such as these, then, no single or unified narrative agency is in control of the novel. As a result, though much energy is expended in the pursuit of knowledge by the narrator, no progress is ever achieved towards that goal. The novel is a story of epistemological disappointment, a deferral of knowledge that loses its way amidst its own uncertainty. The part-time narrator, Jacques, ends up, like the reader, knowing without knowing, lost in self-conscious speculation, but using what partial truth he thinks he does possess to attempt a seduction of Lol. At this point, for Jacques, less means more, and he makes a virtue of his own ignorance: 'Ce fut là ma première découverte à son propos: ne rien savoir de Lol était la connaître déjà' ['That was the first thing I discovered about her: to know nothing of Lol was to know her already', *R*, 81]. This is a seduction that uses knowledge – or its absence – as the principal means of achieving its end; but the little Jacques discovers about Lol leaves him with no clear idea of how to arrive at his goal; finally, he cannot tell whether it is he who is leading her astray or she him. At one point he asks her for the name of the man she has just met, since this meeting seems to have brought her happiness for the first time – at least this is what Jacques's narrative tells us (*R*, 108–9). Readers who remember the incident outside the cinema already know the answer, as Jacques both does and does not himself. Lol replies:

> – C'est vous, vous, Jacques Hold. Je vous ai rencontré il y a sept jours, seul d'abord et ensuite dans la compagnie d'une femme. Je vous ai suivi jusqu'à l'Hôtel des Bois.
> J'ai eu peur. Je voudrais revenir vers Tatiana, être dans la rue.
> – Pourquoi?
> Elle détache ses mains du rideau, se redresse, arrive.
> – Je vous ai choisi. (*R*, 111–12)

> ['You're the one, you, Jacques Hold. I met you seven days ago, first of all on your own and then with a woman. I followed you to the Hôtel des Bois.'
> I was frightened. I would like to go back to Tatiana, or be out in the street.
> 'Why?'
> She removes her hands from the curtain, stands up straight, reaches her destination.
> 'I've chosen you.']

Jacques tells the tale of how another tells him of her love; and the result of this detour of seduction is a kind of vertiginous reciprocity by which the pair become like writers of fiction, or even analysts, irrevocably ensnared within each other's speculative, transferential versions of one another. And it is perhaps not difficult to see here what the attraction of the book may have been for an analyst given to repeating the axiom that man's desire is the desire of the Other ('le désir de l'homme, c'est le désir de l'Autre'), or that the formula for intersubjectivity, as one reads at the end of the seminar on 'The Purloined Letter', was that 'l'émetteur [...] reçoit du récepteur son propre message sous une forme inversée' ['the sender [...] receives from the receiver his own message in reverse form', *É*, 41; *PP*, 53].

After an opening preamble touching on the title of Duras's novel, Lacan's homage, like most things in Lacanian theory, has three important moments.

Lacan rehearses these at the start of his essay. They are, in order, what Lacan describes as the knot (or *nœud* that the novel stages in its opening and subsequent scenes; the logic of the gaze; and the question of sublimation and the origin of the work of art. Each of these terms is given its own ternary articulation, giving the essay a structure of three times three in all. While Lol's fate as a subject is knotted, says Lacan, according to an eternal triangle constituted by Michael Richardson, Anne-Marie Stretter, and herself, with each occupying one of the corners of the inaugural scene in the ballroom, so the logic of the gaze governs her third-party involvement – but not as voyeur, Lacan insists – in the erotic encounter between Jacques Hold and Tatiana Karl. Third, the novel itself – the act of *ravissement* – becomes like an object passed between a writer called Marguerite (Duras) and a reader named Jacques (Lacan) in a closing triangle of aesthetic sublimation.

In what follows I want to explore each of these moments in turn in order to consider Lacan's strategy as reader and analyst when confronted with a text such as *Le Ravissement de Lol V. Stein*. In my own homage to Lacan's precept that the receiver only ever returns to the sender his own inverted message, let me begin my account in corresponding fashion, that is, in reverse, by turning first to the closing section of Lacan's article, the passage on sublimation.

Sublimation, in Freudian theory, by common agreement, remains an underdeveloped and enigmatic notion. What it designates in the first instance is an inhibition of sexual energy, a deflection of libido from its original aim and its re-investment in a non-sexual, culturally more highly valued object or activity, like artistic creation or intellectual inquiry. But this definition, as Jean Laplanche points out, raises many unanswered questions. While the process of aim-inhibition is relatively precise in its formulation, writes Laplanche, Freud also seems to want to envisage sublimation as a process of substitution of one sexual object by another, desexualised and culturally valued one. Here the difficulties arise:

> Si on va au fond des formulations et des exemples freudiens, on arrive à un paradoxe beaucoup plus gênant: il ne s'agit pas simplement de substituer un but à un autre dans un mouvement pulsionnel qui resterait dans l'ensemble le même; il ne reste dans le sublimé *ni* le but, *ni* l'objet, *ni* même la source de la pulsion, si bien que nous sommes supposés retrouver finalement la seule 'énergie sexuelle'; mais une énergie sexuelle ... elle-même 'désexualisée', déqualifiée, mise au service d'activités non-sexuelles. Vous voyez qu'il y a là un énorme problème, celui, tout simplement, de savoir au nom de quoi parler encore d'une conservation d'énergie.[12]

> [If one pursues Freud's own formulations and examples to their logical conclusion, one arrives at a far more awkward paradox: it is not simply a matter of substituting one aim for another within a libidinal movement that largely remains the same; for in that which is sublimated there continues to exist *neither* the aim, *nor* the object, *nor* even the source of the drive, with the result that we are supposed to be left only with 'sexual energy' in general; but this is a form of sexual energy ... that is itself desexualised, emptied of qualities, put in the service of non-sexual activities. You can see that there is an enormous problem with all of this, namely how one can still speak of energy being conserved.]

Sublimation, then, names a process of displacement or translation that shows little respect for continuity or identity. It functions as an index for the enigmatic production of the non-sexual from the sexual, or the cultural from the erotic; but as such, as Laplanche's remarks imply, what it offers is less a theory of cultural production than a myth of origins. Sublimation, it appears, is more like a fable than a concept, and it is not indifferent that the story it tells, as it already does in Freud, and with even greater insistence in the work of Lacan, is a story of erection, elevation, and edification.

Sublimation in Lacan is a key concept with regard not only to the project – which admittedly Lacan never overtly espouses – of developing a psychoanalytic understanding of aesthetics, but also the more fundamental – foundational – task of elaborating an ethics of psychoanalysis, too. The feature that ethics and aesthetics both share, in Lacan's account, is their relationship to the limit, and it is in relation to the theme of the limit, passing, along the signifying chain, between nature and culture, life and death, that the concept of sublimation in Lacan is also deployed. In the seminar on 'L'Éthique de la psychanalyse' he offers the following definition: 'la formule la plus générale que je vous donne de la sublimation', he says, 'est celle-ci – elle élève un objet – et ici, je ne me refuserai pas aux résonances de ce calembour qu'il peut y avoir dans l'usage du terme que je vais amener – à la dignité de la Chose' ['the most general formula for sublimation that I can give you is this: it raises an object – and here let me not refrain from the punning overtones that might be heard in the term I'm about to introduce – to the dignity of the Thing', *S*, VII, 133]. This *Chose*, or Thing, is described, in turn, a few sessions later, as

> ce qui du réel pâtit de ce rapport fondamental, initial, qui engage l'homme dans les voies du signifiant, du fait même qu'il est soumis à ce que Freud appelle le principe de plaisir, et dont il est clair [...] que ce n'est pas autre chose que la dominance du signifiant. (*S*, VII, 161)

> [that of the real which suffers from the fundamental, inaugural relationship that commits man to the paths of the signifier, by virtue of the fact that he is subject to what Freud calls the pleasure principle, and of which it is clear [...] that it is nothing other than the dominance of the signifier.]

The Lacanian Thing, therefore, is a kind of inaugural pre-object, an undifferentiated entity that precedes the separation of real, symbolic, and imaginary in the Lacanian myth of origins. It stands, so to speak, at the point of inception of the signifying chain and as such cannot be assimilated within the symbolic order, merely projected beyond it, into the real, like some kind of originary hallucination. It is also the place occupied, in other, less synchronically-minded analytic theories, like that of Melanie Klein – or Julia Kristeva – by what Lacan calls the mythical maternal body ('le corps mythique de la mère', *S*, VII, 127) and, as Lacan's pun on the word suggests, the other sex.[13] Lacan himself confirms later in the same year:

> Ce champ que j'appelle celui de la Chose, ce champ où se projette quelque chose au-delà, à l'origine de la chaîne signifiante, lieu où est mis en cause tout ce qui est lieu de l'être, lieu élu où se produit la sublimation [...c]'est aussi le lieu de l'œuvre que l'homme, singulièrement, se met à courtiser, et c'est pourquoi le premier exemple que je vous ai donné a été emprunté à l'amour courtois. Avouez que placer en ce point d'au-delà une créature comme la femme est une idée vraiment incroyable. (*S*, VII, 253)

> [This field that I call the field of the Thing, this field beyond which something is

projected, at the origin of the signifying chain, this place in which everything that is the place of being is thrown into question, this prime place at which sublimation occurs, is also the place of the work in which man, singularly, starts courting, and it is for this reason that the first example I gave you was taken from courtly love. You must admit that the very idea of placing a creature like woman at this point of transcendence is really quite incredible.]

This phenomenon of courtly love occurs throughout Lacan as the key paradigm of what a successful sublimation might be (even if, as Lacan reminds us, it may well be a case of desire succeeding by submitting to the failure of the sexual relation). In the example of the medieval courtly lyric, for Lacan, sexual energy is sublimated into the production of poetry, at the same time that the object of love is elevated to a position of lofty inaccessibility, and a rigid and demanding code of prohibitions is imposed on themselves by Lacan's gallant band of lover-poets. The satisfactions enjoyed by way of such sublimation, Lacan insists, are not illusory ones (*MD*, 135) and to this extent the example of courtly love supports the otherwise somewhat precarious thesis that sublimation provides a satisfaction of desire without repression ('satisfaction sans refoulement' (*S*, VII, 340)). The object is indeed changed, says Lacan, but what counts is not the object in itself but the slippage of desire along the purely metonymic chain of signifiers: 'C'est le changement comme tel. J'y insiste – ce rapport proprement métonymique d'un signifiant à l'autre que nous appelons le désir, ce n'est pas le nouvel objet, ni l'objet d'avant, c'est le changement d'objet en soi-même' ['It's change as such. Let me emphasise this – this properly metonymic relation between one signifier and the next that we call desire, this is not the new object, nor the previous object, but the change of the object in itself', *S*, VII, 340]. Freed from a concern for the object in itself, then, courtly love offers a palliative to the tragic insight – on which, Lacan claims, an ethics can be founded – that, as the later Lacan puts it, 'il n'y a pas de rapport sexuel'. As a result, he suggests, 'l'amour courtois, c'est pour l'homme, dont la dame était entièrement, au sens le plus servile, la sujette, la seule façon de se tirer avec élégance de l'absence de rapport sexuel' ['Courtly love, for the man, whose lady was entirely his subject, in the most servile sense of the word, is the only way to deal elegantly with the absence of sexual relation', *S*, XX, 65].

This discussion of sublimation and courtly love might seem to have taken us far from Marguerite Duras and *Le Ravissement de Lol V. Stein*, were it not that, in closing his essay, Lacan doubles the figure of Marguerite Duras with that of yet another Marguerite, a Queen this time, Marguerite de Navarre (though Lacan refers to her as Marguerite d'Angoulême), the author of a collection of stories first published in French in 1559, entitled, after Boccaccio, *L'Heptaméron*.[14] (And it is perhaps symptomatic to find here, as in Lacan's version of 'The Purloined Letter', that a Queen is once more at the origin of the textual permutations Lacan brings into play (*E*, 31–6).) The occasion for the parallel is a reminder to the reader of the account of courtly love given five years previously in the still unpublished seminar on 'L'Éthique de la psychanalyse'. In that seminar, Lacan had conducted the discussion of courtly love only in broad, general terms (*S*, VII, 167–84). In the 'Hommage' to Duras, however, he goes one step further, and cites one particular story from *L'Heptaméron* which serves as an implicit intertextual gloss on Duras's novel.

The story in question is the well-known tenth story from the first day. It concerns a young man, Amadour, who falls in love with a young girl of twelve, Floride. Prevented from considering marriage because of Floride's age and high birth, Amadour decides instead to marry her best friend, Avanturade. After the wedding, Amadour becomes a close and trusted member of Floride's family household. But he has to leave for several years to fight in the wars. On his return, to conceal his enduring love for Floride, he publicly takes a mistress, but then declares his love to Floride, asking her to accept his devotion and not to reveal his secret. Floride agrees, and eventually their – still Platonic – affection for each other prospers. Amadour returns to war again and is taken captive. Meanwhile, to keep faith with her mother, Floride is party to an unhappy arranged marriage. She withdraws with Avanturade to live 'a life that seemed to her little better than death' ('une vie moins belle que la mort', *H*, 69–70; 138). In due course, Amadour returns to Floride and Avanturade, but soon his wife falls downstairs and dies. Amadour is doubly tormented, first by the death of his wife but second because he has now lost the pretext enabling him to pursue his friend-ship with Floride. He decides to play double or nothing, and launches a violent sexual attack on Floride. Passion, he says, justifies all; Floride replies that all he has done is to destroy the foundation of honour and virtue which might have been the basis for their common future. She makes the point with a metaphor that has an almost Freudian ring:

> Sur ceste pierre d'honnesteté, j'étois venue icy, délibérée de y prendre ung très seur fondement; mais, Amadour, en un moment, vous m'avez monstré que en lieu d'une pierre necte et pure, le fondement de cest ediffice seroit sur sablon legier ou sur la fange infame.

> [Thus it was that I came to you, Amador, firmly resolved to build upon this rock of honour. But in this short space of time you have clearly demonstrated to me that I would have been building not on the solid rock of purity, but upon the shifting sands, nay, upon a treacherous bog of vice.] (*H*, 74; 143)

With this, Floride breaks off all contact with Amadour, still in love, but determined to retain her honour. The pair become estranged, but Amadour tries one final time to satisfy his carnal desires by force. Floride resists, and for the first time is able to reveal her troubles to her mother. Eventually, Amadour kills himself in battle, while Floride, for her part, ends up in a nunnery.

This story of Amadour and Floride, then, is both a tale of failed seduc-tion and, as Floride's words to Amadour make clear, a tale of failed subli-mation (though one might want to argue that sublimation is only ever a partial success, always necessarily a mitigated failure). Desire passes from body to body in a metonymic round of sublimation, but not without lurch-ing into disrespect, defusion, and violence at crucial moments in the story. On the level of the plot, at any rate, the process of sublimation is constantly threatened by the spectre of its own failure (the reasons for which may have something to do with the difficulties inherent in the concept of sublimation itself). But despite these problems, Lacan cites the story of Amadour as being somehow exemplary for an understanding of the economy of sublimation. And he offers it as a commentary on *Le Ravissement de Lol V. Stein* in spite of the fact that Duras's novel contains no act of violence nor any hint of sacrificial death. (One could say in passing, though, that what the story does seem to repeat, in its closing scenes of erotic violence and the protagonist's submission to an external authority, is not so much the plot of *Le Ravissement de Lol V. Stein* as – by transference – the final stages of the tale of Lacan's 'Aimée', i.e. the paroxysmal attack on the actress and avantgarde feminist Huguette ex-Duflos and the subsequent imprisonment of the perpetrator, Marguerite Anzieu.)

Why does Lacan cite the story of Amadour in the margins of *Le Ravissement de Lol V. Stein?* Ostensibly, it is to lend psychological plausibility to Duras's plot. It is true that there are superficial analogies between Marguerite Duras's story and that of her namesake. Both explore a series of triangular love relationships and display an interest in the detours and slippages of what Duras elsewhere calls love by proxy (*l'amour délégué*).[15] These similarities, such as they are, allow Lacan to rebuff the suggestion by Lucien Febvre that the stories in L'Heptaméron – and the tenth story in particular – are, for historical reasons, alien and difficult to understand for modern readers.[16] Lacan responds by appealing to the doubled – tripled – name of Marguerite which acts as a rhetorical proof of the historical (though, in fact, anhistorical) permanence of the structure of desire as articulated by Lacanian theory.

However, what is striking about Lacan's remarks is the heroic or edifying status that they claim for the figure of Amadour. There is no mention here of the repeated malfunctioning of the libidinal economy of sublimation that is evident in Marguerite de Navarre's story. Rather, Lacan's reference to the tale translates it into a parable on the virtues of fortitude and self-sacrifice. For Lacan, Amadour, the tale's male protagonist, gives up his life in the cause of an impossible love (*MD*, 136). He is an exemplary hero who dies in the cause of sublimation, rebuffed as he is by a woman whose role it is to represent in the face of Amadour's impatient desires the claims of idealisation and the importance of culture as a bulwark against the treacherous bog – the 'fange infame' – of vice, carnal lust and violence. The fact that sublimation in Amadour's story is only dubiously successful is of course itself proof of the dialectical success of Marguerite de Navarre, who, like Duras, is able to recuperate – as Lacan puts it (*MD*, 135) – the object and sublimate it into a work of art.

I want to claim that Lacan's use of this story as an intertextual gloss or transferential free association is far from indifferent. By the particular reading of the story that he puts forward and by substituting one Marguerite for another in a kind of intertextual daisy chain, what Lacan does is to draw an edifying frame around *Le Ravissement de Lol V. Stein*. And in that frame, Lacan offers the reader a transferential counterplot, a rival version of Duras's novel which secures for the narrator and male protagonist, Jacques, a place of unilateral authority and centrality. Lol is returned to the role of a passive – suffering – object and Jacques becomes the only effective agent of the plot. As we have seen, sublimation in Lacan speaks of elevation or edification; in each case, though, the agent of edification is a male protagonist, and the object of edification a female body. This is where Lacan's retelling of *Le Ravissement de Lol V. Stein* converges with his version of the story of Amadour. Both texts are cited in support of the theory of sublimation; but they are in fact already constituted by Lacan as allegorical models of sublimation. In other words, Lacan does not – oddly enough – read either text with analytic attention to the metonymies and metaphors of desire embedded in the narrative trajectories of the texts, but as parables in which the theory of desire may be found ready-made, in the form of a model narrative. The reason why Duras, for Lacan, turns out already to know Lacanian doctrine in advance, without previously having had the benefit of Lacan's own words of seduction, is to this extent a simple one: it is that Lacan himself, when he reads, looks only for a story that anticipates – and therefore may be construed as confirming – his own theory. In the 'Hommage' to Duras, Lacan finds evidence not of a Lacanian unconscious, but of a Lacanian theoretical fable. *Le Ravissement de Lol V. Stein*, like the story of Amadour, turns into an allegory, seemingly co-authored by Lacan, of the process of sublimation as dramatised by Lacanian theory itself.

But there is a price paid for this allegorical rewriting of Duras. Lacan eliminates from his account, for instance, all the slippages between voice and vision that I have mentioned, all the difficulties of attribution or identity that affect the narrator and each of the characters involved in the text. To make the text conform to his own pre-emptive fable of sublimation, he centres the text around the figure of Jacques Hold, whom he transforms unequivocally therefore into an Amadour look-alike confronted with the anxiety and desire inspired by the other sex, the *Chose* somewhere lodged in the maternal body. The character of Lol becomes mere object, deprived of desire and enjoyment, animated only by the compulsion that forces her to re-enact her past and precipitates her, according to Lacan, into madness. This transformation of Lol into indescribable object and of Jacques into analytic subject can be plotted in Lacan's text. For the purpose of the reference to Marguerite de Navarre's story is to establish how, for Lacan, the figure of Jacques in Duras's novel functions not only as the story's narrator but also as its subject, in the full analytic sense of the word: 'j'ai marqué', says Lacan, 'qu'il remplit ici la fonction non du récitant, mais du sujet' ['I have indicated that the function he fulfils is not that of the narrator, but of the subject', *MD*, 136]. Some pages earlier, the narrative voice of *Le Ravissement de Lol V. Stein*, the voice of Jacques, in other words, had been described by Lacan as its ambivalent anxiety, 'son angoisse', without it being certain, Lacan adds, whether this anxiety belonged to the narrator or the story (*MD*, 132). By the final page of the essay, however, that anxiety has gone, it has been re-absorbed into Jacques as the sole subject of the novel. (And the move is repeated at another level. Lacan begins his essay with a rhetorical flourish that asks whether Lol is subject or object of her '*ravissement*'; the question is one he also asks of Duras's readers: 'nous les ravis', as Lacan phrases it; so is Lacan as reader subject or object of this '*ravissement*'? The answer bounces back from the following page: 'me voici le tiers à y mettre un ravissement, dans mon cas décidément subjectif' ['here I am adding as a third a sense of ravishment, in my case decidedly a subjective one', *MD*, 132]. Lacan's desire, one might conclude, is to forgo ecstatic displacement and reserve his position as reader to secure the objectivity of his analytical vantage point.)

At this point, a second counterplot is introduced into Lacan's analysis: the story of Antigone.[17] She appears here, as in the seminar on 'L'Éthique de la psychanalyse', as a function of the limit, that limit, writes Lacan, 'où le regard se retourne en beauté' ['at which the gaze turns back in beauty'] and which he calls 'le seuil de l'entre-deux-morts' ['the threshold of the between-two-deaths', *MD*, 137]. On this threshold, according to Lacan, Antigone is beyond the cares of men, and to that extent already dead; but she still desires to give her brother Polynices a human burial. Her life henceforth is distinguished only by the tenacious desire to position herself on that limit that passes between life and death, nature and culture, language and aphasia. On that edge, she is what she is, says Lacan; what she embodies is pure desire, the desire for death: 'Antigone', he states, 'mène jusqu'à la limite l'accomplissement de ce que l'on peut appeler le désir pur, le pur et simple désir de mort comme tel. Ce désir, elle l'incarne' ['Antigone pushes to the limit the realisation of what one may call pure desire, the pure and simple desire for death as such', *S*, VII, 329]. And her embodiment of this desire is what allows her to voice a sublime lament: 'son supplice va consister à être enfermée, suspendue, dans la zone entre la vie et la mort. Sans être encore morte, elle est déjà rayée du monde des vivants. Et c'est à partir de là seulement que se développe sa plainte, à savoir la lamentation de la vie' ['her torture is going to consist in being walled up, in limbo, in the zone between life and death. Without yet being dead, she is already banished from the world of the living. And only from there does her complaint develop, that is, her lament for life', *S*, VII, 326].

At this limit, as Antigone's lament bears witness, desire is sublimated and purified. The result is a catharsis that, according to Lacan, offers the only rigorous foundation for the ethics of psychoanalysis. While analysis may have little to say to literature (as Lacan suggests in 'Lituraterre'), and literature (as Lacan implies in his 'Hommage' to Duras) only reveals to analysis what it already knows, it seems that in this figure of catharsis or purification the fate of the two are nevertheless intertwined: literature and psychoanalysis share the same constitutive limit, death, and the same outcome, the same tragic sense that there is nothing beyond the signifier except the inverted and misleading reflections of the imaginary. But it is surely not indifferent here that, like Lol, Antigone is a woman, and a failed Queen, one who, though she may seem, as for Hegel, to embody a dialectical contradiction inherent in human society, in fact turns out for Lacan already to have one foot in the grave. As a result of her position on the limit, the figure of Antigone can provoke a sublime catharsis, the price of which is the place of Antigone as she hovers undecidably between death and death.

Antigone here doubles for the figure of Lol V. Stein, who occupies, according to Lacan, a similar position to Antigone on the limit of human society, within the symbolic order only to the extent that she is already beyond it. This is Lacan's understanding of the final outcome of Lol's desire to revisit her past. It is at this point that she is declared to be mad by Lacan. Readers will recall Lacan's remark to Duras as to the clinical perfection of Lol's delusions. But it is worth noting that Lacan, in order to prove his point, uses this opportunity to make known his own meeting with Duras; indeed Lacan himself now claims – despite the earlier doubts regarding psychobiography –that it was the author who reliably informed him (and not he her) of Lol's actual madness – a possibility that the conclusion of the novel is careful to leave in doubt (*MD*, 135).

As in the story of Amadour, in Lacan's reading of *Le Ravissement de Lol V. Stein*, the stability of the cultural order is preserved and guaranteed, tragically, at the end by a pseudo- or quasi-death, that of Lol looking on as Jacques and his mistress go about their games of love. It is thus that a purification is brought about which endorses a sublime and necessarily feminine principle. What that principle reveals is the double positioning of women in Lacanian discourse: of this world, but somehow also of the next, sublimely guaranteeing the law, but possessed of madness, alive, but also dead, suspended, both a product of culture but representing a strange infringement of the cultural order, the pleasure of their bodies understandable the first time around as phallic enjoyment, but then – at the second time of asking (*'encore'*, as Lacan has it) – only as an event that takes place beyond the symbolic, on the other side, sublime and mysterious, as witnessed by Bernini's version of Saint Teresa. And as Antigone, so Lol: a sublime figure on the margin whose fate, under Lacan, is to be written out of the story that bears her name (and both this elision of a woman from the story and the naming of the story after her are a direct consequence of this need to articulate the place of women as the place of truth). The effects of this move are readable from Lacan's account of the theme of the gaze or look (*le regard*) in Duras's text. This is the second of the key moments in the essay to which I now want to turn my attention.

The concept of gaze is an important one for Lacanian theory and receives its fullest elaboration, shortly before the writing of the 'Hommage' to Duras, in the 1964 seminar on 'Les Quatre Concepts fondamentaux de la psychanalyse'. In Lacan, the gaze is generally described as one of four primordial objects, together with the breast, excrement, and the voice, whose articulation is attendant on the constitution of the subject as the subject of demand (*S*, XX, 114). In the 1964 seminar, Lacan develops the concept of the gaze as a paradigmatic instance of the function of the object as cause of desire, what Lacanian theory knows as the 'objet *a*'.

There is much to be said about the privilege Lacan confers on the gaze in his work. It repeats, of course, a long-standing tradition, according to which seeing is equivalent to believing, and Lacan himself both perpetuates and challenges that tradition with the converse claim that seeing must be understood as belonging to the realm of narcissism and (self-)deception with all the lures and misprisions that derive from the imaginary. In the 'Hommage', a similar suspicion is cast on the activity of looking. I have already mentioned some of the convolutions that affect the relationship between seeing and speaking in Duras's novel, and it is certainly the case, though critics seem reluctant to recognise the implications of this, that many of Duras's women protagonists or narrators spend their time seeing the stories they tell or witness. Lol, for instance, is constantly described by Duras's novel as being one who looks: at the scene of her abandonment, at Jacques emerging from the cinema, at Jacques and Tatiana meeting to make love in their hotel room. But Lol herself, Lacan claims, though she may appear to look in this way, does so with the eyes of another. In fact, though she may give the appearance of looking, Lol cannot see; she is not a voyeur: 'Surtout ne vous trompez pas sur la place ici du regard', Lacan enjoins his reader. 'Ce n'est pas Lol qui regarde, ne serait-ce qu'elle ne voit rien. Elle n'est pas le voyeur. Ce qui se passe la réalise' ['Most of all do not mistake the place of the gaze. Lol isn't the one looking, if only because she sees nothing. She is not the voyeur. What happens fulfils her', *MD*, 134–5].

The passage marks a key moment in Lacan's reading and it echoes (or is echoed by) a similar move in Michèle Montrelay's analysis. Arguing along similar lines to Lacan, Montrelay writes:

> Dans la suite du roman, Lol V. Stein prend figure de voyeuse. Faussement. La perversion, si elle existe, est du côté de Jacques Hold. Le pervers n'est-il pas celui qui veut voir sur l'autre le fading du sujet, qui guette dans son regard, sur son corps, les signes de sa déroute? Celui qui sait que la 'folie' d'une femme le sus-cite au plus vif, parce qu'elle change son angoisse en cette brûlante curiosité qu'est la pulsion épistémologique.[18]

> [In what follows in the novel, Lol V. Stein takes on the appearance of a female voyeur. Misleadingly. Perversion, if it exists here, is on the side of Jacques Hold. Isn't the subject of perversion the one who wants to see the fading of the subject on the other, who tries to catch the signs of defeat in the other's look, and on the other's body? The one who knows that the 'madness' of a woman provokes him most keenly of all, because it changes his anxiety into that burning curiosity that is the drive to know.]

Like Lacan, Montrelay converts Duras's novel into a story about male anx-iety and the desire to know; the hidden truth of Jacques Hold's desire is measured by the extent of his curiosity about the 'madness' of a woman. But in the face of such unanimity and such assertiveness on the part of both Lacan and Montrelay, a number of unavoidable questions persist. Why is it so crucial, one might ask, for Lol to be denied voyeuristic status? And why might we, as non-analysts, none the less wish to deceive ourselves, or sim-ply be deceived, in this regard?

On one level, the reasons for Lol's declared scopic passivity are prescrip-tive: Lol, occupying the place of a woman, cannot be a fetishist since her desire is not sustained by the 'objet *a*' as cause of desire (see *S*, XX, 73). This means Lol is less a subject of seeing than a divided blot on the landscape, a mysterious something that may look but cannot see. Her position in this respect is like the famous sardine can that surfaces in one of Lacan's few funny stories or *Witz*-like anecdotes in the seminar on 'Les Quatre Concepts fondamentaux', and which runs as follows: one day, one of Lacan's Breton fishermen friends, by the name of Petit-Jean, points to something, not quite an object, no longer quite an undifferentiated thing, 'un quelque-chose', says Lacan, bobbing up and down on the waves. Lacan continues:

> C'était une petite boîte, et même, précisons, une boîte à sardines. Elle flottait là dans le soleil [...]. Elle miroitait dans le soleil. Et Petit-Jean me dit – *Tu vois, cette boite? Tu la vois? Eh bien, elle, elle te voit pas!*
> Ce petit épisode, il trouvait ça très drôle, moi, moins. J'ai cherché pourquoi moi, je le trouvais moins drôle. C'est fort instructif.
> D'abord, si ça a un sens que Petit-Jean me dise que la boîte ne me voit pas,

c'est parce que, en un certain sens, tout de même, elle me regarde. Elle me regarde au niveau du point lumineux, où est tout ce qui me regarde, et ce n'est point là métaphore.

[It was a small can, a sardine can. It floated there in the sun [...]. It glittered in the sun. And Petit-Jean said to me – *You see that can? Do you see it? Well, it doesn't see you!*

He found the incident highly amusing – I less so. I thought about it. Why did I find it less amusing than he? It's an interesting question.

To begin with, if what Petit-Jean said to me, namely that the can did not see me, had any meaning, it was because in a sense, it was looking at me, all the same. It was looking at me at the level on the point of light, the point at which everything that looks at me is situated – and I am not speaking metaphorically.] (*S*, XI, 88–9; 95)

What Lacan describes here is again a function of a certain limit: the oddity of the anecdote comes from the fact that the subject – the analyst himself – is somehow looked at by this thing or pre-object that is the sardine tin without being seen by it as by another subject. Prior to intersubjectivity, as it were, there is this uncanny sense of being looked at without being seen. Being looked at, Lacan argues, precedes the act of seeing: 'ce qui est lumière me regarde' ['That which is light looks at me', *S*, XI, 89; 96]. And the displeasure of the incident told in the funny story, Lacan suggests, also comes from being seen by the fisherman not as a fellow subject, but rather as a blot on the landscape, an eyesore or intrusive nuisance.

There is here evidence of a curious analogy between the odd case of the sardine tin and the story of Lol, as rewritten by Lacan. On the one hand, a woman character in a novel who looks but does not see; on the other, a sardine tin that does much the same. In both cases, there is a division or fissure – between the eye and the look – that for Lacan is constitutive of visual and subjective space. In both cases, too, there is the uncanny or uncomfortable sense by which the subject is caught out of place, having somehow become the object of that of which formerly he thought he was merely the subject. One one-eyed Jacques (Lacan) is caught out by Petit-Jean's sardine tin in exactly the same way that, for Lacan, another perverse one-eyed Jacques (Hold) is caught unawares by the enigmatic – 'mad' – machinations of a woman. One might conclude from this equivalence that women are a little like sardine tins (and it is true that they have an equal propensity for suggesting to men the ablation of certain extremities, say, thumbs or fingers or other protuberances); or, more provocatively in the case of Lacan's reading of Duras, that the gaze of the other (sex) is enough to make the subject want to suppress that gaze entirely by dividing it from itself as an object that looks but cannot see.

As a reading of Duras's novel, this refusal to allow Lol the ability to see, in which, as far as Duras's text is concerned, the whole of her desire is concentrated, is, I would like to maintain, little short of an act of excision. Duras, for her part, construes the character of Lol as resting almost exclusively on the desire to see; Lacan, on the other hand, clearly wants to subordinate the act of looking to that of speaking. While *Le Ravissement de Lol V. Stein* itself insists throughout on the incommensurability of seeing and speaking, Lacan attempts to establish a hierarchy such that voice has mastery over vision, in the same way that revealed truth has precedence over the evidence of the senses. The fable of sublimation, once again, as Lacan formulates it, provides him with a story of elevation or erection by which a narrator or analyst called Jacques has the capacity to raise up from a posture of imaginary delusion and misrecognition the woman protagonist or author to whom an act of homage is due and who, by receiving such homage, will be immortalised in words.

This is, I think, clear from Lacan's treatment of the theme of repetition or *remémoration*, as he prefers to describe it, in *Le Ravissement de Lol V. Stein*. In an influential move, Lacan argues that the plot of the novel is structured by a recurring triangular knot. Lol's quest, Lacan says, is motivated by a desire to reconstitute the scene in the dance-hall at T. Beach which, early in the novel, shows Michael Richardson and Anne-Marie Stretter dancing together as an intimate twosome while Lol looks on as a third-party observer. For Lacan, the key to that scene lies not in the doubleness of imaginary repetition but in the ternary or triangular symbolic structure that is the cause of the subject's desire. (It is worth noting, though, notwithstanding Lacan's preference for triangles, that the ballroom scene is not in fact an inaugural scene at all, but already a repetition of the opening scene of Lol and Tatiana dancing together as a same-sex pair of teenagers in the school playground.) But so much has been written about the recurrence of triangular structures in Duras's novel that, in the light of Lacan's analysis, it is worth looking again at the section in *Le Ravissement de Lol V. Stein* in which the initial ballroom scene is reconstructed – by now for the second time – by Duras's as yet anonymous narrator. Here is one part of that account, describing Lol's wanderings through S. Tahla in search, it would seem, for an image of the dance at T. Beach:

> Je connais Lol V. Stein de la seule façon que je puisse, d'amour. C'est en raison de cette connaissance que je suis arrivé à croire ceci: dans les multiples aspects du bal de T. Beach, c'est la fin qui retient Lol. C'est l'instant précis de sa fin, quand l'aurore arrive avec une brutalité inouïe et la sépare du couple que formaient Michael Richardson et Anne-Marie Stretter, pour toujours, toujours. Lol progresse chaque jour dans la reconstitution de cet instant. Elle arrive même à capter un peu de sa foudroyante rapidité, à l'étaler, à en grillager les secondes dans une immobilité d'une extrême fragilité mais qui est pour elle d'une grâce infinie. [...]
>
> Elle se voit, et c'est là sa pensée véritable, à la même place, dans cette fin, toujours, au centre d'une triangulation dont l'aurore et eux deux sont les termes éternels: elle vient d'apercevoir cette aurore alors qu'eux ne l'ont pas encore remarquée. Elle, sait, eux pas encore. Elle est impuissante à les empêcher de savoir. (*R*, 47)

> [I know Lol V. Stein in the only manner that I can, through love. By virtue of that knowledge what I have come to believe is that of all the many aspects of the dance at T. Beach the most important one for Lol is the end, the exact instant of its ending, when the day breaks with unprecedented violence and separates her from the couple that was Michael Richardson and Anne-Marie Stretter, for ever and ever. She even manages to harness a little of its lightning speed, to spread it out and capture each of its moments in a motionlessness of extreme fragility but for her of infinite grace. [...]
>
> She sees herself, and that is her genuine belief, in the same spot, in this

ending, always, at the centre of a triangulation in which the daybreak and the two others are the never-ending terms: she has just seen the daybreak while they have not yet noticed it. She knows already, the others not yet. She is powerless to prevent them from knowing.]

The triangular structure of this scene, presented as it is from Lol's point of view, is in some ways more apparent than real. Lol is not firmly positioned as a spectator midway between Michael Richardson and Anne-Marie Stretter as a third to their couple, as Lacan's account implies and other critics, like Carol Murphy, have since asserted.[19] Lol is placed at the point where an imaginary line from the dawn intersects with one drawn from Michael Richardson and Anne-Marie Stretter. The relation between these points is not simple. The dawn, belonging to the impending day, functions here as a figure of separation; but the couple of Michael Richardson and Anne-Marie Stretter, lingering on in the preceding night, continue to dramatise the possibility of amorous fusion. As it breaks, the dawn signifies a sudden and brutal separation, but what it illuminates is a scene in which separation is suspended. Time, therefore, is poised between what has already happened but not yet taken place. Between day and night, the dawn and the two lovers, between separation and fusion, it is not Jacques Hold who hangs in the balance, as Lacan suggests (*MD*, 132), but Lol; her gaze is less a static vantage point than an oscillating movement, swinging back and forth, Duras puts it, from the couple to the dawn. And in that movement, the reference to the dawn, which Lacan omits, is crucial: it suggests a fundamental indeterminacy regarding positionality in the scenes, and it registers the impossibility of ever closing the triangle.

Lol's moment of happiness in the ballroom falls neither before nor after the moment of separation from the two lovers, but at exactly the point when the distinction between separation and fusion is itself hopelessly blurred, when she herself is already detached from her fiancé but at one with the sight of the lovers before her, apparently loving them still, like an ageing mother (*MD*, 18). The scene is one of loss and desire, but, as Lol shows when she endeavours to restage it later, with the help of Jacques and Tatiana, its meaning is not fixed; for Lol seems not to want to re-enact the scene passively as though it were no more than a pathological or hysterical symptom, but rather to transform it by substituting for the dawn – as she does in the rye field – a different half-light, the half-light of evening, which, as elsewhere in Duras, promises a return to darkness but also the hope of a different kind of dawn. (And as though to deliver this promise, *L'Amour*, written seven years later, ends with the coming of an apocalyptic dawn and the perplexing news that shortly the woman in the novel – a re-embodiment of Lol V. Stein – will hear the sound of God: 'vous savez ... ? de Dieu? ... ce truc ...?' ['you know ...? God? ... that thing...?].[20])

What repeats itself for Lol, then, as the object of her desire, is less a static triangle, with its unchanging repertoire of male and female participants (as Lacan's analysis implies), than a dynamic, flickering scenario in which there are no fixed positions but a series of shifting relationships. Duras's text is better seen, therefore, as a rhetoric of figural multiplicity than as a calculable geometry (the view suggested in Lacan (*MD*, 132)). Indeed, what is at stake in the scene of the ballroom, governing the whole theme of sight in the novel, is the act of looking not as illusory misrecognition but as a mode of erotic participation or identification, an undecidable interplay of proximity and distance founded on the constant merging together and coming apart of bodies.

Let me conclude briefly at this point. The claim is often made that there are many close affinities between the writing of Duras and the psychoanalysis of Lacan, and that because of this Lacan's account of *Le Ravissement de Lol V. Stein* deserves to be seen as an authoritative explication of Duras's text. What I hope to have shown, however, is that there are real and substantial differences between what is at issue in Duras's writing and the account of *Le Ravissement de Lol V. Stein* put forward by Lacan in his essay. Lacan stages his reading, with an element of self-conscious irony, as a tongue-in-cheek or back-handed homage to Duras, but it is not at all clear, any more than it is with Jacques Hold within Duras's novel itself, that Lacan is able to maintain control over that irony, for as Lacan pays homage, he does no more than repeat a voice – that of Jacques Hold – which has already preceded him. So, as the theory of Lacan strives to frame Duras's novel, it is itself framed by it. This is no doubt the reason why Lacan's own reading turns out to be a covertly transferential one; failing to dominate the text of the novel, Lacan is dominated by it, forced to repeat it by repeating a story of his own, adducing in his own text a whole range of associations, both explicit and implicit, that turn on the name of Marguerite in its multiple embodiment. In behaving like this, of course, Lacan is acting no differently from any other reader, but the effect is to raise major questions about the claims of Lacanian theory to deliver transmissible truths in its dealings with literature. The issue becomes particularly acute when, as in the case of Duras, Poe, Shakespeare, and all the others, what Lacanian theory seems to be asking of literature is for it to provide a fund of ready-made model narratives or myths that will serve to repeat and endorse the theoretical constructions of Lacanian doctrine and sustain it in its own constantly denied yet perpetual passion for narrative.

Notes

1. The texts I am referring to here are as follows: Sigmund Freud, 'Delusions and Dreams in Jensen's *Gradiva*', *Standard Edition of the Complete Psychological Works of Sigmund Freud*, trans. and ed. by James Strachey, 24 vols, London: The Hogarth Press, 1953-74, IX, 7-95; 'The Uncanny', *S.E.* XVII, 218-56; Marie Bonaparte, *Edgar Poe, sa vie, son œuvre', étude analytique*, Paris: PUF, 1933; and Jacques Lacan, 'Séminaire sur "la Lettre volée"', in *Écrits*, Paris: Seuil, 1966, pp. 11–61. (Further references to the French text of *Écrits* will be given in the text, preceded by the abbreviation: *É.*) On Lacan's reading of 'The Purloined Letter' and the various different responses it has provoked, see John P. Muller and William J. Richardson, eds, *The Purloined Poe: Lacan, Derrida, and Psychoanalytic Reading*, Baltimore, MD: The Johns Hopkins University Press, 1988. This volume contains, in a translation by Jeffrey Mehlman, the most readily available English version of Lacan's paper and it is this printing I shall be using when referring to Lacan's seminar in what follows (preceded by the abbreviation *PP*).

2. See Freud's essay entitled, 'Creative Writers and Day-Dreaming', *S.E.* 9, 141–53.

3. See, for instance, Jacques Lacan, 'Lituraterre', *Littérature*, October 1971,

4. The texts I am referring to are as follows: Marguerite Duras, *Le Ravissement de Lol V. Stein*, Paris: Gallimard, 'folio', 1964. References to Duras's novel will be to this edition and given in the text, preceded by the abbreviation: *R*. Lacan's 'Hommage à Marguerite Duras, du ravissement de Lol V. Stein' first appeared in *Cahiers de la compagnie Renaud-Barrault*, 52 (December 1965), 7–15; it is reprinted in: François Barat and Joël Farges, eds, *Marguerite Duras*, Paris: Éditions Albatros, [1975] revised edition 1979, pp. 131–7; all references will be to this edition and given in the text, preceded by the abbreviation: *MD*. (The essay is available in English in a translation by Peter Connor in: *Duras on Duras*, San Francisco: City Lights Books, 1987, pp. 122–9.) A revised version of Montrelay's original presentation is published in her book *L'Ombre et le nom: sur la féminité*, Paris: Minuit, 1977, pp. 7–23. Other analysts who have written about Duras after Lacan include Daniel Sibony, in his *La Haine du désir*, Paris: Christian Bourgois, 1978, pp. 81–141; Julia Kristeva, in an essay collected in her *Soleil noir: dépression et mélancolie*, Paris: Gallimard, 1987, pp. 227–65, also available in English in a translation by Katharine A. Jensen under the title 'The Pain of Sorrow in the Modern World: The Works of Marguerite Duras', in *PMLA*, 102, 2, March 1987, 138–52; and François Peraldi in his 'Waiting for the Father', in Sanford Scribnmer Ames, ed., *Remains to be Seen: Essays on Marguerite Duras*, New York: Peter Lang, 1988. pp. 31–50.

5. Marguerite Duras, 'La Destruction de la parole', interview by Jean Narboni and Jacques Rivette, *Les Cahiers du cinema*, 217, November 1969, 45–57 (p. 65); Duras mentions the meeting again in an interview by Catherine Francblin, in *Art Press International*, 24, January 1979, 4, adding that the bar was in the rue Bernard Palissy, not far from the offices of the Éditions de Minuit.

6. Marguerite Duras and Xavière Gauthier, *Les Parleuses*, Paris: Minuit, 1974, p. 161. The review by Jacqueline Piatier that Duras is referring to here appeared in *Le Monde*, 25 April 1964; Hélène Cixous's famous footnote can be found in 'Le Rire de la Méduse', *L'Arc*, 61, 1975, 39–54 (p. 42).

7. See Jacques Lacan, *De la psychose paranoïaque dans ses rapports avec la personnalité*, Paris: Seuil, 1975. On the figure and story of 'Aimée', see Elisabeth Roudinesco, *La Bataille de cent ans: Histoire de la psychanalyse en France*, 2 vols, Paris: Ramsay/Seuil, 1986, II, 124–38 (available in English in a translation by Jeffrey Mehlman as *Jacques Lacan and Co., a History of Psychoanalysis in France 1925–1985*, Chicago: University of Chicago Press, 1990, pp. 109–24); and Jean Allouch, *Marguerite ou l'Aimée de Lacan*, E.P.E.L., 1990. Allouch articulates in some detail the nature of the transferential relationship between Lacan and his patient; incidentally, in retracing Marguerite Anzieu's family tree, he reveals (p. 149) that, like her own dead sister, who was tragically killed some eighteen months before she herself was born, she was named after her maternal grandmother, Marguerite Donnadieu (*née* Maisonneuve). It was of course well known in Paris after the war that the name Duras was a pseudonym, adopted by the writer in 1943, after the small town in Southern France where her father had died. By an odd – no doubt transferential – coincidence, Duras's own original family name was... Marguerite Donnadieu.

8. See Jacques Lacan, *Le Séminaire: Livre VII: L'Éthique de la psychanalyse*, Paris: Seuil, 1986, henceforth: *S*, VII; *Le Séminaire: Livre XI: Les Quatre Concepts fondamentaux de la psychanalyse*, Paris: Seuil, 1973. In English as *The Four Fundamental Concepts of Psycho-Analysis*, trans. Alan Sheridan, Harmondsworth, Penguin, 1979, henceforth: *S*, XI; *Le Séminaire: Livre XX: Encore*, Paris, Seuil, 1975, henceforth: *S*, XX. Further reference will be to these editions and given in the text, preceded by the abbreviations indicated. (Where two figures appear, the first will be to the standard French text, the second to the available English translation. Unless otherwise indicated, all translations are my own.) Lacan's account of *Hamlet* is contained in

the unpublished seminar series of 1958–9 on desire and interpretation; extracts from the sessions are available in *Ornicar?*, 24 (1981), 7–31; 25 (1982), 13–36; and 26–7 (1983), 7–44.

9. Accounts of *Le Ravissement de Lol V. Stein* tend to fall into several distinct camps. Among those sympathetic to Lacan, for instance, are Philippe Boyer, *L'Écarté(e)*, Paris: Seghers/Laffont, 1973), pp. 187–205; Christiane Rabant, 'La Bête chanteuse', *L'Arc*, 58, 1974, 15–20; Elisabeth Lyon, 'The Cinema of Lol V. Stein', in Constance Penley, ed., *Feminism and Film Theory*, London: BFI and Routledge, 1988, pp. 244–71; Carol J. Murphy, *Alienation and Absence in the Novels of Marguerite Duras*, Lexington: French Forum, 1982, pp. 95–102; Michèle Druon, 'Mise en scène et catharsis de l'amour dans *Le Ravissement de Lol V. Stein*, de Marguerite Duras', *The French Review*, LVIII, 3, February 1985, 382–90; Susan Cohen, 'Phantasm and Narration in Marguerite Duras' *The Ravishing of Lol V. Stein*', in Joseph Reppen and Maurice Charney, eds, *The Psychoanalytic Study of Literature*, Hillsdale, NJ: The Analytic Press, 1985, pp. 255–77; Sharon Willis, *Marguerite Duras: Writing on the Body*, Urbana and Chicago: University of Illinois Press, 1987, pp. 63–95; Bernard Alberti and Marie-Thérèse Mathet, 'Le "Ravisement" de Lol V. Stein', *French Studies*, XLIV, 4, October 1990, 416–23; and Deborah N. Glassman, *Marguerite Duras: Fascinating Vision and Narrative Cure*, Cranbury, NJ: Associated University Presses, 1991, pp. 34–61. Among readers of the novel more critical of Lacan, Marcelle Marini, in *Territoires du féminin: avec Marguerite Duras*, Paris: Minuit, 1977, adopts a view closer to Luce Irigaray; in *Gynesis: Configurations of Woman and Modernity*, New York: Cornell University Press, 1985, pp. 172–7, Alice Jardine draws attention to the gender politics implicit in Lacan's reading; while Martha Noel Evans, in her chapter on Duras in *Masks of Tradition: Women and the Politics of Writing in Twentieth-Century France*, Ithaca, NY: Cornell University Press, 1987, pp. 123–56, argues, contra Lacan, that 'in confronting Lol's architecture of pre-varication, Jacques comes face to face with radical otherness' (p. 137). Trista Selous, in *The Other Woman: Feminism and Femininity in the Work of Marguerite Duras*, New Haven, CT and London: Yale University Press, 1988, condemns both Lacan and Duras for their supposed essentialism and anti-feminism. A more rigorous study of *Le Ravissement de Lol V. Stein* which demonstrates some of the shortcomings of Lacan's analysis on textual rather than ideological grounds is provided by Marie-Claire Ropars-Wuilleumier in *Écraniques: le film du texte*, Lille: Presses universitaires de Lille, 1990, pp. 57–83; and Susan Rubin Suleiman, in her book *Subversive Intent: Gender, Politics and the Avant-Garde*, Cambridge, MA: Harvard University Press, 1990, pp. 88–118, examines how Lacan's essay and Duras's novel can each be read as a commentary on the other.

10. See Jacques Lacan, *Télévision*, Paris: Seuil, 1974, p. 9.

11. See Jacques Lacan, 'Le Canevas', *Ornicar?* (1981), 24.

12. Jean Laplanche, *Problématiques III: La Sublimation*, Paris: PUF, 1980, p. 122. See also the article on sublimation in Jean Laplanche and J.-B. Pontalis, *Vocabulaire de la psychanalyse*, Paris: PUF, 1967.

13. Compare here, for instance, Kristeva's own account of 'la Chose' in her *Soleil noir, dépression et mélancolie*, pp. 22–5.

14. Marguerite de Navarre, *L'Heptaméron*, edited by Michel François, Paris: Garnier, 1967. Further references will be to this edition and given in the text, preceded by the abbreviation: *H*. The book is available in English in a translation by Paul Chilton under the title *The Heptameron*, Harmondsworth: Penguin, 1984. References to this version will be given in the text immediately following the original.

15. See Suzanne Lamy and Andre Roy, eds, *Marguerite Duras à Montréal*, Montreal: Éditions Spirale, 1981, p. 19.

16. See Lucien Febvre, *Autour de l'Heptaméron*, Paris: Gallimard, 1944.

17. On Lacan's reading of Sophocles' Antigone, see Philippe Lacoue-Labarthe, 'De l'éthique: à propos d'Antigone', in *Lacan avec les philosophes*, Paris: Albin Michel, 1991, pp. 21–6.
18. Michele Montrelay, *L'Ombre et le nom*, p. 21.
19. In *Alienation and Absence in the Novels of Marguerite Duras*, Carol Murphy refers, for instance, following Lacan, to 'the triangular dance of desire in *Le Ravissement de Lol V. Stein*, in which Lol's ravishing consists both of her exclusion or absence from the dance of Anne-Marie Stretter and Michael Richardson and of her necessary presence during this seduction' (pp. 137–8).
20. Marguerite Duras, *L'Amour*, Paris: Gallimard, 1971, p. 143.

11

Jacqueline Rose, 'She', in *The Haunting of Sylvia Plath*.

London: Virago Press, 1991, pp. 11–28.

Editor's Introduction

Jacqueline Rose's chapter deals with the (often hostile) critical reception given to Sylvia Plath and her poetry. Rose's question is not only: Why does Plath 'become the horror of which she speaks'? but also: How does Plath become this horror? In this regard, Rose's text pivots around two psychoanalytic terms: 'projection' and 'transference'.

Projection occurs when people (for instance, readers) project their own fantasies or fears on to an external object without recognising that this is what they are doing. Projection is a one-way process: the person projecting is oblivious of the possibility that the other might constitute an obstacle to the projector's certainty. The racist thus projects his or her own unacknowledged desires or fears on to the hated group. Paranoia, and certain phobias, are other examples of projection.[1]

Transference, on the other hand, may be understood in the Lacanian sense as the 'actualisation of the unconscious', in so far as – unlike the projector – the analysand places the analyst in the position of the 'one who is supposed to know'. In doing this, however, the analysand places the analyst in the position of a love object. For it is precisely the lack of indifference that the analysand has for the analyst – and subsequently, as Kristeva has shown, the lack of indifference of the analyst – towards the analysand, that provides the analytic situation with its internal dynamic. Without transference (which entails the recognition of a certain reciprocity), there can be no analysis.

Evoked here – and evoked by Rose in her discussion of the reception to Plath – is a structure of intersubjectivity: a relationship between self (reader) and other (text) in which the text can never be entirely mastered by any reading. At least, no text can be mastered if this means that its essential truth is to be discovered. Nor can any text be mastered if it is presumed to be a symmetrical version of the reader's own psyche – which is an entirely imaginary position. In effect, the text is always other, always resistant to complete domination, always capable of saying something 'other than it says'.[2]

As Shoshana Felman's work[3] (cited by Rose) has shown, projection and transference have been insightfully 'transferred' to the field of literary criticism, acknowledgement of them serving to heighten the reader's powers of reflexivity. Like Felman, who challenges (among others) Edmund Wilson's supposedly Freudian claim that Henry James's story 'The Turn of the Screw' is a story of madness caused by frustrated sexual desire, Rose shows how responses to Sylvia Plath's poetry have often been unable to do justice to its relative textual autonomy, so helplessly have critics become embroiled in the very fantasy structure they are supposed to be analysing. In particular, certain male readers have either demonised or pathologised Plath's writing, thus repeating what the text(s) had already anticipated.

Notes

1. See J. Laplanche and J. B. Pontalis, 'Projection', in *The Language of Psychoanalysis*, trans. Donald Nicholson-Smith, London: Karnac Books and Institute of Psycho-Analysis, 1988, pp. 349–56.
2. This structure of intersubjectivity and its limits is articulated by Lacan in his reading of Poe's 'The Purloined Letter'.
3. See Shoshana Felman, 'Turning the Screw of Interpretation', in Shoshana Felman, ed., *Literature and Psychoanalysis. The Question of Reading: Otherwise*, Baltimore, MD and London: Johns Hopkins University Press, 1982, pp. 94–207.

'She'

We have been told that there is a Plath fantasia which deforms the truth of her writing, distorts the facts of her life.[1] To begin with, at least, it might be worth taking this argument at its word. What happens if we ask, not what truth does the Plath fantasia *conceal*, but what truth does it *express*? Not about Plath herself in this first instance, but about the discourse of literary criticism. I want to start by looking at the worst of what has been done to Plath – not simply to castigate it, nor to repeat, with the ultimate desire of bypassing it, the truism that she has so endlessly been constituted as a myth. If it seems appropriate to start here, it is because no writer seems to reveal so clearly, so grotesquely, the forms of fantasy, of psychic and sexual investment, that can be involved in the constitution of literature itself.

Here are three quotations from different critics. The first is from Edward Butscher describing his attempt to write his biography of Plath in an essay called 'In Search of Sylvia'. He is referring to the friends, teachers and classmates he tracked down as 'witnesses' for the book:

'witnesses' is appropriate as I soon came to view myself as a literary Lew Archer in pursuit of another violated little girl, another doomed Oedipal victim, who had been as contradictory as she had been gifted.[2]

The second is by Richard Howard in an essay, 'Sylvia Plath: "And I Have No Face, I Have Wanted To Efface Myself" ', in Charles Newman's 1970 anthology *The Art of Sylvia Plath*:

> There is no pathos in the accents of these final poems ... only a certain pride, the pride of an utter and ultimate surrender (like the pride of O, naked and chained in her owl mask, as she asks Sir Stephen for death).[3]

The third is from Hugh Kenner in an article called 'Sincerity Kills' from Gary Lane's 1979 collection *Sylvia Plath: New Views on the Poetry*:

> As who should say, 'The price of absorption in pornography is an incremental deadening of the spirit, an attenuation of the already frail belief in the sanctity of personhood. I shall now show you a pornographic film.' All her life a reader had been someone to manipulate.[4]

I came across these quotations at random when I was preparing for the first time to teach Sylvia Plath. If in one sense they seem to require no commentary, it might none the less be worth trying to uncover something of their logic in order to pull them back, and our own reaction to them, from the realm of the safely outrageous or joke. Jokes they indeed are, but precisely by being so they reveal a particular economy of fantasy, one which passes from a recognition of the woman as ultimate victim, sexualised through that very recognition (the Lew Archer hunt), through the pornographic scenario of the woman's utter surrender, to arrive finally at the accusation of the woman as pornographer (the trajectory can equally work the other way round). Thus Plath becomes the ultimate manipulator (crudely, the artist of the hand job), accountable for – or even guilty of – the different sexual scenarios that these male critics have generated to meet her.

But what each of these quotations also suggests is that the drama rests in the relationship between the writer and her audience in a very specific way. It is a crisis of *address* that Plath produces in the critic, as if to accuse: 'Who is she talking to?' or 'By what right does she speak?' or 'What is it that she is doing to, or withholding from, me?' What matters, therefore, is not just the sexuality of these responses to Plath and their too easily predictable misogyny, but the way that the sexuality and the misogyny belong on the boundary between the literary text and its reader. As Shoshana Felman puts it, in her analysis of Henry James's short story 'The Turn of the Screw' and its critics, the scandal provoked by the text belongs in the realm of a 'reading effect'.[5] It resides not just inside the work but in our relationship to it – in how it gets to us, as we might say. The outrage of Plath – what, at least partly, calls up the intensity of sexual reaction – may therefore have something to do with a crisis privileged at the furthest edge of the literary, at that point where the literary work recognises, situates and delimits itself, or in this case fails in that delimitation.

This might become clearer if we go back to the quotations and note how, if they do have a logic, it is one which in each case is based on a contradiction. In Butscher's case, it is the contradiction between the image of a violated little girl and the image of an Oedipal victim, or rather between that 'Oedipal' and that 'victim'. For it was precisely the concept of the Oedipus complex in Freud's work that shattered the image of the hysteric as victim by introducing childhood fantasy into the understanding of psychic disturbance, and thus throwing into question his earlier belief that hysteria could best be understood in terms of the violation of little girls (this is Freud's famous relinquishment of the seduction theory of hysteria, which has been the object of much recent critique[6]). But that Butscher wants his little girl violated *and* Oedipal is a way of having your cake and eating it too. Let her be utterly done over and somewhere desiring it at the same time (the classic pornographic scenario).

The same contradiction is there in the Howard example, which precisely activates that scenario through the explicit reference to *The Story of O*. The *Ariel* poems are totally without pathos, expressive only of a certain pride, which may seem the more active emotion, except that this same pride is the pride of total surrender asking (the man, inevitably) for death. So the quotation makes the same move, gets into the same muddle as to where sexuality and desire can be located. What is the sexual distribution of roles? Active male, passive female, or the female active in her pursuit of the ultimate passivity (death)? Who, finally, is accountable to whom? Only in the Kenner quote is that contradiction subordinated to the idea of a self-knowing and willed manipulation. Plath disavows her intention to do it to the reader, and then does it all the more viciously all the same. If I, the critic, cannot sort out, define, control what it is that this woman is doing sexually in her writing, then it must be that she is doing it (the critical confusion) to me.

Psychoanalysis would recognise in this the mechanism of projection, to be distinguished from that of transference, which has become current in recent discussion of psychoanalysis and literature. In Henry James's story, it is not clear to the reader whether the governess is the saviour of the children in her charge, or whether she hallucinates the very evil she thinks she is protecting them against. This is the question the text holds in suspense. By trying to answer it, critics have simply repeated the drama of the governess herself, entering into the argument that the writing is having with itself. The implications of this are far-reaching. By repeating the demand of the governess that the events in which she is implicated should, in terms of their origin and destination, unequivocally make sense, these critics have acted out one of the central demands of a whole tradition of literary critical thought which rests its authority in the clarity of its own activity as well as on the aesthetic unity it looks for in the literary text.

For Shoshana Felman, this is the mechanism of transference, first restricted by Freud to the field of neurosis, where patients transfer on to the analyst during the course of treatment their unconscious fantasies and desires. In relation to literature, transference refers to the way critics read their unconscious into the text, repeating in their critical analysis the structures of meaning called up by the writing. Thus transference suggests a process of mutual implication (the critic repeats and enters into the text). In the case of projection, on the other hand, that same repetition works by exclusion – a structural incapacity, that of psychosis, to recognise your relation to something which seems to assail you from outside. The subject expels what he or she cannot bear to acknowledge as his or her own reality, only to have it return even larger, and more grotesquely, than reality itself (this is, of course, also the subject of 'The Turn of the Screw' – do the ghosts belong inside or outside the mind?).

Melanie Klein describes one form of this mechanism as 'projective identification', the model or prototype of later aggressivity, a mechanism which aims to protect the ego but which – in an ironic twist – finally weakens it because what has been evicted is intimate, bound up with the 'power, potency, strength, knowledge and many other desired qualities upon which the ego relies'.[7] Apply this concept of projection to literary analysis, and what you would expect to discover is a criticism once again caught up in the writing, but this time in the form of deadly struggle *against* it. In the course of this struggle, the text itself must be evicted by the critic. Above all, what must be got rid of is any trace of the critic's own relationship to, or implication in, the writing as such.

Would it be going too far to suggest that Plath has generated a form of 'psychotic' criticism? And not only because of the speed with which critics have rushed to apply the labels 'psychotic' and 'schizophrenic' to her work? (Anne Stevenson's biography – the most recent – is saying nothing new in this context, it simply rejoins the very point of origin of the Plath myth.[8]) It is more that the stakes seem to be so raised in response to Plath's writing: from the question posed by James's story as to whether the governess hallucinates (desires) sexuality or is defending the children against it (an issue of sexual innocence or guilt), to the issue of a sexuality conceived of as so violent that it can only be repudiated – the question the critic then repeatedly asks being whether he (never mind Plath) can survive. Thus Plath puts the whole enterprise of criticism – 'its power, potency, strength, knowledge' – at risk.

This is David Holbrook's epigraph to his book *Sylvia Plath: Poetry and Existence*, published in 1976, one of the first full-length studies of Plath.[9] The quotation comes from George MacDonald's *Lilith*, written in 1895, which belongs, along with Rider Haggard's *She*, to that genre of late-nineteenth-century imperialist texts in which the Christian conquest of other worlds takes the form of an encounter with a deadly female principle:

> The strife of thought, accusing and excusing, began afresh, and gathered fierceness. The soul of Lilith lay naked to the torture of pure interpenetrating inward light. She began to moan and sigh deep sighs, then murmur as if holding colloquy with a dividual self: her queendom was no longer whole; it was divided against herself. One moment she would exult as over her worst enemy, and weep; the next she would writhe as if in the embrace of a fiend whom her soul hated and laugh like a demon. At length she began what seemed a tale about herself, in language so strange, and in forms so shadowy, that I could but here and there understand a little...
>
> Gradually my soul grew aware of an invisible darkness, a something more terrible than aught that had yet made itself felt. A horrible Nothingness, a Negation positive infolded her; the border of its being that was yet no being, touched me and for one ghastly instant I seemed alone with Death Absolute! It was not the absence of everything I felt, but the presence of Nothing. The princess dashed herself from the settle to the floor with an exceeding great and bitter cry. It was the recoil of Being from Annihilation...[10]

Note how this evokes its own pornographic scenario: 'She began to moan and sigh deep sighs.' Note too how it is beginning to take on the form of diagnosis: 'a dividual self' (a self dangerous because divided, as opposed to a self which does not threaten because it is integrated and whole). In his introduction, Holbrook reports that his book was circulated in manuscript form among analysts working on schizophrenia, and that it was already being used in clinical work (a literary interpretation of Plath thus acquires the status of a clinical case).[11] This idea of a 'dividual self' also carries its own aesthetic values. We will see at various points the extent to which the opposing idea of authenticity, integrity, psychic and aesthetic wholeness has appeared as the standard against which Plath has been measured. Speaking in the name of that wholeness, criticism thus establishes its own sanity through the distance it strikes from her work.

Above all – and nowhere more transparently than here – it is the critic's implication, or possible identification with this drama, which must at all costs be denied. Accordingly, Holbrook's quotation from *Lilith* cuts these lines from right out of the middle of the passage as it appears in the original text: 'Yet the language seemed the primeval shape of one I knew well, and the forms to belong to dreams which had once been mine, but refused to be recalled.'[12] It is a staggering instance of projection on the part of Holbrook – in fact, with the missing part back in, the passage from the novel can be read as a description or analysis of projection in itself. The spectator in the novel acknowledges the relation between his own unconscious and the horror ('dreams which had once been mine'); acknowledges too the resistance to acknowledgement itself ('refused to be recalled'). Holbrook then acts out this resistance by taking out the moment of recognition, thereby propelling the horror outside and away from himself.

Already, in this quotation, the pornographic scenario can also be read as a fantasy of literary criticism: 'naked to the torture of pure interpenetrating inward light'. Somewhere the opposition 'woman' versus the 'logos' is at stake. The critic takes up the position of witness to a form of the terrible, to the terrible as form. As witness, he cannot be the source of the terror which displays itself to him (or at least not in Holbrook's version), but he is no less threatened by it – he is perhaps even more threatened – for all that. If the violence of Plath presents itself (to reuse Felman's expression) as the violence of a reading-effect, then in this case the experience of reading operates like the sight of the Medusa, a full-frontal assault. The witness survives this display of evil by the woman, in the Lilith story at least, only in so far as he stands squarely in the place of God.

If all this seems extravagant, untypical, in the order of excess, compare the basic trope or rhetorical figure of this passage with the first lines of the epigraph to Anne Stevenson's biography, *Bitter Fame*: 'There was a tremendous power in the burning look of her dark eyes; she came "conquering and to conquer"' (the quotation from Dostoyevsky's *The Devils* continues more kindly, but it unquestionably starts in the same place).[13] Similarly, Stephen Spender, in his essay on Plath, 'Warnings from the Grave', describes her as a 'priestess cultivating her hysteria', a hysteria which seems to refer outwards to history (the prophetess), but finally refers only to femininity itself: 'her femininity is that her hysteria comes completely out of herself'.[14] He is comparing her with Owen, whose poetry, he argues, comes out of the concrete experience of the war. From prophecy back into the hysterical body of femininity, Spender's move is strikingly similar to the reversal at the centre of D. M. Thomas's *The White Hotel*, in which the woman seems to have foreknowledge of the impending Holocaust but in fact, through her sexuality, she *is* it.[15] Spender's diagnosis offers the perfect image of male literary critical chauvinism – a point made by Mary Ellman in her book *Thinking About Women*, in 1969.[16] Ellman rightly objects to the removal of the woman from history, this turning-in-on-herself of all historical and literary process. I would go further, and suggest that it is basic to this fantasmatic scenario that the woman becomes the horror of which she speaks.

Holbrook may be ridiculous, exaggerated and excessive, but at the same time he is supremely representative of the sexual imaginary precipitated by Plath's work. His reading merely inflates a dynamic which repeats itself across a range of responses to her writing. From the Oedipal little victim, to the hysteric, to O, to Lilith, we watch the standard figures of femininity transmuting themselves one into the other along the axis of a violence whose logic seems finally to be that of sexual difference itself. According to this logic, it is the fact of femininity which appals. Sexuality is horrifying because of the gap which it wrenches open in the order of things. The specific scenarios of victimisation, pornography and apocalypse merely embody as visual dramatisation the lapse from certainty which occurred when sexuality first ushered evil into the world. There is one account of Freud which states that the boy child *recognises* that moment in the body of the woman, but there is a better one which says that he *projects* it *on to* her, endlessly staging and restaging an accusation against her for a difference of which, by definition, she cannot be the single source.[17] According to Julia Kristeva, it is this structure of projection that can be recognised as the mechanism at the basis of the writings of Céline in their monstrous depiction of the woman as both source and destroyer of life.[18] Plath, however, is herself the producer of words. The problem she poses as a woman does not belong only to the images inside the text, but hurtles back to the origins of writing. Femininity becomes accountable for what went wrong in the beginning – but also, as we will see, for the end of the world.

Taking Holbrook as merely symptomatic, we can then expect to find, alongside this degraded and abused image of femininity, the idealisation to which it is almost invariably attached. This idealised femininity is set up as the principle whose task it is to hold the original evil in check. There is a famous article by the psychoanalyst D. W. Winnicott, 'Creativity and its Origins', which starts by describing the instability of sexual identity and ends with a mythical image of femininity and masculinity which he more or less lifts out of Robert Graves.[19] A whole school of psychoanalytic literary criticism has been founded on the celebration of the female principle of pure being that surfaces in this mystified ending to Winnicott's text.[20] It is this 'female-element-being quality' to which Holbrook appeals. The schizoid woman, he writes, tries to 'unite the disparate elements of her identity', but all she can find is 'two death-male-elements, neither male with a female component, nor female with a male component'.[21] This is the 'secret of the schizoid woman, who has within her an impulse to annihilate the male – the animus which becomes malevolent because it cannot find itself "female-element-being" quality' (this is the kind of thing that gives psychoanalysis a bad name).[22] The worst evil in woman is a masculinity untempered by an essentially female modification. Maleness becomes evil in the woman, who then seeks to annihilate men.

I think what Holbrook believes he is doing in this reading of Plath is describing the failure of her femininity. What I think he is actually doing, however, is projecting on to Plath a familiar fantasy of femininity which makes it accountable for the destruction or salvation (one or the other) of mankind. Similarly, Ruskin argued in the nineteenth century that woman's sphere was not political, historical – 'The man, in his rough work in the open world, must encounter all peril and trial' – but that she was none the less responsible for all evil in the outside world: 'There is not a war in the world, no, nor an injustice, but you women are answerable for it.'[23]

It has to be acknowledged, however, that it is not only male critics who have turned on Plath in relation to femininity in this way. In her essay on Plath, 'The Death Throes of Romanticism', Joyce Carol Oates writes on 'Magi' from *Crossing the Water*: 'its vision is exclusively Plath's and, in a horrifying way, very female', although later in the same article she suggests that, if there is any horror of femininity, it is Plath's own: 'a woman who despises herself as a woman obviously cannot feel sympathy with any other woman'.[24]

Holbrook's account of Plath's femininity also has another significance. We can recognise in it a classic description of projection on to the feminist. The lines about the 'two death-male-elements' ends with a parenthesis: '(And this apparently makes her ideal for Women's Liberation!)'.[25] Repeatedly he juxtaposes his image of Plath's failed femininity with feminism: 'One can see how Sylvia Plath appeals to the women's liberators ... Sylvia Plath could scarcely find anything within her that was feminine at all . . . she is sadly pseudo-male, like many of her cultists.'[26] It is the all too familiar stereotype of the feminist as failed woman and then (the one as a consequence of the other) as destroyer of men. If Holbrook is important here, it may also be because his writing on Plath reveals so starkly the economy of sexual fantasy which underpins one form of attack on feminism by the Right.

The sexual issue is therefore a political issue in the fullest sense of the term. This account of Plath is weighted with the responsibility for the global survival of culture in our time. We are living at a moment of 'extremism, violence, gross indecency', when we are 'being urged to cultivate our psychoses and endorse decadence and moral inversion'.[27] What Plath has to say about 'male and female and other subjects' is 'grossly distorted and false'.[28] Holbrook's image of true femininity reveals itself as part of a pedagogic project in which literature occupies the privileged place: 'culture is primary in human existence', 'the reading of literature refines the emotions and helps to civilise us'.[29] Plath must not be taught in schools or, if she is, she must be taught only in order to establish the essential falseness of her vision. She seems to occupy roughly the place of the homosexual in relation to the recent legislation of Clause 28 – homosexuality can be acknowledged in schools, but only if it is condemned (the term 'moral inversion' appears no fewer than four times in the introduction to Holbrook's book alone[30]). If we fail in this task, then 'what values can we invoke to condemn those who blow up children with terrorist bombs or harm their consciousness with cruel exploitation?'[31]

This account of the civilising and humanising mission of culture has come to be associated in the twentieth century with the work of F.R. Leavis, who articulated it most clearly in the 1930s and then again after the war. It has become a commonplace of recent Marxist literary criticism to point to its élitism, its assumption and creation of cultural privilege, its anti-democratic politics, and its defence of a tradition of Englishness founded in an imperialism which was still – and continued for some time (many would say continues) to be – in place. The role of culture was to transcend all materialism – meaning socialism on the one hand, the rise of a consumerist and commodity culture on the other. The authority and influence of this school (Leavis and the journal *Scrutiny*, which he founded in 1932) rested, to a great extent, on the way it succeeded in elevating this vested political account of culture to a realm outside all historical time.[32]

To this extent, Holbrook is merely continuing an established tradition whose reactionary implications at the level of our cultural life were starting to be unravelled at about the same time as he was writing his book on Plath. What is distinctive about this later version, however, is the place it assigns to feminism and the woman writer. It is as if the argument 'for' culture was being forced to acknowledge its investment in something that can be called the symbolic order, meaning the implicit rules which govern our language and sexuality, and the forms of fantasy, especially in the sexual field, on which such ordering relies. Sexuality – or, more precisely, a dread of femininity – reveals itself as one of the sub-texts of Holbrook's vision of culture. That vision may be transcendent and mythic in its terms, but it is rooted in a specific historical configuration in which 'feminism' (and/or 'failed femininity') and the 'survival of the culture' are pitted against each other from remarkably similar positions to those occupied by 'socialism' (and/or 'consumerism') versus the 'literary' in the *Scrutiny* battles of the decades before. In this new battle, I would argue, Sylvia Plath comes to occupy a crucial place, one in which the question of cultural survival is sexualised and the woman writer who might be said to have made survival the stake of her own writing becomes somehow accountable for those who blow up children with terrorist bombs.

If it is tempting to dismiss this reading as pathological, it might be worth turning from Holbrook, who wants Plath out of the educational system, to A. Alvarez, the critic in England who did most in the early stages for the promotion of her work (he could almost be described as her impresario). Alvarez places Plath, along with Robert Lowell, at the forefront of a new movement of poetry which he calls 'Extremism'. He sets this movement against what he sees as the middle-class, welfare-state gentility of Britain after the war. Plath and Anne Sexton were the only women poets included in Alvarez's 1966 revised edition of his anthology, *The New Poetry*, first published, as part of his definition of this type of writing, in 1962.[33]

At first glance Alvarez seems to be writing from a position diametrically opposed to everything we have seen so far. If psychoanalysis appears in his discourse, it is as much part of a collective as individual diagnosis, which means it is not being used to hold the psychically disturbing at bay: 'it is hard to live in an age of psychoanalysis and feel oneself wholly detached from the dominant public savagery'.[34] Certainly he never turns against Plath the violence that he reads in her poetry, and he was attacked by Holbrook for promoting her work.[35] And yet despite that immediate difference of assessment, what is most striking is the remarkable similarity of the language in which, at key moments, this defence of Plath is expressed. Perhaps more than any other critic, it is Alvarez who most clearly demonstrates the extent to which Plath becomes part of – is almost produced as a literary object in response to – a battle about the limits and survival of culture.

Again, this is criticism in the apocalyptic mode. For Alvarez, true – read 'high' – culture has been destroyed. Extremist poetry stands as the last bastion against a general cultural mediocrity. Along with B movies, television and spectator sports, a pseudo avant-garde panders to the middle classes. Relegated to a 'subdivision of the entertainments industry', the arts have become, in Saul Bellow's words: 'something to goose the new middle class with'.[36] Compare Holbrook: 'Does not a great deal of our commercial and avant-garde culture ... rape us, even at the heart of our being?'[37] Alvarez constantly demands that the artist speak of the worst of social evils, but it is clear that his apocalyptic vision rests at least as much with this notion of cultural degeneration as it does with the forms of contemporary political horror (the 'dominant public savagery') to which he repeatedly refers: '[The Extremist style] may, after all, have less to do with the prognosis of a nuclear holocaust than with the relatively simple understanding of the fact that the traditional basis of the arts has been smashed.'[38] In this context, Plath herself becomes the very image of poetic vision concealed inside, or wrestling with, the crude trappings of a commodity culture:

> She was a tall, spindly girl with waist-length sandy hair, which she usually wore in a bun, and that curious, advertisement-trained transatlantic air of anxious pleasantness. But this was a nervous social manner; under it, she was ruthless about her perceptions, wary and very individual [the opening lines of the article published by Alvarez in *The Review* at the time of Plath's death].[39]

The Extremist artist stands for the due intensity of highbrow art in an increasingly commercialised world. Plath's intensity is what ensures that the world (that she) is not *cheap*: 'there is always the delicate question of how common common sense should be'.[40]

For this image of culture, the philosophy is Social Darwinism. A last survivor, the Extremist artist emerges as the 'creatively fittest' through a process of natural selection: 'Art always depends on a principle of natural selection ... Extremism, however, is based on a form of psychic Darwinism that is far beyond the most stringent usual demands of talent' (the remark immediately follows a reference to Plath).[41] Similarly, Holbrook appeals to a 'philosophical biology' with its 'primary realities of the evolutionary process'.[42] Extremism then appears as the culmination of a Leavisite aesthetic: art as the ascendancy over (the aesthetic-cum-political containment of) the many by the few.

Paradoxically, the only art that can survive in this world is that which knows the present impossibility of art: 'They survive morally by becoming, in one way or another, an imitation of death in which they share.'[43] Alvarez insisted that he was not offering Plath as the 'sacrificial victim offering her-self up for the sake of her art', but it is clear that suicide (her suicide) rep-resents the truest state, and measure, of the art: 'In following this black thread [suicide], I have arrived at a theory which, for me, in some way, explains what the arts are about now' (preface to *The Savage God*, Alvarez's study of literature and suicide).[44] Plath is the prologue, Alvarez's own failed suicide attempt the epilogue, of this book: 'I want the book to start, as it ends, with a detailed case-history.'[45] For all the denials, that 'case-history' indicates the pathologising of art, or the romanticising of art as pathology. Alvarez had to add a qualifying note to the essay he had written on Plath at the time of her death: 'I was *not* in any sense meaning to imply that break-down or suicide is a validation of what I now call Extremist poetry.'[46] The comment seems to imply that the very concept of Extremism emerged only after (in response to?) Plath's death. Thus Plath engenders a literary move-ment constituted in the very image of her death. Either the woman destroys the culture, or her self-immolation is the precondition for culture to sur-vive.[47]

If, therefore, Holbrook identifies Plath with the inversion and degener-acy of cultural value, Alvarez lays on her the weight of reparation for the same collapse of the moral and cultural world. She is either beneath or above culture: 'beneath' as in 'hidden behind' or 'accountable for', 'beneath' as in 'low'; 'above' as 'superiority' or 'higher forms', 'above' as 'transcen-dence'. The second may be the more favourable judgement, but it effec-tively removes the writer from historical and cultural time. Alvarez was undoubtedly the critic who, in the earliest stages, allowed Plath to take off. Rereading Plath's beginnings as a cultural icon today gives us a unique opportunity to watch the cultural politics of this still influential vision of cul-tural ascendancy. As we will see, however, Plath herself took pleasure in the multifarious forms of the culture, both high and low, crossing over the limit which she has so repeatedly been used to enforce.

It could be argued that Alvarez's writing on Plath is remarkable for how little attention it pays to the fact that she was a woman. As Alan Sinfield has pointed out, this can be seen as a form of political denial in itself.[48] Sexual difference has to be ignored in order to secure that universalism, or transcendence, of aesthetic terms: 'She steers clear of feminine charm, deli-ciousness, gentility, supersensitivity and the act of being a poetess. She sim-ply writes good poetry.'[49] But this does not mean that his account of the end of culture has nothing sexual at stake. Note that link between gentility and feminine charm. Plath's access, or condition of entry, to the highest form of culture is that she leaves her femininity *behind*. In his article 'Literature of the Holocaust', Alvarez asks, alluding to Matthew Arnold: 'How do *people* measure up to it as *men* [*sic*]?'[50] On the subject of Lowell: 'A poem suc-ceeds or fails by virtue of the balance and subtlety of the man himself.'[51] By virtue of his manhood – the traditional aesthetic qualities of balance and subtlety migrate and find their last refuge in the image of masculinity itself. Sandra Gilbert and Susan Gubar have commented on the pervasiveness of this masculist image of writing, but it is not restricted to male critics alone.[52] Joyce Carol Oates opens her essay on Plath: 'Tragedy is not a woman, how-ever gifted, dragging her shadow around in a circle ... tragedy is cultural, mysteriously enlarging the individual.'[53] The association of woman/shadow/circle is a conventional one (it is taken from Plath's poem 'A Life'[54]). But which body, and which part of that body, mysteriously enlarges itself? Compare too Oates's critique of lyric poetry for not coming up to size: 'How quickly these six-inch masterpieces betray their creators!'[55] I think this has to be an (intended) joke.

Alvarez and Holbrook finally have in common this sexualisation of the cultural stakes. A decadent culture is onanistic and impotent. In the first issue of *The Review*, in a discussion with Donald Davie, Alvarez compared aestheticism to masturbation on the ground of their shared relinquishment of the realities of life.[56] Compare Holbrook: 'our essential cultural experiences (gramophone, television set, wireless or cinema) are not celebrative, they are, rather, onanistic'.[57] He then spends a great deal of time on the line 'Masturbating a glitter' from Plath's poem 'Death and Co.', arguing that it establishes her psychosis via a reference to a case-study of a German boy who shot a prostitute and, apparently surrounded by shining objects, used to masturbate a lot.[58] It is easy, however, to follow this logic: the weakening of the culture, the dissipation of sexual energy, a kind of premature sexual-cum-nuclear waste (the sexual and political terrors are closely linked).

The dispute over Plath is therefore aesthetic as well as sexual and cultural-political in scope. If she is hysterical prophetess for Spender, it is at least partly because her poems are lacking in form: 'they don't have "form". From poem to poem they have little principle of beginning or ending, but seem fragments, not so much of one long poem, as of an outpouring which could not stop with the lapsing of the poet's hysteria' (Plath's poetry is the 'emotional–mystical' extension and continuation of hysteria).[59] But we should not expect Alvarez's praise of Plath to involve in any way a validation of this image of a writing, part hysteric, part onanistic, spilling out of itself. Despite his argument for extremity and his critique of literary convention, Alvarez speaks finally in the name of a very traditional aesthetic, visible in his rejection of the avant-garde, in his ideal of a language transparent to the world and to the man ('the poems since *Life Studies* have gained a kind of transparency: you see through them to see the man as he is'), in that image of the unity, identity and coherence of the poetic which counters the holocaust of culture.[60] Extremism is not a challenge to form but the final securing of its possibility, the art of an identity which asserts itself against the odds. For Alvarez, the task of the artist, faced with the failure of 'all our traditions and beliefs', is to secure 'his own identity' from scratch.[61] This identity, forged – self-engendered – by the writer, is thus proposed by Alvarez as a solution to a 'post-modern' predicament which many today would see as a challenge to the category, and the pretensions, of singular identity as such.

Plath is not, therefore, being sponsored as an artist of the irrational. Extremism never means letting up the essential artistic control: 'Like Coleridge's Imagination', it reconciles 'a more than usual state of emotion with a more than usual order' (a type of D. H. Lawrence and T. S. Eliot combined).[62] This is extremism in the rationalist mode, a mode that Alvarez opposes to fascism, although today we might see those very terms of supreme control, identity and aesthetic heroism as just as likely to be part of fascism itself – ' marshalled… and ordered', to use Alvarez's own expression from his 1963 essay on Plath.[63] Kristeva's account of Céline as a fascist writer suggests that what is involved is not irrationalism but a highly regulated fantasy world subject to a super-competent ego that controls and distributes, according to a rigid sexual economy, the worst of its terms. Already it is clear, however, that – in relation to Plath (although not only in relation to her) – we need a conception of writing as neither marshalled nor fragmented, neither surplus order nor a hysterical body pouring out of itself.

The main point of this chapter has been to show how Sylvia Plath is constituted as a literary object on the battleground of cultural survival. Through the intensity of their investment in her, and beyond any immediate differences of appraisal, she becomes for Holbrook and Alvarez (and not only for them) an object of desire. Alvarez makes little of Plath as a woman, but his account of the last months of her life in *The Savage God* follows the conventions of the narrative/sexual pursuit. Plath has become – the point has been made before – the Marilyn Monroe of the literati: with this difference – that it is not only the survival of manhood (the manhood which survives by fetishising the woman) but the very capacity of culture to symbolise its own lineage and perpetuity which is at stake. This is not the first time the concept of culture has been invested with the future of civilisation. Doesn't the very definition of the classic rest on the question of whether a text will *survive*? Only this time, we can clearly see that the cultural object is not simply the refuge from a larger terror, but also embodies it. For good or for evil, Plath has come to symbolise that terror for a literary discourse which, according to the most traditional valorisation of its own high social function, is still asking literature to carry the privileged weight of the future of man. In these terms, Sylvia Plath is either the apotheosis or the apocalypse (or both together) of art.

A difficult aesthetic question remains. For some time now, feminist criticism has seemed to be divided between a reading of women writers which bemoans the lack of – or attempts to retrieve for them – a consistent and articulate 'I', and one which celebrates linguistic fragmentation, the disintegration of body and sexual identity, in the name of a form of writing which has come to be known as '*écriture féminine*'.[64] The first is expressed most clearly by Sandra Gilbert and Susan Gubar:

> For all literary artists, of course, self-definition necessarily precedes self-assertion: the creative 'I AM' cannot be uttered if the 'I' knows not what it is. But for the female artist the essential process of self-definition is complicated by all those patriarchal definitions that intervene between herself and herself.[65]

The second can be related to a number of French feminist writers, amongst them Hélène Cixous:

> If there is a 'propriety of woman', it is paradoxically her capacity to depropriate unselfishly, body without end, without appendage, without principal 'parts' … This doesn't mean that she's an undifferentiated magma, but that she doesn't lord it over her body or her desire… Her libido is cosmic, just as her unconscious is worldwide. Her writing can only keep going, without ever inscribing or discerning contours.[66]

We can recognise the awkward proximity of these conceptions to Alvarez's consistency of representation on the one hand, and, on the other, to Spender's disintegration of writing as a femininity spilling out of itself.[67] In fact, these early responses to Plath provide an early version of a still unresolved drama about femininity and writing. As we read them, we can watch unfold the stark alternative between, on the one hand, a masculist aesthetic and, on the other, a form of writing connoted feminine only to the extent that it is projected on to the underside of language and speech.

But there is also, I would argue, a strange proximity between these two accounts of women's writing, in the way that they each situate the woman inside an exclusively personal struggle to express either the self or the non-self. Both seem to remove the woman writer from historical process, the first through the image of a sustained lineage of women writers across all historical differences (cultural perpetuity for women), the second by dissolving the very possibility for women of any purchase on historical time. And both seem attached to the same valorisation of high culture, whether in its coherent 'realist' or its fragmented 'modernist' mode (it has been pointed out that the argument between them inherits the terms of the realist/modern dispute[68]). We should also ask – since this will be such a central issue in relation to Plath – what image of sexual relations these different accounts of women's writing seem to imply – a battle of the sexes, meaning a battle between unequivocally gendered and sexually differentiated egos,[69] or a disintegration into a body without identity, shape or purpose, where no difference, and no battle, can take place.

And what, finally, is this image of the body in language? When feminism takes up, and valorises for women, the much-denigrated image of a hysterical outpouring of the body, it has often found itself doing so, understandably, at the cost of idealising the body itself. According to this argument, writing castigated as hysterical is writing where the passage of the body through language is too insistently present; it is writing in which a body, normally ordered by the proprieties of language and sexual identity, gets too close. Fragmented and disorderly, this writing refuses to submit to the aesthetic norms of integration and wholeness against which it is diagnosed and judged. Its body can be called feminine to the precise degree that it flouts the rigidity (the masculinity) of the requisite forms of literary cohesion and control.

In a classic feminist move, this argument inverts a traditional devalorisation of women. But in the very process of this inversion, what is most discomforting about the body disappears. The body must be positive, it must figure as pure (aesthetic and moral) value if its low-grade ideological colouring is to be removed. Thus uplifted, this body often seems remote from sex and substance, strangely incorporeal, suspended in pure fluidity or cosmic time. Ironically, then, this celebration of the woman's body in language seems partly to share with the criticism it answers the image of a body that repels. No writer more than Plath has been more clearly hystericised by the worst of a male literary tradition. No writer more than Plath, as we will now see, demonstrates the limits of responding to that tradition, and its barely concealed repulsion, by cleaning up the woman writer, thereby re-repressing one part of what that tradition so fiercely, and with such ceaseless misogyny, expels.

Notes

1. In a long letter to the *Guardian* on the subject of the defacement of Plath's grave and the surrounding controversy, Ted Hughes wrote: 'A rational observer might conclude (correctly in my opinion) that the Fantasia about Sylvia Plath is more needed than the facts.' Ted Hughes, 'The place where Sylvia Plath should rest in peace', *Guardian*, 20 April 1989. For a full discussion of this controversy, see Chapter 3 of my book *The Haunting of Sylvia Plath*.
2. Edward Butscher, 'In Search of Sylvia: An Introduction', in Butscher, ed., *Sylvia Plath: The Woman and the Work*, New York: Dodd, Mead and Company, 1977, p. 5.
3. Richard Howard, 'Sylvia Plath: "And I Have No Face, I Have Wanted to Efface Myself" ', in Charles Newman, ed., *The Art of Sylvia Plath*, Bloomington and London: Indiana University Press, 1970, pp. 77–88 (p. 87). The passage is cited by Richard Howard as a 'casual remark that seems to me to be a provocative way into a better understanding of Sylvia Plath's "mythic" structure', in Richard Allen Blessing, 'The Shape of the Psyche: Vision and Technique in the Late Poems of Sylvia Plath', in Gary Lane, ed., *Sylvia Plath: New Views on the Poetry*, Baltimore: Johns Hopkins University Press, 1979, pp. 57–73 (p. 69).
4. Hugh Kenner, 'Sincerity Kills', in Gary Lane, *Sylvia Plath*, pp. 33–44 (p. 35).
5. Shoshana Felman, 'Turning the Screw of Interpretation', in Felman, ed., *Literature and Psychoanalysis: The Question of Reading Otherwise*, New Haven: Yale University Press, 1977, pp. 94–207; also in Felman, *Writing and Madness*, Ithaca: Cornell University Press, 1986.
6. For the critique of Freud, see Marie Balmary, *Psycho-Analysing Psycho-Analysis*, Baltimore: Johns Hopkins University Press, 1982; Marianne Krull, *Freud and His Father*, London: Hutchinson, 1986; Jeffrey Masson, *Freud: The Assault on Truth – Freud's Suppression of the Seduction Theory*, London: Faber, 1984; for replies, see Ann Scott, 'Feminism and the Seductiveness of the Real Event', *Feminist Review*, Special Issue: *Family Secrets: Child Sexual Abuse*, 28, Spring 1988, pp. 88–102; Jean Laplanche, *New Foundations for Psychoanalysis*, Oxford: Blackwell, 1989.
7. Melanie Klein, 'Notes on Some Schizoid Mechanisms', 1946, in Juliet Mitchell, ed., *The Selected Melanie Klein*, Harmondsworth: Penguin, 1986, pp. 176–200 (p. 183).
8. Anne Stevenson, *Bitter Fame: A Life of Sylvia Plath*, Boston: Houghton Mifflin, London: Viking, 1989.
9. David Holbrook, *Sylvia Plath: Poetry and Existence*, London: Athlone, 1976. The only previous full study of Plath was the short book by Eileen M. Aird, *Sylvia Plath*, published by Harper & Row in the United States and by Oliver & Boyd (a branch of Longmans) in Edinburgh in 1973.
10. George MacDonald, *Lilith*, 1895, London: Gollancz 1962, pp. 374–5; H. Rider Haggard, *She*, London: Longmans, Green & Company, 1887. Interestingly, the passage from MacDonald (up to 'divided against itself') also forms one of the two epigraphs to Sandra Gilbert and Susan Gubar's study of the nineteenth-century woman writer, *The Madwoman in the Attic: The Woman Writer and the Nineteenth Century Literary Imagination*, New Haven/London: Yale University Press, 1979. The second epigraph is the passage from Laura Riding's 'Eve's Side of It': 'It was not at first clear to me exactly what I was, except that I was someone who was being made to do certain things by someone else who was really the same person as myself – I have always called her Lilith. And yet the facts were mine and not Lilith's.' For Gilbert and Gubar the myth of Lilith and women's response to, reappropriation of, it forms in some sense the frame of the nineteenth-century literary imagination.
11. Holbrook, *Sylvia Plath: Poetry and Existence*, p. 7.
12. MacDonald, *Lilith*, p. 374.
13. Stevenson, *Bitter Fame*.
14. Stephen Spender. 'Warnings from the Grave', in Charles Newman, ed., *The Art*

of Sylvia Plath, pp. 199–203 (p. 203), first published in a review of *Ariel in The New Republic*, vol. 154, no. 25, 18 June 1966.

15. D. M. Thomas, *The White Hotel*, London: Gollancz, 1981.

16. Mary Ellman, *Thinking About Women*, 1969, London: Virago, 1979, Chapter 3, 'Feminine Stereotypes', pp. 84–5.

17. Sigmund Freud, 'The Dissolution of the Oedipus Complex', 1924, 'Some Psychical Consequences of the Anatomical Distinction Between the Sexes', 1925, *Standard Edition*, vol. XIX, pp. 171–9, 241–58; Pelican Freud, 7, pp. 313–22, 323–43.

18. Julia Kristeva, *Powers of Horror*, New York: Columbia University Press, 1982.

19. D. W. Winnicott, 'Creativity and its Origins', in *Playing and Reality*, London: Tavistock, 1971, pp. 65–85. The reference to Robert Graves is pointed out by Masud Khan in discussion when the paper was originally presented as 'Split-Off Male and Female Elements Found Clinically in Men and Women: Theoretical Inferences', 1966, in J. Linden, ed., *Psychoanalytic Forum*, vol. 4, New York: International Universities Press, 1972, pp. 362–93 (p. 386). Interestingly, Masud Khan is the analyst Holbrook refers to when describing his book's circulation in analytic circles.

20. See, for example, Murray M. Schwartz and Coppélia Kahn, eds, *Representing Shakespeare: New Psychoanalytic Essays*, Baltimore/London: Johns Hopkins University Press, 1980.

21. Holbrook, *Sylvia Plath: Poetry and Existence*, p. 172. Holbrook also refers to R. D. Laing, Harry Guntrip and W. R. D. Fairbairn.

22. ibid., p. 180.

23. John Ruskin, *Sesame and Lilies*, first published 1885: London: Allen & Unwin, 1919, pp. 108, 136.

24. Joyce Carol Oates, 'The Death Throes of Romanticism', in Paul Alexander, ed., *Ariel Ascending*, New York: Harper & Row, 1985, pp. 26–45 (pp. 31, 41).

25. Holbrook, *Sylvia Plath: Poetry and Existence*, p. 172.

26. ibid., p. 179; compare also: 'a heroine of women's liberation movements. Her rejection of certain kinds of femininity (and, as I would put it, her hatred of certain aspects of woman)', p. 2.

27. ibid., pp. 20, 5.

28. ibid., p. 2.

29. ibid., pp. 19, 2.

30. ibid., pp. 2, 19 (twice), 20.

31. ibid., p. 2.

32. *On Scrutiny*, see Frances Mulhern, *The Moment of Scrutiny*, London: Verso, 1979; on its prehistory in relation to imperialism, see Chris Baldick, *The Social Mission of English Criticism 1848–1832*, Oxford: Oxford University Press, 1983.

33. *The New Poetry*, selected and edited by A. Alvarez, Harmondsworth: Penguin, 1962.

34. Alvarez, 'The New Poetry, or, Beyond the Gentility Principle', Introduction to *The New Poetry*, p. 27. For a discussion of the ethnocentrism of this cultural use of psychoanalysis, see Alan Sinfield, *Literature, Politics and Culture in Postwar Britain*, London: Routledge, 1989, Chapter 7, 'Cultural plunder and the savage within', pp. 116–51.

35. The circle is, however, a close one. Holbrook is included as a poet in *The New Poetry*, and Hugh Kenner (see 'Sincerity Kills', above) is one of the two writers to whom Alvarez dedicated his book *The Shaping Spirit* in 1958 (Alvarez, *The Shaping Spirit*, London: Chatto, 1967). Holbrook sees Alvarez's promotion of Plath (and Hughes) as 'menacing' the very 'shaping spirit' he claims to support: see Holbrook, *Lost Bearings in English Poetry*, London: Vision, 1977, p. 239: 'but he does not discuss the essential problem of the loss of the shaping spirit in our time, and indeed in his influence on Sylvia Plath and Ted Hughes menaced it'.

36. Saul Bellow, cited Alvarez, 'Beyond All This Fiddle', in *Beyond All This Fiddle*,

London: Allen Lane, 1968, pp. 3–21 (p. 6).

37. Holbroook, *Human Hope and the Death Instinct: An Exploration of Psychoanalytic Theories of Human Nature and Their Implications for Culture and Education*, London: Pergamon, 1971, p. 240.

38. Alvarez, 'Beyond All This Fiddle', in *Beyond All This Fiddle*, p. 21.

39. Alvarez, 'Sylvia Plath', in *Beyond All This Fiddle*, pp. 45–58 (p. 45). The article was originally transmitted as a radio broadcast in 1963, and was subsequently published in *The Review*, 9, October 1963, pp. 20–6.

40. Alvarez, 'The New Poetry', *The New Poetry*, p. 25.

41. Alvarez, 'Beyond All This Fiddle', in *Beyond All This Fiddle*, p. 17.

42. Holbrook, *Sylvia Plath: Poetry and Existence*, p. 3.

43. Alvarez, *The Savage God: A Study of Suicide*, London: Weidenfeld & Nicolson, 1971, p. 216.

44. ibid., p. 33, p. xiii.

45. ibid., p. xi.

46. Alvarez, 'Sylvia Plath', in *Beyond All This Fiddle*, p. 57.

47. Alvarez is one of the few critics not to take Plath to task for identification with the Jew in her late poetry. But Jewishness as a concept in his writing is no less caught up in the selection and privileging of distinct classes and cultural forms. Judaism, he writes, is the only religious tone present in the modern arts: 'a force working perennially on the side of sanity'. Jewishness is 'worldliness': 'a precondition of survival'. But 'worldliness' is also a negative value, associated with cinema, which is 'corporate', 'technological', 'commercial' ('since the less we believe in minority culture the more we believe in audience ratings and box office returns as a criterion of excellence'), 'disposable', and 'cynical', and cinema is 'that exclusively twentieth-century and dominantly Jewish art form'. Jewishness is therefore cause or symptom (a dangerous and cynical materiality) *and* cure (only its worldliness will survive). Alvarez, 'Beyond All This Fiddle', in *Beyond All This Fiddle*, pp. 7, 18.

48. Sinfield, *Literature, Politics and Culture in Postwar Britain*, p. 226.

49. Alvarez, comment on the back of Sylvia Plath, *The Colossus*, London: Heinemann, 1960: see Sinfield, p. 226.

50. Alvarez, 'Literature of the Holocaust', in *Beyond All This Fiddle*, pp. 22–33 (p. 31).

51. Alvarez, 'Beyond All This Fiddle', in *Beyond All This Fiddle*, p. 14.

52. Sandra Gilbert and Susan Gubar, *The Madwoman in the Attic*, especially Chapter 1, 'The Queen's Looking Glass: Female Creativity, Male Images of Women, and the Metaphor of Literary Paternity', pp. 3–44.

53. Joyce Carol Oates, 'The Death Throes of Romanticism', p. 26.

54. *CP*, 1960, pp. 149–50, first published in *Crossing the Water*, London: Faber & Faber, 1971.

55. Oates, 'The Death Throes of Romanticism', p. 38.

56. Alvarez and Donald Davie, 'A Discussion', *The Review*, 1, April–May 1962, pp. 15–21. Davie comments: 'Of course I refuse the masturbation analogy', p. 18.

57. Holbrook, *English for Maturity: English in the Secondary School*, Cambridge: Cambridge University Press, 1961, p. 45.

58. Holbrook, *Sylvia Plath: Poetry and Existence*, pp. 167–73.

59. Spender, 'Warnings from the Grave', p. 202.

60. Alvarez, 'Beyond All This Fiddle', p. 14.

61. ibid., p. 11.

62. Alvarez, 'The New Poetry, or, Beyond the Gentility Principle', p. 32.

63. Alvarez, 'Sylvia Plath', p. 52.

64. Gilbert and Gubar, *The Madwoman in the Attic*, p. 17; Hélène Cixous, 'The Laugh of the Medusa', *Signs*, 1, Summer 1976, reprinted in Elaine Marks and Isabelle de Courtivron, eds, *New French Feminisms*, Brighton: Harvester, 1981, pp. 245–64.

See also Luce Irigaray, *This Sex Which Isn't One*, Ithaca: Cornell University Press, 1985. For a discussion of the two accounts, see Toril Moi, *Sexual/Textual Politics: Feminist Literary Theory*, London/New York: Methuen, 1985; Rachel Bowlby, 'Flight Reservations', *Oxford Literary Review*, vol. 10, 1988, pp. 61–72; on French feminism, Ann Rosalind Jones, 'Writing the Body: Toward an Understanding of l'Écriture féminine', in Elaine Showalter, ed., *The New Feminist Criticism: Essays on Women, Literature and Theory*, London: Virago, New York: Pantheon, 1985, pp. 361–77.
65. Gilbert and Gubar, *The Madwoman in the Attic*, p. 17.
66. Hélène Cixous, 'The Laugh of the Medusa', p. 259.
67. Interestingly, Oates's reading of Plath sits right in the centre of the two. The death throes of Romanticism which she reads in Plath's writing are the death throes of the post-Renaissance 'very masculine, combative, ideal of an "I" set against all the other "I"s', but Oates explicitly sets herself against the aesthetic of the fragment, looking to a future in which the unified and total will be restored: 'Hopefully a world of totality awaits us, not a played-out world of fragments.' Oates, 'The Death Throes of Romanticism', pp. 30, 44.
68. See Toril Moi, *Sexual/Textual Politics: Feminist Literary Theory*.
69. The first chapter of the first volume of Gilbert and Gubar's three-volume study of twentieth-century women's writing is called 'The Battle of the Sexes', and it opens with a discussion of Plath and Hughes. Gilbert and Gubar, *No Man's Land: The Place of the Woman Writer in the Twentieth Century*, volume 1, *The War of the Words*, New Haven/London: Yale University Press, 1988.

12

Julia Kristeva, 'Is Sensation a Language?', in *Le Temps sensible*: *Proust et l'expérience littéraire*.

Paris: Gallimard, 'NRF essais', 1994, pp. 280–306.

Editor's Introduction

Through an interpretation of Freud's 'Project for a Scientific Psychology', as well as a close reading of Proust, Kristeva explores the relation between sensation and perception, experience and speaking, flesh and signs, style and meaning. Or, more accurately, Kristeva shows how sensation and experience actually enter and become an intimate part of language. She thus challenges the reigning view which sees sensation and language as binary opposites, and thus incompatible with one another. Through Proust's writing, sensation enters language – this is Kristeva's most important and salient thesis. To affirm this, she takes seriously Merleau-Ponty's arguments about the reversibility of sensation: to touch is inseparable from being tangible, to see is inseparable from being visible, and so on.

Experience – sensation – is *sui generis*, yet it is knowable: this is the nub of Kristeva's argument in this very important chapter. For with it she challenges the Lacanian shibboleth that there is only articulated language. For Lacan – as for certain cognitivist psychologists – there is no prediscursive domain; there is always judgement – the sensation of red here means: 'I experience red.' Kristeva, then, is concerned to look at sensation in its autonomy. True, access to sensation does require 'an enlarged and subtle rhetoric ... capable of naming the unnameable'. But this does not alter the fact that it is accessible, and even communicable.

Through a re-examination of Plato's cave theory which hides another cave of sensation (hence Kristeva's discussion of a 'sensory cave'), and through a detailed analysis of Proust's writing, where sensation becomes located in a 'second apartment', Kristeva is able to make a case for the autonomy of sensation, just as, in previous studies, she was able to make a case for the relative autonomy of the semiotic.

What is of special interest here, for the reader of this collection on writing and psychoanalysis, is that Kristeva, as well as returning to Freud's theory of experience as a kind of transcription, also examines the way Proust's writing becomes a transcription of his sensations – a transcription charged with therapeutic effects. Proust writes the better to appreciate his experience, just as he engages in experiences (viewing of a flagellation scene) to boost the emotional charge of his writing: 'lived experience slides into the representation'. Instead of an opposition, and thus a discontinuity, between lived experience and writing, Kristeva argues for a continuity between the two realms – to the point, perhaps, where one can speak of a 'transubstantiation'. It is the dynamic of Proust's writing, we find, which is also reminiscent of analytic listening in so far as such listening must try to identify with the analysand's *experience*, just as Proust's writing of the flagellation scene – including, and especially, the rhythm of the sentence structure – is a result of his identification with the experience of M. de Charlus. Memory – experience – is embodied in the rhythm of Proust's sentences.

Particularly with regard to the notion of the other's experience, Kristeva is able to refer to Merleau-Ponty's philosophy of perception. What interests her here is Merleau-Ponty's view that we are not, as individuals, each locked in our own experience and thus totally cut off from the experience of another. Instead, the philosopher argues, experience – which so often results from something external – is inseparable from a certain form of communication based on the 'becoming-thing' of words – that is, on a form of transubstantiation. People who suffer from autism, Kristeva notes, experience words becoming things to an extraordinary degree, so that words and sensations intermingle, almost to the point where words *are* sensations, and vice versa. Autistic experience indeed underpins a significant part of Kristeva's analysis of sensation and language.

Is Sensation a Language?

Everyone who has read Proust has been awakened to an unsuspected, unheard-of sensibility, the pursuit of which, whether in their memory, readings, or meetings, never comes to an end. Everyone who knew Proust was bedazzled by the fineness and intensity of his perceptions and his passions:

From his childhood, Proust must have been, for experiences of feeling, a marvellous subject: he offered no barrier to its instability; with him there was always somewhere for the inner bird to alight. He was capable of all the ideas that passion can give: none was stopped or stifled along the way by any conscious decision....[1]

Proust himself, forgetting for a moment that he was going to look for a style in order to capture lost time, declared that a genius is quite simply a sensitive being:

It may be that, for the creation of a work of literature, *imagination* and *sensibility* are interchangeable qualities, and that the latter may with no great harm be substituted for the former.... A man born with sensibility but without imagination might, in spite of this deficiency, be able to write *admirable* novels.[2]

Of course, Proust was not forgetting the time he spent studying Plato, and he declared that from the very outset everything was 'interpreted by the intellect': 'one does not know what feeling is so long as it is not brought within the range of the intellect'.[3] However, through what is 'intellectualised', another reality is perceived: 'One distinguishes, and with what difficulty, the lineaments of what one has felt.'[4]

Here Proust summarises and reopens a philosophical debate whose origin is in fact lost in the beginnings of metaphysics, one that phenomenology – contemporary with Proust but apparently unknown to him – was to reformulate in terms close to his intuitions.

For the moment, let us briefly take up the question again at the point to which psychoanalysis took it. Before Lacan inscribed it within a theory of language, psychoanalytic theory clearly did not neglect sensation. But the Freudian conception of sensation[5] seems at the very least ambiguous, if not ambivalent. Indeed, by listening to patients' words, does the analyst have access to their sensations? How can interpretation imagine and reconstruct a psychical reality which reveals itself through language without being identical with it?

1. Perception and Consciousness According to Freud: Difficulties of Identity and Difference

As we know, the notion of sensation is not central in Freud's work. He nevertheless speaks of it in his *Letters to Wilhelm Fliess* (1887–1902), in the 'Project for a Scientific Psychology' [1895],[6] in *The Interpretation of Dreams* (1900), and in the very dense and much-commented-upon short 'Note upon the "Mystic Writing-Pad" ' (1925). Despite the mutations in Freud's thought, some constant features throughout this series of texts may be noted.

Thus, perception is from the outset associated with the perception–consciousness system which, being incapable of retaining traces, is without memory.

However, in the beginning were perceptions. What is a perception?: '*W* [*Wahrnehmungen* (perceptions)] are neurones in which perceptions originate, to which consciousness attaches, but which in themselves retain no trace of what has happened. For *consciousness and memory are mutually exclusive.*'[7]

Then follows the '*Wz* [*Wahrnehmungszeichen* (indication of perception)]', which 'is the first *registration* of the perceptions; it is *quite incapable of consciousness*, and arranged according to associations by simultaneity'.

'*Ub* (*Unbewusstsein* [unconscious]) is the second registration, arranged according to other (perhaps causal) relations.'

Let us keep in mind that perception 'registers' 'simultaneity', while the unconscious registers 'causality'.

'*Ub* traces would perhaps correspond to *conceptual memories*; equally inaccessible to consciousness.'

As regards the *preconscious*, it is a

> third transcription, attached to word-representations and corresponding to our official ego ... [T]his *secondary thought consciousness* is subsequent in time, and is probably linked to the hallucinatory activation of word-presentations, so that the neurones of consciousness would once again be perceptual neurones and in themselves without memory.

And further on: 'I explain the peculiarities of the psychoneuroses by supposing that the *translation* of some of the material *has not occurred*.'[8]

We can return to these passages – not for their neurological basis, which is no doubt unsustainable in the present state of research, but to take up the *model of strata* (Perception, Unconscious, Preconscious), structurally differentiated owing to the presence or absence in them of language and memory. As proposed by Freud, this model necessitates a *translation* of these strata as the condition of normal psychical functioning.

In addition, it is necessary to guard against an abusive and inattentive reading of the term 'perception-consciousness' which could lead us into thinking that Freud is postulating some kind of *identity* between Perception and Consciousness. On the contrary, the whole Freudian project seems to be geared to keeping apart the poles Perception-Consciousness. Notably this is so in Freud's insistence on the *late* coming of word-presentations in the Preconscious, and on '*secondary* thought consciousness', linked to the reactivation of verbal hallucination.

What Freud calls the *Wahrnehmung* (*W*), 'perception',[9] is then set in motion by quantities, as small as possible, so as to allow the change from quantity to quality. This third system of neurones, called 'perceptual neurones',[10] is inserted between ϕ-permeable and ψ-impermeable neurones: *W* transmits neither quantity nor quality to ψ, and only excites it.

> In the case of every external perception a qualitative excitation occurs in *W*, which in the first instance, however, has no significance for ψ. It must be added that the w excitation leads to w discharge, and information of this ... reaches ψ. *The information of the discharge from ω is thus the index of quality or of reality for ψ.*[11]

At a second stage, both logically and chronologically, when the function of judgement is instituted, 'perceptions, on account of their possible connection with the wished-for object, are arousing interest, and their complexes are dissected into an unassimilable component (the thing) and one known to the ego from its own experience (attribute, activity) – what we call *understanding*'.[12] Let us note the simultaneous emergence of the *desirable* (and unassimilable) object and of *understanding* clearly distinguished from the prior sensation-perception articulated 'information' and 'indices'.

Things could not be clearer: perception (*Wahrnehmung*) 'excites' understanding which only happens secondarily, and this thanks to *two types* of contact with verbal expression. Important here is the dissimilarity of these distinct semiologies which, according to Freud, govern the accession of perception to expression.

On the one hand, painful objects make one *cry out*, and these cries give the object its specific character as an object of suffering capable of leaving behind a conscious memory; by contrast, perception which is not inscribed in verbal expressions (whether *cries* or not) is not memorisable. With these objects which make one cry out, Freud associates a second category of objects which constantly emit certain noises: complex perceptive objects where sound plays an original role.

On the other hand, a secondary process occurs: 'In virtue of the trend towards *imitation, which emerges during judging*, it is possible to find the information of movement [carried out by the ego itself] attaching to this sound-image.'[13] Thus the series of movements may become conscious and, furthermore, sounds associated with perceptions can be freely emitted. In observing these auditory signs, the subject sees memories well up within him and become conscious like perceptions which can be cathected by the ψ system.

Freud notes: 'Thus we have found that it is characteristic of the process of *cognitive thought* that during it attention is from the first directed to the *indications* of thought-discharge, to the indications of speech.'[14]

Here Freud takes a logical short cut that we cannot pass over in silence, for the *indications* of thought discharge no doubt *initiate* the process of *cognitive* thought, but are not identical with it. Similarly, the auditory *imitation* or the cry is not to be confused with the *indications of speech*, as Freud brusquely assumes, forgetting that he himself had used the term *index* to specify perception and its expression. The liaison between a sensation (whether painful or sonorous) and a vocal utterance (of distress or of an imitation of an object) puts the subject, who is its support, into what Freud will call[15] *Representations of things*, and not into the *Representation of words*. These are 'symbolic equations' (cry, imitation) - if we return to Klein–Segal's terminology[16] – belonging to a register of significance other than that of verbal representation (or the linguistic signifier). This is the register of the mnemic trace, of 'figurability', of 'container' or 'fetish', without there being any distinction between the thing represented and the representing ego. It can develop or be integrated into a sign-judgement, as it can remain at its own specific level, without acceding to representation or to a signifier.

In reality, what allows the Freudian model of the psychical apparatus to function as a cognitive apparatus is the *unconscious*, the import of which is to be seen in the metaphor of the magic writing-pad.

The psychical perceptive apparatus has two layers: one external (the protective shield against stimuli), the other internal (the surface receiving the stimuli), called the Perception–Consciousness system. As a result, the celluloid and the waxed paper are compared to the Perception–Consciousness system with its protective shield against stimuli, while the wax on which the trace is scratched is compared to the Unconscious. It is because the Unconscious is a receptive surface protected from both internal and external perceptual excitations that traces can be recorded such that they imitate motor activity and become, in time, judgements. This model presupposes several conditions:

• a stocking and a reactivation of preconscious verbal representations;
• a diminution of the quantity of perceptual excitation and possibly the intervention of a pharmacological agent;
• the intervention of a *third* factor at the heart of this dual interaction, serving simultaneously as a shield protecting from excitation and as a link with the universe of signs. This would be somewhat like a pre-Oedipal, paternal function, a support for primary identification. Freud was to consider these conditions of 'thirdness' necessary for the advent of signs and thought only when he abandoned the neurological perceptive model in order to commit himself resolutely to the successive developments in his discovery of psychoanalysis. The result of this discrepancy is that Freudian theory seen as a whole bequeathes to us a conception of sensation–perception *separated* from properly analytical considerations about identification or the Oedipus complex as conditions of mental functioning.

In addition, after having isolated the *Wahrnehmung W* system from the φ exogenous system and the ψ endogenous system, Freud identifies Perception with Consciousness. To do this he uses a paradox or a rush to logic (which Lacan will cultivate) that consists in identifying pre-language with language (cry and imitation = judgement). This step places before us two possibilities. Either we take account of the rush to logic (with the confusion?), which amounts to disregarding the stratification of the psychical apparatus clearly evident in the magic writing-pad, or, alternatively, we rehabilitate this 'foliated' functioning of the psychical apparatus in trying to restore to the logical order of judgement, to which psychical functioning aspires, the prior or deeper stages of *quasi-signs*. Among the latter, in my own terminology, is 'the semiotic';[17] that which, according to the Freud of *The Origins of Psycho-Analysis*, is 'cries', 'imitations' and 'perception-excitations'. They can become conscious only by being linked to language and to unconscious desires, while relating to a different register.

If one accepts the second hypothesis, one sees that access to the speaking subject's sensation requires the possibility of an enlarged and subtle rhetoric. This would have to be capable of naming its unnameable experiences, on condition of not reducing things to a 'pure signifier' but utilising the capacity for perceptive and sensory regression. Whether therapist or writer, the one who is committed to bestowing signs or even a style on this sensory cave which, for the majority of people, is unnameable is called to a true experience (*Erlebnis* and *Erfahrung*[18]). Having identified with both perceived and perceiver, he/she becomes more than just 'decoder' – indeed, the 'encoder'. A 'nomothete', as Plato puts it in the *Cratylus*, a Homer as poet and legislator, creator of a language for a singular experience.

Before returning to this *poiesis* of sensory nomination, let us pause briefly on the cognitive aporias with regard to sensation–perception.

2. The Cognitivists' Appropriate Sensation

The cognitivists are the only modern theorists to be interested in the series sensation–perception–emotion. For the most part they take the view that sensations are *attributive judgements* (the sensation of red is equivalent to the proposition 'I experience [*sens*] red: 'red' is an *objet*, a *logical attribute*) or *adverbial* (I feel [*sens*] *as if* it was red': here 'red' is an *adverb*), accompanied or not accompanied by emotion, which, in their turn, are *evaluative judgements*. Whether it be at the centre of perception or simply its condition, *cognitive appreciation* is omnipresent in sensation, according to these authors.[19]

However, a critique of this position has been initiated starting from phylogenetic and ontogenetic considerations: fear in animals when perceiving certain circumstances is rooted not in an evaluative *judgement* but in an initial *impulsion*; the facial expression of an infant affected by perceived colour or sound becomes evident *before* the acquisition of evaluative logic, and so on. In psychology since 1980, R. B. Zajonc (in *American Psychologist*) has emphasised the fact that olfactory or gustative stimuli, as with the infant's reaction to sound, provoke immediate emotional reactions which do not necessitate any judgement. Affective and sensory states can be induced by drugs and hormones (without taking account of the evaluation that the subject makes of the information received, Valium changes the perceptual and emotive state). Also important is the fact that emotions can be stimulated, in animals as in man, without using the neocortex implied in judgement.[20] Furthermore, in many species a direct route has been observed running from the retina to the hypothalamus: this retino-hypothalamic route allows the organism to generate emotions by purely sensory 'input'. In man, there is not sufficient evidence for this to be established, but it would explain the 'non-cognitive preference' for tones and polygons, spontaneously picked out in certain tests, even when they are jumbled up beyond recognition.

Consequently, many researchers conclude that sensations–emotions are 'susceptible' to rational evaluation, but the propositional attitude *is not* a necessary condition for them. Accordingly, authors like S. G. Clarke[21] have proposed considering sensations *and* feelings ('feelings as sensations') as units of information *insufficiently complex* either to have a propositional form, or to be judgements (of threat, danger, defeat, etc.). '(Evaluative) cognitive penetration' can occur at different levels in sensation, but it is not absolutely necessary.

In fact, certain sensations are 'cognitively impenetrable': akrazia (emotional retardation or lag) persists, even if affective judgement changes and becomes dynamic; in other words, the rational control of sensations is not enough to change them. However, the author concludes that constraints of normativity and signification weigh on perceptions and emotions before they come under control; but these constraints are of *another order* and must not be confused with propositional attitudes such as 'belief' or 'evaluation', and they cannot be described by means of syntax, semantics or argument.

3. The Platonic Cave Hides a Sensory Cave

Let us leave open this debate about whether a sensation is a thought. This is a sharp debate in current philosophy, but it goes back to the sources of philosophy itself. We will try in what follows to show that it can be at the heart of diametrically opposed conceptions of psychical life. This is an original debate if ever there was one, for we find the trace of it – or rather, its scar – in Plato when, in the *The Republic*, he evokes the *cave*, its prisoners and the shadows projected on to its wall. These 'shadows' are the '*symbol of sense experience*', which means that they are, from that moment on, intelligible realities. The shadows are of two kinds: either original and primary, or secondary. Both, however, must be illuminated by the Fire located beyond the wall as a symbol of the Sun, itself a symbol of Good and Evil. Of the external world the prisoner perceives only shadows, but were he to leave the cave, he would be dazzled by the Sun. He must therefore move to an intermediate reality, which – being neither a sensory illusion nor an invisible secret, but a mathematical construction of forms – allows access to true knowledge. We are thus caught, since these Greek beginnings, in an *aporia of sensation*: irreducible to Ideas yet always dependent on them, sensation cannot be adequate to the Intelligible (since the Intelligible precedes it, posited as it is from the beginning), and yet it exists only by making itself intelligible. The cave of Platonic 'shadows' retains from sensations only the idea of a rudimentary stage of representation: the realm of illusion. Trapped by deception, sensation is necessarily false, for it is always dependent on the Intelligible and flawed in relation to it.

The difficulty of approaching sensation impels me to make an abrupt leap in the therapeutic relation which faces up to it. Modern psychiatric, neurological, psychoanalytic clinical practice is challenged by an enigmatic affection: *autism*, the symptom of which is increasingly supposed to consist in the subject's failure to acquire language, while an often complex sensory life underlies this mutism.[22] If we allude to this dramatic affection and to the debates it raises for specialists, this is due to the theoretical resonances to which it gives rise in an examination of sensation and its link with language.

From the drama of autism, we are led to push philosophical trial and error still further so as to present the hypothesis of what should indeed be called *another cave*. Even more profound and untranslatable, because it is deprived of the intelligible and evaluative Fire–Sun, this would be a *sensory cave bereft of symbols* (bereft of 'shadows' in the Platonic sense). There, sensory experience (*Erlebnis*), not yet informed by cognitive experience (*Erfahrung*) and often definitively rebellious towards it, can nevertheless find *Representations of things* in which it forms and arranges itself, and acts. This sensory experience, brought by Representations of things, is an essential part of the psychic experience of every speaking subject. *Representations of words* do not necessarily translate it. If it is true that we have a *sensory cave*, some of us live it as psychical catastrophe (autistic people are the extreme limit), while others derive *jouissance* from it (hysterics complain of the discrepancy between *feeling* and *speaking*), while yet others try to bring it to a *normative* discourse, producing this coalescence of sensations and linguistic signs called style.

In proposing the hypothesis of the omnipresence of the sensory cave and of its greater or lesser irreducibility to language, are we in the process of subscribing to the thesis of an endogenous *universal autism* anterior to the 'depressive position' at the edge of psychical life as postulated by Melanie Klein? Not exactly. In a rather more 'economic' perspective, not based on evolution or on stages of development, we can situate the sensory cave as a constitutive part of the psychical apparatus in so far as it is *heterogeneity*. The psychical apparatus is a stratified *signifiance*[23] that linguistic and cognitive imperialism has a tendency to conceal and to restrict to the single dimension of language seen purely in terms of the Idea.

The autistic person is withdrawn in this sensory cave in a way that is tragic for those close to him, and probably for himself as well. He fixes this cave and renders it untranslatable. Frances Tustin[24] has broadened the notion of autism in uncovering a pocket of autism in the neurotic personality, the avatar of an autism overcome – unless this be, precisely, the index of something universal and permanent, constitutive of the psyche. The question can be envisaged differently. If sensation–perception, the essential and archaic domain of psychical experience, is not absorbed by language and remains, in all subjects, more or less irreducible to it, then this irreducibility between the sensory and the cognitive is not necessarily lived in the distressing form of an autistic residue, but in other ways as exemplified by, among other things, perversion, art and psychoanalysis.

4. The 'Second Apartment'

In finding a language for this opaque, non-verbal sensory experience that is deep sleep,[25] just as he also finds one for the sensations of perverse pleasure, Proust succeeds where the autistic person fails.

'I have always said – and have proved by experience – that the most powerful soporific is sleep itself',[26] the narrator maintains in *Sodom and Gomorrah*, having explored a strange and complex space. In passing from conscious wakefulness to a sleep which 'does not dwell under the tutelage of foresight, in the company, even latent, of reflexion', he arrives at *deep sleep*.[27]

'Perhaps each night we accept the risk of experiencing, while we are asleep, sufferings which we regard as null and void because they will be felt in the course of a sleep which we think [*croyons*] is without consciousness.'[28]

The sleep that we think (*croyons*)[29] is without consciousness strangely resembles Plato's cave of shadows, yet it is even deeper and even more inaccessible: a 'dark and indefinable area'. For, initially lit and then stopped by the fire (the reference to which in Plato's *Republic* was noted earlier), this deep Proustian sleep takes over when the fire (of all intelligibility?) dies down. Without light, it is only the intensity of sensations that suffuses and overwhelms the sleeper. More than 'another stage', this sleep is a closed space without a stage (*scène*): a 'second apartment', writes Proust: 'and I entered the realm of sleep, it being like a second apartment that we would have, and where, abandoning our own, we would go to sleep'.[30]

We let go, draw away, dive under. This is an enclosed space, shut off – a closed apartment. Here the audible universes of sound unfold; disembodied sounds with no one there: 'It has noises of its own, and we are sometimes violently awakened by the sound of bells, perfectly heard by our ears, although nobody has rung.'[31]

Hallucination without an object, without an other (neither object nor other person). Nothing but the sensation in the ears. And even if, now and then, the sleeper thinks he can see servants or visitors pass by, Proust insists that 'the room is empty ... nobody has called'. There is an excessive, extraordinary permanence to this sonorous solitude. Who lives in the empty apartment? Here, Proust becomes Freudian: the dreaming subject is ambivalent, ambiguous and reversible. 'The race that inhabits it, like that of our first human ancestors, is androgynous. A man in it appears a moment later in the form of a woman. Things in it show a tendency to turn into men, men into friends and enemies.'[32] For the sleeper the flow of time stops....

Here is the logic of the moment, of the simultaneity of contraries, outside time and outside any project: in this apartment of sleep: 'we descend into depths in which memory can no longer keep up with it, and on the brink of which the mind has been obliged to retrace its steps'.[33] We are then at the ultimate point of time regained where no memory may venture, where there are no mnesic traces, split off from the mind. Have psychoanalysts ever read such a precise description of psychic regression and the autistic 'hole'?

A Platonic metaphor reappears, that of 'harnessing', but as though diverging from Plato. For the harnessing of sleep – similar, according to Proust, to that of the sun – goes much further here, much deeper again, in an 'atmosphere in which there is no longer any resistance'. Neither the light of memory nor that of time can put up any resistance – unless 'some little meteorite extraneous to ourselves'[34] were to put an end to the journey and bring us back to waking consciousness.

Is this meteorite constituted by an unusual word, by a traumatic image or, by contrast, by a banal signifier apt to extract us from a dark sensory dive? Proust does not specify it, but in the following sentences he resumes his description of the paradoxical state that is deep sleep. There we can decipher the standard experience of the 'sensory cave' well before it turns into the cave of Platonic illusion:

> we awake in a dawn, not knowing who we are, being nobody ... the brain emptied of that past which was life up until then.... Then, from the black storm through which we seem to have passed (but we do not even say *we*), we emerge prostrate, without a thought, a *we* that is void of content.[35]

This *we* without content is described also as a 'being' or a 'thing' traumatised by unknown pleasure or pain: without traces or memory, without psychic unity; no ego (*moi*), no self (English in the text), no subject. Nothing but an 'azur' or an 'unknown', transformed by the dream story, remade, or, at a pinch, invented: 'What hammer-blow has the person or thing that is lying there received to make it unaware of everything, stupefied until the moment when memory, flooding back, restores consciousness or personality?'[36]

This loss of self at the heart of the sensory cave is still more clearly imagined in what follows:

Moreover, when sleep bore him so far away from the world inhabited by memory and thought, through an ether in which he was alone, more than alone, without even companionship of self-perception, he was outside the range of time and its measurements.[37]

There is no replica of self, no double, no *alter ego*. With this zero degree of alterity, 'I' is not. It is outside time: 'Perhaps indeed more than another time: another life.'[38] And yet this empty solitude is not bereft of sensations and emotions. Proust brightly calls them 'pleasures' – incommensurable pleasures, incompatible with erotic pleasures, for the pleasures of sleep hark back to another 'budget':

> We do not include the pleasures we enjoy in sleep in the inventory of the pleasures we have experienced in the course of existence.... We have had pleasure in another life which is not ours. If we enter up in a budget the pains and pleasures of dreams (which generally vanish soon enough after our waking), it is not in the current account of our everyday life.[39]

Nevertheless, this deep dreaming is not without 'thought': reflection accumulates upon waking and, passing through a voice promising a pleasant dinner, it takes the form of a sudden reminder: ' "My grandmother has only a few weeks to live, so the doctor assures us." He rings, he weeps at the thought that it will not be, as in the past, his grandmother, his dying grandmother, but an indifferent valet that will come in answer to his summons.'[40]

In this way, then, a *dream thought* arises from the 'ether' of the unnameable sensory solitude in which the 'meteorite' of anguish and desire is condensed: grandmother (and mother) are going to die. Incestuous desire mixed with aggressive ambivalence constitutes, in the same movement, the *object* of the dream (which was until then without an object), its *thought* and its *signs*. They interrupt the sensory pleasure and pain enclosed in the depths of the dream.

And yet, faced with this dichotomy between deep sleep-pleasure and ambiguous dream-desire, a question inevitably arises. Was the first 'apartment' of deep sleep, this sensory cave, a defence against deathly, incestuous desires, a regression from the confrontation with Eros and its homosexual extensions (let us note that the grandmother is replaced by a valet)? Or, on the contrary, might this remote room of inexpressible sensation, this camera obscura, figure, not as a defence against the libido, but as the archaic traces of its non-differentiation, of its fusion with the container of this not-yet *other* that the autistic person probably also experiences in his way?

Here we are faced with two theoretical options, and nothing allows for the privileging of the one rather than the other, except for the fact of Proust's insistence on lost time, on lost language. The point is to make the latter happen through writing at any price. Why this urgency of an aesthetic, metaphysical and, plainly, therapeutic nature? Maybe because there was another time, another experience, where time–thought–language *had not taken place*. If this were the case, regaining time would not simply mean being reconciled with whatever was the sense of the stimulus and was repressed (a desire, an object, a sign). Regaining time would be to make it come to pass: to extract feeling from its dark apartment; to snatch it from inexpressibility; to provide the sign, meaning and object they were lacking.

Regaining memory would be to create it by creating words and thoughts anew. In confronting an immemorial sensation and inscribing it in memory, Proust succeeds where the autistic person fails. And what if we were to reread the texts which deeply move us in this perspective?

5. To See Suffocation: A Flagellation

This enclosed space of incommunicable pleasure and of deep sleep finds an echo in the eroticism that Proust's narrative genius, reaching a rare compositional and stylistic lucidity, stages in *Sodom and Gommorrah*. Sensoriality and sexuality alternate and cohabit once again, refinding – but only in excess – the violence which scours the ego, which language is sure it can contain.

Many biographers (G. Painter, J. E. Rivers, and many others[41]) recount Proust's perverse experiences, in particular his frequenting of the male brothel run by his young friend Le Cuziat. There, the writer would watch scenes of flagellation through a hole made in the wall. To Céleste Albaret, his housekeeper, indignant at these extravagances, Proust confirmed: 'But I can only write things as they *are*, and to do that I have to *see* them.'[42] This insistence on the *gaze*, and the permanence of the visible in perception, could not hide the fact that the act is a sadomasochistic one:

> My dear Céleste, what I saw this evening was unimaginable. I arrived at Le Cuziat's, as you know. He indicated to me that there was a man who visited him in order to be flagellated. Through a tiny window in the wall of another room, I witnessed the whole scene. I tell you it was incredible! I had my doubts; I wanted a way of checking; I had one. It was a big industrial type who had made the trip specially from the North of France. Imagine this man there, in the room, chained and padlocked to a wall with this type of dirty individual, picked up from who knows where, and paid for it, beating him from above with a whip until blood was running everywhere. And it was in this way that the unfortunate man took delight in all his pleasures....[43]

It is also said that Proust searched for excitement with butchers' boys, who gave him the sensation of carnage; and that he liked to stick hatpins into rats, until they squealed and blood appeared; and that he delivered up the family furniture as well as family photographs of his mother to the profanation of the brothel. The voyeurism of the flagellation scene is therefore deeply rooted in his sadomasochism, and the inexpressible sensory experience of a painful *jouissance* must be seen as indispensable to his life. Thus, the well-known symptom of his life-threatening asthma, lacerating his lungs and his heart, chaining him to his bed and to his mother, makes him live art in the flesh, a struggle that could not be said to be simply erotic, for it is eminently thanatoid. It bears the unconscious, auditory and spasmic memory of the primal scene – somatically, of course, but one often forgets that it is a paroxysmic, and thus solitary, sensation.

Unless, more archaically, asthma is the memory of an impossible individuation, of precisely a sensory cave where mother and child, like relentless lovers, wind themselves around each other. The narrator can escape only through this violent – and sensory – wrench which is asthmatic self-flagellation. After the death of his mother, he manages to establish some temporary distance between himself and his own body through recourse to voyeurism, this time enjoying another's flagellation.

6. Writing as Sensory Cave Therapy

Yet beyond this limit between the sensory violence of the mother–child bond, the asthmatic symptom, voyeurism and sadomasochism, the strictly Proustian effect is nothing other than the passage from the ordeal of *experience* to *expression* (*formulation*). Céleste Albaret provides us with evidence of it. Having given the factual story of the flagellation scene, Proust speaks of it in a detached tone. Benefiting from an intermediary – that is, from a transference on to the serene, not desirable but satisfying housekeeper–mother – he detaches himself from felt experience and settles into another universe. This world – for which Proust had had a 'vocation' since childhood, and which his writings before *In Search of Lost Time* ceaselessly explore – is not necessarily cold, but it is made up of representations. It is a universe of *spectacle* where words become – more than signs – conventions and fetishes which crystallise a dramatic sensibility, here finally captured, arranged, appeased: 'The strange thing is that every time he came back from the flagellation scene he would talk to me about the visit just as if he'd come back from an evening at Count de Beaumont's or Countess Greffuhle's. What interested him was the *picture* of what he'd seen, nothing else.'[44]

Céleste's perspicacity is astonishing, over and above what might seem like the prudish repression of a housekeeper blinding herself to the pleasure of her master by recalling only the 'picture', the image, or the representation.

We can have confidence in Céleste for at least one thing: she is a 'steadying' influence. Proust relies on her, and on the first sensory account that he entrusts to her, in order to arrive at a second verbal experience, this time dissociated from the sensation. The Representations of things, identical with sensations in the initial account, are displaced into Representations of words. These in their turn are emptied of the sensory sadomasochistic pleasure which underlies them. They obtain an autonomous, or perhaps even defensive, consistency, but only on condition of admitting that another pleasure quickly comes to replenish them. No longer the pleasure of *seeing* flagellation to the point of experiencing it, but the pleasure of *manipulating* sounds, the throat, breathing, at the same time as logic and syntax. The immense Proustian sentence, breathless and majestic, flagellated and contented, sent to sleep with the profound dream of *Sodom and Gomorrah* but nevertheless remaining perfectly lucid, passes from one (sadomasochistic, voyeuristic) sensation to another. Up to, indeed, the 'pleasure of the text' which, passing through language henceforth nourished by all these sensations, becomes music, style and flesh.

Writing, this therapy of the sensory cave, often needs to give itself a pseudo-object – the object of perversion – in order to pass through its autistic enclosure (that evoked by deep sleep) and reach the contagious auto-eroticism which is the construction of a sensory *fiction*.

Proust thus begins by describing the perverse scene. Immediately, he seizes the signifiers that have emerged and repeats them, turns them into things, manipulates them, flagellates them, and thereby finds his own wind: 'Anyway, we talked about the horrible flagellation scene for hours that night, me still horror-struck and he going over it as though not to forget anything, and no doubt thinking aloud, as usual, of what he was going to write.'[45]

The reader will have noted that Céleste is 'crushed' and 'struck', whereas Proust breathes pictures, represents, models, survives. We see him repeating his words and arranging them, harassing Céleste, using her, forgetting her, sacrificing her, thus liberating himself from the pleasure tying him to the brothel and to the housekeeper. He counts on the participation–indignation of this fine woman in order to retrace the scene at a distance, as a quasi-comedy, to laugh about it, to free himself finally from his sensation, and only then to create for himself the companion he lacked in the dream. This *alter ego*, who stabilises our identity in so far as it destines it for others, is ... the *narrator*: the double of the one who inhabits deep sleep, the double of the one who frequents the brothel, a passion which can be spoken.

In this sublimatory remodelling a pseudo-other will simultaneously figure: the *novelistic character*. In this regard Proust takes upon himself the excesses of the oversensitive author; he both exhibits and dissimulates them. This other is *real*, no doubt (for example, we recognise the features of the decadent Montesquiou and of some anonymous factory owner who is a lover of unusual sensations), but is also an essential part of the narrator himself: the character shows up an indecent facet of the oversensitive one surmounted by the stylist. In this case the character will be the Baron de Charlus, whom we thus meet in *Time Regained*:

> Suddenly [*Tout d'un coup*] from a room situated by itself at the end of a corridor, I thought I heard stifled groans. I walked rapidly towards the sounds and put my *ear* to the door. 'I beseech you, mercy, have pity, untie me, don't beat me so hard,' said a voice. 'I kiss your feet, I abase myself, I promise not to offend again. Have pity on me.' 'No, you filthy brute,' replied another *voice*, 'and if you *yell* and drag yourself about on your knees like that, you'll be tied to the bed, no mercy for you,' and I *heard* the noise of the crack of a whip, which I guessed to be reinforced with nails, for it was followed by *cries* of pain. At this moment I *noticed* that there was a small *oval window* [*œil-de-bœuf*] opening from the room on to the corridor and the curtain had not been drawn across it; stealthily in the darkness I crept as far as this window and there in the room, chained to a bed like Prometheus to his rock, receiving the blows that Maurice rained upon him with a whip which was in fact studded with nails, *I saw*, with blood already flowing from him and covered with bruises which proved that the chastisement was not taking place for the first time – *I saw* before me M. de Charlus.[46]

The Baron soon entered the ante-room, walking with difficulty on account of his injuries, though doubtless he must have been used to them. Although his pleasure was at an end and he had only come to give Maurice the money which he owed him, he directed at the young men a tender and curious glance which travelled round the whole circle, promising himself with each of them the pleasure of a moment's chat, platonic but amorously prolonged. And in the sprightly frivolity which he exhibited before this harem *which* [*qui*] appeared almost to intimidate him, I recognised those jerky movements of the body and the head, those languishing glances *which* [*qui*] had struck me on the evening of his first visit to

La Raspelière, graces inherited from some grandmother *whom* [*que*] I had not known, *which* [*que*] in ordinary life were disguised by more virile expressions on his face but *which* [*qu'y*] from time to time were made to blossom there coquettishly, when circumstances made him anxious to please an inferior audience, by the desire to appear a great lady.[47]

Abruptly, suddenly, (*tout d'un coup*) – the scene begins with a 'blow' (*coup*). It takes us into a room (let us recall the darkened room of the dream) from which 'stifled groans' are coming: this is a world of noises, cries, voices and yells which evokes the suffocation and the panting – perhaps of the asthmatic, or, if one likes, of coitus, of a sonorous, nocturnal hallucination, or, finally, of suffering without a sufferer, of suffering as such. Whip cracks, evil without mercy, an entire invisible *sound effect*. Only afterwards does the *gaze* appear: by way of an 'oval window' [*œil-de-bœuf* – literally: 'ox's eye' (TN)], animality being hardly disguised: I *notice*, I *see*, I *see*. Also caught in a panting repetition (I *see*, I *see*), visual perception continues the flagellation scene. Without softening it, but transposing from the auditory into the visual register, the gaze seems to relativise it. From loud breathing to the sight of blood, opening up a series of expressive means or markings, which can vary, be linked together, or substituted for one another. As a result, lived experience (*le vécu*) slides into representation, pain slides into the spectacle, and feeling slides into imagery or the symbol.[48]

The hurting body is already entirely in the affectation of the spectacle: still covered with bruises, the Baron meets his Platonic loves, in 'sprightly frivolity'; his body is no longer chained or sick, but waddling along like a puppet; some strange, decidedly feminine charm animates him, that of a grandmother (here the dead woman returns, maternal time is regained). Yet, in this world henceforth made of artifice, the stifled panting does not cease to resonate. Is it the panting of the invalid, or of the sick, or of the victim? Here, subordinate propositions accumulate: 'whom I had not known', 'which ... were disguised by more virile expressions', 'which in ordinary life [still another subordinated proposition] ... were made to blossom there coquettishly, when circumstances made him anxious to please an inferior audience, by the desire to appear a great lady'.[49] From peripeteia to peripeteia, the sentence draws breath and loses it, thought becomes confused even while it aspires to clarity: who is this *who*? (*qui est ce qui*), what is this *that* (*quel est ce que*)?[50] There are multiple embeddings which become blurred and indefinite, at the limit of the grammatical.[51]

Thus is a protean identity outlined. It is no longer non-existent, as it is in the deep dream: for in the perversity scene, solitude is abolished and the non-person of the dream in the other apartment here becomes a prestigious baron. However, by dint of commentaries, discourses and meta-discourses, Charlus's speech meets the undecidable. His personality is analogical and continues in the *sensations* it covers with and we have encountered in sleep, particularly in the precious play with *codes* that the Baron in turn respects and misuses, like a master of the art, having once been a slave of the senses.

Casualness alternates with detachment, irony with satire. We will come to know everything about *Action française* and *L'Action libérale*, about snobbery and Germanophilia, about Sarah Bernhardt and about the French who no longer want war, about the Baron's whims in which aristocratic contempt is mixed with amorous dependence. The 'social whole' is vaporous, easy, nonchalant. Breath in Proust is regained just like time, stands open to the winds just like time, in this free and interminable association of *In Search of Lost Time* that only death can interrupt.

Might torture be the obligatory way to embodiment? The narrator gives us to understand that although it is necessary, passion is not enough:

> 'How unfortunate it is that M. de Charlus is not a novelist or poet! Not merely so that he could describe what he sees, *but because the position in which a Charlus finds himself with respect to desire* causes scandals to spring up around him, and compels him to take life seriously, to load pleasure with a weight of emotion. He *cannot get stuck* in an *ironical and superficial view of things* because a current of pain is perpetually reawakened within him.'[52]

A man of pain, Charlus is 'this consenting Prometheus [who] had had himself nailed by Force *to the rock of Pure Matter*';[53] but nothing guarantees that he will accede to 'embodied time', for, being a simple 'dilettante', he 'never dreamt of writing and had no gift for it'.[54] Would embodied time – transubstantiation – then require, in addition to martyrdom, a momentary pause, 'an ironical and superficial view'? – 'A slap in the face or a box on the ear helps to educate not only children but poets.'[55]

Provided that one becomes immobilised, laughs at it and writes. From this perspective, the sadomasochistic experience would be like a kind of *reading*:[56] it prefigures sensory time, but does not constitute it.

7. Interpretation between Words–Signs and Words–Fetishes: A Beauty

The dynamic of writing that we have just observed in Proust is reminiscent of analytic listening and interpretation. If writing is memory regained – from signs to flesh and vice versa – through an intense identification with and a dramatic separation from a loved, desired, hated, indifferent other, so is interpretation. It is so at least in the rare moments of grace where the countertransference responds to the logic of the transference and allows remodelling of the psychical map of the analyst and analysand. What happens when we name the often unspeakable sensations of our patients?

An *identification* with the analysand is required which mobilises the whole of my psychical apparatus: an identification with his or her biography, supposed memory – even with the transgenerational memory – and with imagined sensation. The countertransference is an imaginary yet real operation: a *transubstantiation* (this term from the Catholic liturgy is claimed by Joyce, another sensory writer, in order to describe the subjective economy of writing as the advent of new signs and a new body[57]). Whether it be primary, secondary, projective or in all its other variants, it would be desirable to understand this identification with a paroxysmic intensity. Insufficient weight is placed upon it by classical psychoanalytic theory, preoccupied as it is, originally and above all, with the neurotic, whereas depressions, psychoses – and, of course, autism – attract attention to it with renewed force.

To gain access to this paroxysmic intensity of identification, which is incontestably necessary in certain treatments, it is as well that the psychoanalyst remember Merleau-Ponty's thoughts on the involvement of the body with the external world as well as with the bodies of others. The philosopher calls this involvement *reversible* and *chiasmic*, for the toucher is aways tangible, the seer, visible, matter, a body, the same, an other. Merleau-Ponty's objective was to combat metaphysical dichotomies in philosophy and psychology. In fact, both naïve and scientific experience consider that an X perceives a Y from which it is supposed to be always-already separated. Now it is precisely the self-evidence of this separation which is put in question by the French philosopher's phenomenological operation, which is a radicalisation of Husserl. It seems to me legitimate to transpose this *interpenetration* and this *reversibility* of perceiving and the perceived, of feeling and the felt, not only in psychoanalysis but also in the reading of literary texts. Merleau-Ponty gives this transposition the highly charged term of 'flesh':

> It is said that the colors, the tactile reliefs given to the other, are for me an absolute mystery, forever inaccessible. This is not completely true; for me to have not an idea, an image, nor a representation, but as it were the imminent experience of them, it suffices that I look at a landscape, that I speak of it with someone. Then, through the concordant operation of this body and my own, what I see passes into him, this individual green, as the customs officer recognizes suddenly in a traveler the man whose description he had been given. There is here no problem of the *alter ego* because it is not *I* who sees, because an anonymous visibility inhabits both of us, a vision in general, in virtue of that primordial property that belongs to the flesh, being here and now, of radiating everywhere and forever, being an individual, of being also a dimension and a universal.[58]

> Once again, the flesh we are speaking of is not matter. It is the coiling over of the visible upon the seeing body, of the tangible on the touching body ... this pact between them [things] and me according to which I lend them my body in order that they inscribe upon it and give me their resemblance, this fold, this central cavity of the visible which is my vision....We must not think the flesh starting from substances, from the body and spirit – for then it would be the union of contradictories – but we must think it, as we said, as an element, as the concrete emblem of a general manner of being.[59]

> We touch here the most difficult point, that is, the bond between the flesh and the idea, between the visible and the interior armature which it manifests and which it conceals. No one has gone further than Proust in fixing the relations between the visible and the invisible.[60]

These reflections, whose problematic difficulty is easily grasped, along with their mystical impact, are of interest to the reader of Proust because they signal the pregnancy of figurability in the felt, torn between the two spheres of world and thought. This bi-faced sensoriality is a 'manner of being' which characterises the experience of writing in the sense of 'time regained'. It is this that the philosopher seeks to make burst forth in the world, whereas the analyst experiences it in the transference and countertransference. A *state of flesh* seems to underpin the therapeutic act, but it can truly become a *therapeutic act* only on condition of driving this reversible and chiasmic sensation into language, which is supported by it.

The becoming flesh is an aspect of the analytic process that it is important to restore without limiting oneself exclusively to it. For to signal the sensory aspect presupposes a distance, even a split, in which resides, as it were, the professional perversion of analysts. The act of naming consists in abandoning the pleasure and pain of carnal identification and textuality in order to dissociate Representations of things and Representations of words. Interpretation fixes the Representation of words in their arbitrary autonomy to the extent that these are signs distinct from perceptions–sensations. It even constitutes them as fetishes, leads the patient to play with these words–signs–fetishes, restores them to him as the mother does to her child – that is, to begin with, as toys. From her flesh that we shared, we make Representations of words; but in setting them up, repeating and punctuating them, we give these words the consistence of thingly symbols, and thus bring them closer to being Representations of things. Like a writer, repeating, loving and arranging his text. In this way, therefore, from sensory *fixations*, the analysis first of all works through sensory *games*, then *words*, *pleasures–words*, *things–words*, and *fetishes–words*. Starting from the flesh of signs, we can call this a naming where the therapist is engaged in the art of making transitional objects. In the treatment of narcissistic affections, this art is more essential than any other. The becoming-thing (*chosification*) of the word, its fetishisation, seems to be an obligatory movement from sensation to the idea, and thence to a softening of the logical order where it is called upon to deploy itself in order to become a thought.

Therapists of autistic patients[61] have noted the aesthetic pleasure such patients take in using their first words, words loaded more with sensations than with ideas. Beauty would be necessary for psychical growth and for the blosssoming of thoughts, but it could not exist were the analyst directing this process not capable of creating, for himself and for the other, this same beauty and enjoyment. Thus, if I have been attentive to Proustian pleasures, this is not only to share my obviously questionable interest in the excitation underlying the art of the man who continued to be called, until his death as a famous writer, 'little Marcel'. In the light of his work, it would be important to reflect on the sadomasochistic dimension of the aesthetic performance which is disguised *in analytic interpretation* in general, but still more so when faced with psychosis and autism. Here we have the unconscious, sadomasochistic pleasure unaware of identifying with a bound soul, with this palpitating and mute sensation, which is unaware of me as an *other*, all while including me in its touch, its saliva, its breathing, and in its dull, fleeting or striking gaze. This word that I neither hear nor see but generate is also a violent pleasure. I watch, through a hole in my consciousness, a fettered psyche provisionally opened up in flesh. I fuse with it, but know that it needs me to distance myself from it. Thus this other flesh will perhaps be able, on the basis of my named pleasure, to become someone else, a *subject*.

Freud notes the banal and anodyne genesis of the saving violence of naming in the cotton-reel game, the Fort–Da.[62] He brings it to light in the *Verneinung* (Negation): this celebrated and ambiguous negativity which rejects erotic value, at the same time as it presents an originary symbolism in the dialectic of an incessant drive repression (*repoussement*).[63] Parents see it in the so-called emotional crisis of the young infant during its acquisition of language and/or its Oedipal positioning.... The violence of sensory naming is obligatory; it is also, and above all, beneficial within the treatment. For how can one create from discontinuity? How can a *sign* be carved out for an *object*, which is constituted only when it becomes an object of desire, bursting into the continuous and analogical sensoriality of the patient – without imposing our own desire for a name, and therefore for an object? Desire, which removes, can only do harm, can only hurt. Kindness and tact are, then, all the more necessary, notably in treatments which mobilise the split in the analyst and which, beyond their aesthetic pleasure, are based on the analyst's own sadomasochistic latencies.

Much remains to be done if analysts are to perfect their rhetorical art. Reading Proust suggests models able to shape the flesh of our intense identifications with those who neither speak nor think their sensations. But let us not be too taken in by the phenomenological beatitude; let us, rather, remain analysts attentive to the sadomasochistic logic of sensory *identification* as well as that of *nomination*. Why? To utilise them better, not as the threshold of *jouissance* for us, but as care of the other in those domains where the specificity of the human being as a speaking being seems to become lost. For beyond the autistic symptom of the sensory cave, what is at stake here is a border region of our psyche, recalled by aesthetic experience, where analytic interpretation itself is resourced, without being reduced to it.

Translated by John Lechte

Notes

1. Jacques Rivière, 'Quelques progrès dans l'étude du cœur humain', in *Cahiers Marcel Proust*, no. 13, Paris: Gallimard, 1985.

2. Marcel Proust, *In Search of Lost Time, VI: Time Regained*, trans. Andrew Meyer and Terence Kilmartin, revised by D. J. Enright, London: Chatto & Windus, 1992, pp. 260–1. Emphasis added.

3. ibid., p. 255. Translation modified.

4. ibid. Translation modified.

5. We will sometimes use the terms 'sensation' and 'perception' indifferently, while admitting, like many authors, that they play at the interface of a common operation where sensation is orientated towards the object, whereas perception concerns the impact of this object for the subject.

6. Sigmund Freud, *Gesammelte Werke* (*GW*), XIV, pp. 3–8; *Standard Edition* (*S.E.*) 19, pp. 227–32; see Sigmund Freud, *The Origins of Psycho-Analysis: Letters to Wilhem Fliess, Drafts and Notes: 1887–1902*, ed. Marie Bonaparte, Anna Freud and Ernst Kris, London: Imago Publishing Company, 1954.

7. Freud, 'Letter to Fliess of 6.12.1896', *S.E.* I, p. 234; Freud, *The Origins of Psycho-Analysis*, p. 174.

8. Freud, 'Letter to Fliess of 6.12.1896', p. 235; Freud, *Origins of Psycho-Analysis*, p. 175. Emphasis added.

9. Freud, 'Project for a Scientific Psychology', *S.E.* I, p. 309. We should note that Freud distinguishes between '*Wahrnehmung*' ('*W*'), perception in general, and perceptual neurones. Occasionally this distinction is lost in Kristeva's text. (TN)

10. ibid.

11. ibid., p. 325. Translation modified.

12. ibid., p. 366.

13. Freud, 'Project for a Scientific Psychology', p. 367; first emphasis original, second emphasis added.

14. ibid. First emphasis original; subsequent emphases added.

15. In *Zur Auffassung der Aphasien*, 1891, English trans. *On Aphasia*, London, 1953, and Appendix C of the metapsychological works, in *S.E.* 14, pp. 109–215.

16. See Hanna Segal, 'Note on Symbo͟ Formation', *International Journal of Psycho-Analysis*, XXXVII, 1957, p. 393 and *passim*.

17. See Julia Kristeva, 'The Semiotic and the Symbolic', in *Revolution in Poetic Language*, trans. Margaret Waller, New York: Columbia University Press, 1984.

18. Kristeva examines the difference between these two terms in 'L'Expérience du temps incorporé' [The Experience of Embodied Time], Chapter IV of *Le Temps sensible*, esp. p. 239. Generally speaking, *Erlebnis* is immediate experience as lived, while *Erfahrung* is the accumulated body of memories of experience as having been lived. (TN)

19. W. Sellars defends adverbial theory, whereas according to J. Searle the content of perception is a proposition. E. Wright raises the issue of the passive component of the sensory process – its non-epistemic or non-intentional character – against A. Ben-Zeev; whereas C. S. Peirce, while seeing an 'inference' in sensation, as in every mental phenomenon, had already drawn attention, even in own his time, to the 'irreducible vagueness' specific to sensation. See here, too, R. C. Salomon, *The Passions*, New York: Doubleday, 1976; W. Lyons, *Emotion*, Cambridge: Cambridge University Press, 1980; also Lazarus, Greenspan, and others.

20. Guy Lazorthes, *L'Ouvrage des sens*, Paris: Flammarion, 1986, recalls that this type of reaction belongs not to the neocortex but to the reptilian brain, situated in the axial structures of the cerebral trunk; it regulates the major elements of vegetative behaviour and ensures adaptation to the environment. Since it is functional from birth, the stimulation which reaches it determines specific and global reactions: the reflexes of flight and aggression, and so on.

21. S.G. Clarke, 'Emotions: Rationality Without Cognitivism', *Dialogue* (Canadian Philosophical Review), 1986, vol. 25, 4, pp. 663–74.

22. See, among others, Francis Tustin, *Austistic Barriers in Neurotic Patients*, London: Karnac Books, 1986.

23. For a definition of this term see Kristeva, *Revolution in Poetic Language*, p. 17. (TN)

24. See Tustin, *Autistic Barriers in Neurotic Patients*.

25. Marcel Proust, *Sodom and Gomorrah*, in *In Search of Lost Time*, IV, trans. C. K. Scott Moncrieff and Terence Kilmartin, revised by D. J. Enright, pp. 439–43.

26. ibid., p. 442.

27. ibid., p. 440.

28. ibid., p. 439. Translation modified.

29. Here 'think' seems closer to 'hold to be true' than to 'suppose'.

30. Proust, *Sodom and Gomorrah*, p. 439. Translation modified.

31. ibid.

32. ibid.

33. ibid.

34. ibid., p. 440.

35. ibid.

36. ibid. Translation modified.

37. ibid., p. 441.

38. ibid.

39. ibid., pp. 441–2.

40. ibid., p. 441.

41. See G. Painter, *Marcel Proust: A Biography*, New York: Random House, 1959; J. E. Rivers, *Proust and the Art of Love*, New York: Columbia University Press, 1980.

42. Céleste Albaret, *Monsieur Proust* (As Told to Georges Belmont), trans. Barbara Bray, London: Collins and Harvill Press, 1976, p, 196. Emphasis added.

43. ibid.

44. ibid.

45. ibid., p. 198.

46. Proust, *Time Regained*, in *In Search for Lost Time*, VI, p. 154. Emphasis added. The terms which Kristeva will discuss are given in French in square brackets when they do not have an immediate equivalent in the English translation. (TN)

47. *Time Regained*, p. 165. Emphasis added.

48. ibid., p. 166.

49. ibid., p. 165.

50. Kristeva's point is difficult to render into English for, as can be seen, the distinction in English between 'who' (relative pronoun referring to persons) and 'which' (relative pronoun referring to things) is lost in the French. On the other hand, French still uses '*que*' ('that') when the subordinate clause precedes the main clause in a sentence, and '*qui*' ('which') when the main clause precedes the subordinate clause, whereas in English this is less marked. (TN)

51. This is examined later in 'La Phrase de Proust' ['The Proustian Sentence'], Chapter VIII of *Le Temps sensible*, pp. 341-55.

52. Proust, *Time Regained*, p. 173. Emphasis added.

53. ibid., p. 182. Emphasis added.

54. ibid., p. 174. See also *Le Temps sensible*, Part I, Chapter VII, 'Charlus: tout sexe et hors sexe' ['Charlus: All Sex and Outside Sex'], pp. 110–29.

55. Proust, *Time Regained*, p. 173.

56. 'Reading is at the threshold of spiritual life; it can introduce us to it, it does not consitute it…. Books then play for it [a lazy mind] a role similar to that of psychotherapists for certain neurasthenics.' Marcel Proust, *On Reading*, trans. Jean Autret and William Burford, London: Souvenir Press (Educational and Academic), 1972, p. 39.

57. See my 'Joyce the Gracehoper or the Return of Orpheus', in Bernard Benstock, ed., *James Joyce: The Augmented Ninth* (Proceedings of the Ninth International James Joyce Symposium), Syracuse, NY: Syracuse University Press, 1988, pp. 167–80. For Proust's use of this term, see my discussion in *Le Temps sensible*, pp. 241, 264 ff.

58. Maurice Merleau-Ponty, *The Visible and the Invisible*, trans. Alphonso Lingis, Evanston, IL: Northwestern University Press, 1968, Second Printing, 1975, p. 142. See also Chapter VII, 'Proust philosophe' ['Proust as Philosopher'], in *Le Temps sensible*, pp. 331–54.

59. Merleau-Ponty, *The Visible and the Invisible*, pp. 146–7.

60. ibid., p. 149.

61. See Donald Meltzer and Meg Harris Williams, *The Apprehension of Beauty: The Role of Aesthetic Conflict in Development, Art and Violence*, Bellinluig, Scotland: Clunie Press for the Roland Harris Trust, 1988, who lay stress on 'the sufficiently beautiful mother with her sufficiently beautiful baby' as necessary conditions for the appearance of psychical life.

62. Freud, *Beyond the Pleasure Principle* (1920), *G.W.* XII, pp. 3-69; *S.E.* 18, pp. 3–64.

63. Freud, 'Die Verneinung' (1925), *G.W.* XIV, pp. 11–15; 'Negation', *S.E.* 19, pp. 233–9.

Select Bibliography

The following is a selection of bibliographical items around the theme of writing, madness and psychoanalysis.

Abraham, Nicolas and Maria Torok, 'The Wolfman's Magic Word: A Cryptonymy', trans. Nicholas Royle and Ann Wordsworth, eds, in 'Psychoanalysis and Literature, New Work', special number of *The Oxford Literary Review*, vol. 12, nos 1–2, 1990.
Berman, Emanuel, *Essential Papers on Literature and Psychoanalysis*, New York: New York University Press, 1993.
Bowlby, Rachel, *Still Crazy After All These Years: Women, Writing and Psychoanalysis*, London and New York: Routledge, 1992.
Breger, Louis, *Dostoevsky: The Author as Psychoanalyst*, New York: New York University Press, 1989.
Felman, Shoshana, ed., *Literature and Psychoanalysis: The Question of Reading – Otherwise*, Baltimore, MD and London: Johns Hopkins University Press, 1982.
—— *The Literary Speech Act: Don Juan with J. L. Austin, or Seduction in Two Languages*, trans. Catherine Porter, New York: Cornell University Press, 1983.
—— *Writing and Madness: Literature/Philosophy/Psychoanalysis*, Ithaca, NY: Cornell University Press, 1985.
—— *Jacques Lacan and the Adventure of Insight: Psychoanalysis in Contemporary Culture*, Cambridge, MA and London: Harvard University Press, 1987.
Freud, Sigmund, *Art and Literature*, The Pelican Freud Library, vol. 14, Harmondsworth: Penguin, 1985.
Hogan, Patrick and Lalita Pandit, eds, *Criticism and Lacan: Essays and Dialogue on Language, Structure, and the Unconscious*, Athens, GA: University of Georgia Press, 1990.
Kristeva, Julia, *Tales of Love*, trans. Leon S. Roudiez, New York: Columbia University Press, 1987.
—— *Black Sun: Depression and Melancholia*, trans. Leon S. Roudiez, New York: Columbia University Press, 1989.
Kurzweil, Edith and William Phillips, eds, *Literature and Psychoanalysis*, New York: Columbia University Press, 1983.
Muller, John P. and William J. Richardson, eds, *The Purloined Poe: Lacan, Derrida and Psychoanalytic Reading*, Baltimore, MD: Johns Hopkins University Press, 1988.
Shamdasani, Sonu and Michael Münchow, eds, *Speculations After Freud: Psychoanalysis, Philosophy and Culture*, London: Routledge, 1994.
Skura, Meridith-Anne, *The Literary Use of the Psychoanalytic Process*, New Haven, CT: Yale University Press, 1981.

Smith, Joseph H. and William Kerrigan, eds, *Taking Chances*: *Derrida, Psychoanalysis and Literature*, Baltimore, MD: Johns Hopkins University Press, 1987.

Splitter, Randolph, *Proust's Recherche*: *A Psychoanalytic Interpretation*, Boston, MA and London: Routledge & Kegan Paul, 1981.

Wright, Elizabeth, *Psychoanalytic Criticism*: *Theory to Practice*, London and New York: Routledge 'New Accents Series', 1985.

Žižek, Slavoj, *Looking Awry: An Introduction to Jacques Lacan Through Popular Culture*, Cambridge, MA: MIT Press, 'An October Book', 1991.

Index